Farmer's Son Who Dared to Fly

Farmer's Son
Who Dared to Fly

Harbans Singh Sahota

ZORBA BOOKS

ZORBA BOOKS

Publishing Services by Zorba Books, October 2020

Website: www.zorbabooks.com
Email: info@zorbabooks.com
Contact: 0124-4259579/8800509579

Cover Design @ Sathish

Copyright © Harbans Singh Sahota

ISBN Print Book - 978-93-90011-19-3
ISBN eBook - 978-93-90011-20-9

All rights reserved. No part of this book may be reproduced or transmitted in any form or by any means, electronic or mechanical, except by a reviewer. The reviewer may quote brief passages, with attribution, in a review to be printed in a magazine, newspaper, or on the Web—without permission in writing from the copyright owner.

The publisher under the guidance and direction of the author has published the contents in this book, and the publisher takes no responsibility for the contents, it's accuracy, completeness, any inconsistencies, or the statements made. The contents of the book do not reflect the opinion of the publisher or the editor. The publisher and editor shall not be liable for any errors, omissions, or the reliability of the contents of the book.

Any perceived slight against any person/s, place or organization is purely unintentional.

Zorba Books Pvt. Ltd. (opc)
Sushant Arcade,
Sushant Lok 1,
Next to Courtyard Marriot,
Gurgaon – 122009, India

I would like to dedicate my book to my father who was a great visionary for his children while leading a simple life himself.

ਦੇਹਿ ਸਿਵਾ ਬਰੁ ਮੋਹਿ ਇਹੈ ਸੁਭ ਕਰਮਨ ਤੇ ਕਬਹੂ ਨ ਟਰੋਂ ॥ ਨ ਡਰੋਂ ਅਰਿ ਸੋ ਜਬ ਜਾਇ ਲਰੋਂ ਨਿਸਚੈ ਕਰਿ ਆਪਨੀ ਜੀਤ ਕਰੋਂ ॥ ਅਰੁ ਸਿਖ ਹੋਂ ਆਪਨੇ ਹੀ ਮਨ ਕੌ ਇਹ ਲਾਲਚ ਹਉ ਗੁਨ ਤਉ ਉਚਰੋਂ ॥ ਜਬ ਆਵ ਕੀ ਅਉਧ ਨਿਦਾਨ ਬਨੈ ਅਤਿ ਹੀ ਰਨ ਮੈ ਤਬ ਜੂਝ ਮਰੋਂ ॥੨੩੧॥

Deh siva bar mohe eh-hey subh karman te kabhu na taro. Na daro arr seo jab jaye laro nischey kar apni jit karo. Arr Sikh ho apne he mann ko, eh laalach hou gun tau ucharo. Jab aav ki audh nidan bane att he rann me tabh joojh maro.

Meaning:

O Timeless God give me this boon that I never refrain from doing the righteous act. Therefore, I shall have no fear of the enemy when I go into battle and with determination I will be victorious. That, I may teach my mind to only sing your praises. And when the time comes, I should die fighting heroically on the field of battle

CONTENTS

Foreword by Anil Yashwant Tipnis   *xv*

Foreword by Raghunath Nambiar   *xix*

Introduction   *1*

1. Family and Childhood   3

2. Fragments from Simpler Days   6

3. Looking Back at the Teenage Years   17

4. Games I Grew Up Playing   27

5. Some Things Mundane and Something Marvellous   34

6. Preparation for District Inter-School Tournament   42

7. College and its Many Facets   52

8. A Share of My Wisdom   57

9. Joining the Indian Air Force   62

10. Thrills and Trials   76

11. Sky Is the Limit   84

12. Being a Pilot Officer   94

13. *'Saat Samunder Paar'*   99

14. Escaping Death   107

15. Indo-Pak War, 1965   110

16. Beginning of a New Chapter   113

17. Risks and Rewards of an IAF Officer
    And Indo-Pak War 1971   119

18. The Journey from One Base to Another   124

19. Finding the Leader Within   139

20. How Yogasanas Changed My Life   189

21. Retirement and Life Thereon   192

22. How I Became a Homoeopath   211

23. Life with Family in USA   217

Epilogue   *220*

ACKNOWLEDGEMENTS

My dream of completing this book was greatly fulfilled with the initial encouragement by Sardar Preet Mohan Singh Kapoor. His motivation and critical comments helped me put in my best of efforts to add more punch to the manuscript. Sardar Preet Mohan Singh Kapoor is highly qualified in IT field, Hydel power Projects and expert in Equity business. He along with his business partner digitized Sri Guru Granth Sahib - the central religious scripture of the Sikhs, to make the English translations available to non-Punjabi speaking population both in India and the Western World. This was a first of its kind, a CD ROM. There was serendipity in this idea and Preet Mohan Singh humbly accepted the responsibility as being the 9th direct descendant of the illustrious poet laureate bhai Nand Lal Goya who was a devout disciple in the court of Guru Gobind Singh ji. Preet Mohan Singh lives with his wife Harvinder Kaur, his son Shivpreet Singh, his daughter-in-law Dashminder Kaur and his three grandchildren, Gobind Singh, Jania Kaur and Geet Kaur in San Ramon, California, USA.

I would like to thank former Chief of Air Staff, Air Chief Marshal AY Tipnis, PVSM, AVSM, VM, for his whole-hearted encouragement and support by penning down the foreword. He was the Air Officer Commanding-in-Chief of the Western Air Command from Aug 1995 to March 1997 and later he commanded the Air Force to distinction during the Kargil War, when the Air Force flew air superiority and close air support missions at heights of over 18,000 feet It was his leadership that ensured India came victorious in the Kargil conflict. He has been an inspiration for me and many others.

I would also like to thank former Air Officer Commanding-in-Chief of the Western Air Command Air Marshal Raghunath Nambiar, PVSM, AVSM, VM & Bar, for his support in writing the foreword of my book. He was the first fighter pilot in IAF to hit the Pakistani infiltrators at Tiger Hill during the Kargil War **with a precision-guided bomb. A test-pilot, who flew the Mirage 2000, dropped five** of the eight Laser Guided Bombs (LGB) during the Kargil War and was awarded the Vayu Sena

Medal (Gallantry). I cherish warm memories of young Namby at No.21 Sqn where I met him first and all along his successful career in the Air Force.

For illustrations and sketches I would like to thank a young and talented artist Mr Gurpreet Singh. His free hand sketches made the story more meaningful. Gurpreet Singh is studying in school at Garhdiwala, Hoshiarpur, Punjab, India.

The typing of my hand written initial manuscript was done by Mr. Jaswinder Singh a computer expert at Garhdiwala. He not only typed half of the manuscript but also taught me to type the rest of it as I was not confident to do it myself initially. Jaswinder after completing a Post graduation Diploma in Computer Application, is managing his own business enterprise known as Cyber City in Garhdiwala , Hoshiarpur, Punjab, India.

Now my sincere gratitude to all my family members who have been by my side all along the process of getting this book together and I would like to start with my wife Gian, who has supported me all along and has been a pillar of strength for the whole family.

Next in the list is my son Tejpal Singh Sahota, who inserted all the pictures in the manuscript with great precision. He also edited some portion of the script and most of the technical details. He is Bachelor of Electrical Engineering since 1996. He did his Post graduation and has been working for various semiconductor Blue Chip companies for the last 22 years in Sillicon Valley covering manufacturing, component qualification, reliability and engineering process.

I would also like to thank my daughter in law Puneet Randhawa for being a great source of support for all of us. She efficiently manages housework and her job. She is currently working as Sr Director Global Commercial Operations, GE Digital. She has worked in the Silicon Valley for various companies in computer SW industry.

The last step in the ladder was editing of the manuscript. This work was taken over by my daughter Tejinder Kaur Basra. She helped me string the story together from a disjointed one and gave it the shape of a book in a chronological order.

Tejinder Basra –Life Coach, Heartfulness Meditation Trainer, Quantum Healer and Reiki Master. BSc (Phy, Math), MEd, MBA (HR). She is currently a Philosophy research scholar at Sahaj Marg Spirituality Foundation, Research Center, University of Mysore.

I would also like to thank my son in law Air Commodore Harpreet Singh Basra (Retd), AVSM, VM for his assistance in editing the flying specific technical terminology mentioned in the book. He also helped in the publishing details and planning of the book launch.

Last but not the least the future of my family, my five grandchildren who have kept me young and energetic to complete my dream. Spending time with them has been the motivation to write my memories which I hope will be an inspiration for them. Thanks to my lovely grandchildren; Anaika, Ahana, Angad, Keerath and Amanat.

My heartfelt thanks and gratitude to the above mentioned individuals and personalities. Completion of my Book "Farmer's Son Who Dared to Fly" was made possible with their dedicated contribution.

FOREWORD

I met Air Commodore Harbans Singh Sahota, the author of A FARMER'S SON WHO DARED TO FLY, for the first time more than fifty years ago. We were both stationed at Adampur, a premier fighter base of the Indian Air Force. I was then in the only MiG 21 Squadron of the IAF. At that time the MiG 21 was the cynosure of all eyes of the Air Force. That was to be expected; it was the IAF's first fighter of Russian (USSR) origin with a number of other firsts to its credit. And to crown its  novelty, the pilots wore pressure suits! There would be a regular stream of pilots from the co-located Mystere squadrons, eager to have a close look at the aircraft. On a hot summer day, as I came down the aircraft ladder after a sortie, I was greeted more formally than was the norm, by a very smart-looking flying officer, "Sir, may I look into the cockpit?" Hot and sweaty as I was in my pressure suit, the pleading look and the flattering "sir" had me acquiesce. Flying Officer Harbans Singh Sahota (that's how he introduced himself) was absolutely delighted to be allowed into the cockpit. Once inside, just a look was not enough, he wanted to know everything, unmindful of his own starched uniform getting soaking wet. He was effusively grateful.

That image of Harbans has stayed with me over all these years. His turnout was always perfect: nothing out of place on uniform, beard, turban; posture perfectly erect, manner formal, correct. He was inquisitive to know the why of things, learning a passion for him. Over the years he became an equally dedicated instructor, whether in the briefing/classroom or the cockpit. He shouldered his responsibilities with maturity; a few did think that he was a tad too serious. But Harbans continued to do as he thought fit, and he did it well!

Harbans and I never served together in any unit, institution or headquarters, but our paths did cross sporadically. The Air Force grapevine had me stay aware of his progress in the service. Post 1962 War, as part of the US military training programme, he was one of several young pilots who had proceeded to the US for tactical and air gunnery training. All our pilots, including Harbans, had conducted themselves with elan, both on ground and in air, impressing the Americans.

From just one MiG 21 squadron, the IAF had expanded its strength with this formidable aircraft to more than 15 squadrons, upgrading its capabilities progressively with newer versions every few years. Harbans was one of several IAF stalwarts who helped exploit its utilisation well beyond its designed envelope. He served in the field as an operational pilot, a flight commander, a squadron commander, as chief of station operations and finally as the commander of a major MiG 21 base. His excellent performances all along earned him many accolades.

In between he had opportunities to proceed to Nigeria on deputation as a flying instructor; attend the prestigious Fighter Combat Leader Course. Besides his operational experiences of the 1965 and 1971 Wars, he was in command of the Indian Peace Keeping Force (IPKF) air base in Sri Lanka. An enviable experience under fire.

Harbans rose to the rank of air commodore with many accomplishments and without a blemish in his service record. He had within him what would have been expected of him in higher ranks and appointments. But as is often observed as the years go by, life does not always appear to be fair. Service regulations on age limitations had Air Commodore Sahota retire before the rank of air vice marshal could be conferred on him.

The reader will discern the unexpressed disappointment that the author felt at leaving the Air Force, when he still had the passion to do much more for the service that he loved so much. Not the one to look back on what could have been, Harbans Singh Sahota marches forward confidently to chalk out a new career for himself. Given his capacity for hard work, his vast experience as a pilot, administrator, as an organiser, and bereft of false ego, he makes a success as an executive pilot and as aviation administrator and planner.

All of the foregoing was known to me in varying detail, albeit as second-hand information. Yet, having known him throughout his service career, I was totally oblivious of the difficult conditions of his growing up years and the odds against which he, a Farmer's Son Dared to Become a Pilot! It is truly a tale of a young boy with enormous grit, determination and self-belief. I have no doubt that every reader will be filled with as much awe and respect for our author as I am! It is an inspirational chronicle that will fire the ambition of young people, irrespective of their background, to make their dreams come true!

I first met Harbans precisely 55 years ago in 1965 as I familiarized him with the MiG 21 cockpit, answering a spate of queries from him. My last "encounter" with him while we were still in service was 28 years later in March 1993 in the Operations Centre of Headquarters Southern Air Command. I was then Assistant Chief of Air Staff for Inspection; I had been tasked by the Chief to report on the preparedness of the Command to undertake fighter operations in its area of responsibility. As the Air 1, Harbans gave a detailed well-prepared briefing and responded to all my enquiries with alacrity and confidence, unable to mask his obvious pride in the command's ability to fulfill Air Headquarters directions, yet making no bones about what additional support was needed in its perspective plans. It was a joy to see that Harbans had lost none of his youthful enthusiasm while maturing into a competent senior staff officer.

As Harbans left service from Southern Command Headquarters I did not get to meet him again. So I was astonished and delighted to be phone-called by him, from halfway across the Globe from USA. Both astonishment and delight were heightened when he disclosed that he had penned his autobiography. For all their application of mind and hard work, fighter pilots are notoriously shy to write about themselves and yes, a tad too lazy to tap away at the computer for the length of a full book. But then Harbans, like many other challenges in his life's journey, Harbans has overcome both these traits, and proved that even writing his story was not beyond him!!

Harbans, my friend, I congratulate you for your fine effort. I am confident that all air warriors, the serving, the aspiring, the veterans, as well as admirers of warriors will enjoy partaking of your remarkable journey through life.

It is educative, inspirational and motivational. It will be a most welcome addition to the slowly, but steadily growing list of biographical works by veteran air warriors.

Wishing Happy Book-journey to All Readers!

Anil Yashwant Tipnis
Air Chief Marshal
Former Chief of the Indian Air Force

FOREWORD

I take great honour and pride in writing this Foreword for the Autobiography of Air Commodore Harbans Singh (Herbi) Sahota Sir, my first Commanding Officer. I was posted to 21 Squadron in June 1982, one year after commissioning. The Squadron was then located in Pune, equipped with Mig-21 (Bis) aircraft, which was the best Fighter the IAF had in its inventory. We were so proud and thrilled to be posted to this type,  and that too in a happening and cool city like Pune. Herbi Sir had taken over the Squadron three months previously after a stint in Nigeria, where he had been an instructor.

I was part of a bunch of six Pilot Officers posted together to the Squadron, and formed the lowest rung of the pecking order. Despite our junior position our CO made it a point to often call us home and Mrs. Sahota made it a point to host us with great affection and Squadron spirit. I vividly recall the first time she prepared tea from a Microwave Oven, which magically heated up the water in a jiffy. Remember, this was in 1982, and a microwave oven was something we had not even heard of, much less seen.

One of the most endearing qualities of Herbi Sir was his innate simplicity. This clearly comes across in this book, which reveals his life story from his birth in a village in Hoshiarpur, and his many stellar achievements over the years, both in and out of uniform. Being among the junior most in the Squadron I used to closely observe the way Herbi Sir used to deal with issues, be they simple or "prickly" ones. He was always direct and to the point.

Herbi Sir was a practitioner of meditation and insisted the entire Squadron would spend 5 minutes meditating every day after the Squadron briefing. On days we were hard pressed for time, such as when a TOT (Time over Target) was to be met, he would oxymoronically insist that we complete our 5 minutes quickly!

Herbi Sir has been overtly modest in describing his various achievements and often has Ascribed it to "Waheguru" or to luck. The fact is that he was talented and had worked long and hard to achieve his skills and talents.

One of the important traits of a great man is his ability to write about his mistakes and faults and describe them without guile or rancour. Herbi Sir possesses this quality and has not hesitated to get into details about the ups and down of a life well lived in this book.

This book would be an inspiration to the many people who desire to join the IAF and strive to succeed in life.

Raghunath Nambiar
Air Marshal
PVSM, AVSM, VM & Bar.
Former Deputy Chief of Indian Air Force

INTRODUCTION

Hide not your talents. They for use were made.
What is a sundial in the shade?

–Benjamin Franklin

I had no idea that an ordinary man could experience and achieve so much in life. I think it was God's gift laid out on a plate as a reward for my sincerity, hard work, faith in myself and a disciplined approach to become an achiever in all my vocations. Besides being an Indian Air Force officer (fighter pilot), corporate pilot and a doctor of alternative medicines (MD), I had been a good student and a sportsman. Varied circumstances, incidents and happenings and above all—may be my luck—kept me pushing for excellence in all fields and walks of life.

My journey of life—right from school, farming and college to air force, civil flying and doctor of medicine (alternative medicines)—was full of hardships, excitement, tremors and strange experiences. While in school, my practise of throwing a stone to procure ripe mangoes along with my basketball practise sessions sometimes in the moonlit nights not only made me nearly perfect, but also boosted my confidence and created in me a spirit of competence, clarity, certainty and success. My air force career was also full of wondrous pitfalls and achievements beyond my own imagination. Becoming a Marksman of the Indian Air Force was only possible due to the mindful and deliberate armament firing practises with utmost dedication, discipline, clarity and a spirit to win. I always felt that some 'godly power' was guiding me in all my endeavours and accomplishments.

1

FAMILY AND CHILDHOOD

Imust tell you brief history of my village Garhdiwala. It came into existence in 1440. Its founding fathers were Singhhota brothers from Bharatpur (Rajasthan). Singhhota is a Sanskrit word, meaning sons of a brave lioness-like mother. They were, in fact, Rajputs. Their Kulpurohit Sanga Bhatare Kain came with them and settled here. Their elder brother also settled here and built Devi Mandir of Mahsasur Mardangani Devi, and so this town was named as Garh Devi wala, now Garhdiwala. With the passage of time, Singhhota were called Sahota, which is a dominant caste in the area. Garhdiwala is situated in the foothills of Shivalik Hills. It is 30 km from Hoshiarpur on Dasuya Garhdiwala, leading road to Chandigarh via Hoshiarpur.

I was born on 1st February 1943, in a village in Punjab known as Garhdiwala. My Bapuji[1] was Shri Udham Singh Sahota and my Bibiji[2] was Mrs Charan Kaur. After my birth, I was looked after by my Bhuaji[3], Joginder Kaur—my father's younger sister. She was staying with us evenafter her marriage since we were a joint family and her husband, in INA (Indian National Army), was away on duty. There was no contact or communication with him and his whereabouts remained unknown to the family for a long time. However, he returned home safely once independence was declared. To our horror, he was sent to Kala Pani (Andaman and Nicobar Islands), where the British jailed him for quite some time. Anyway, that is a different story altogether. My Bhuaji, Joginder Kaur, took care of me and brought me up till I was four years of age as Bibiji was busy helping my Bapuji in farming.

---

[1] Father
[2] Mother
[3] Aunt

FAMILY TREE

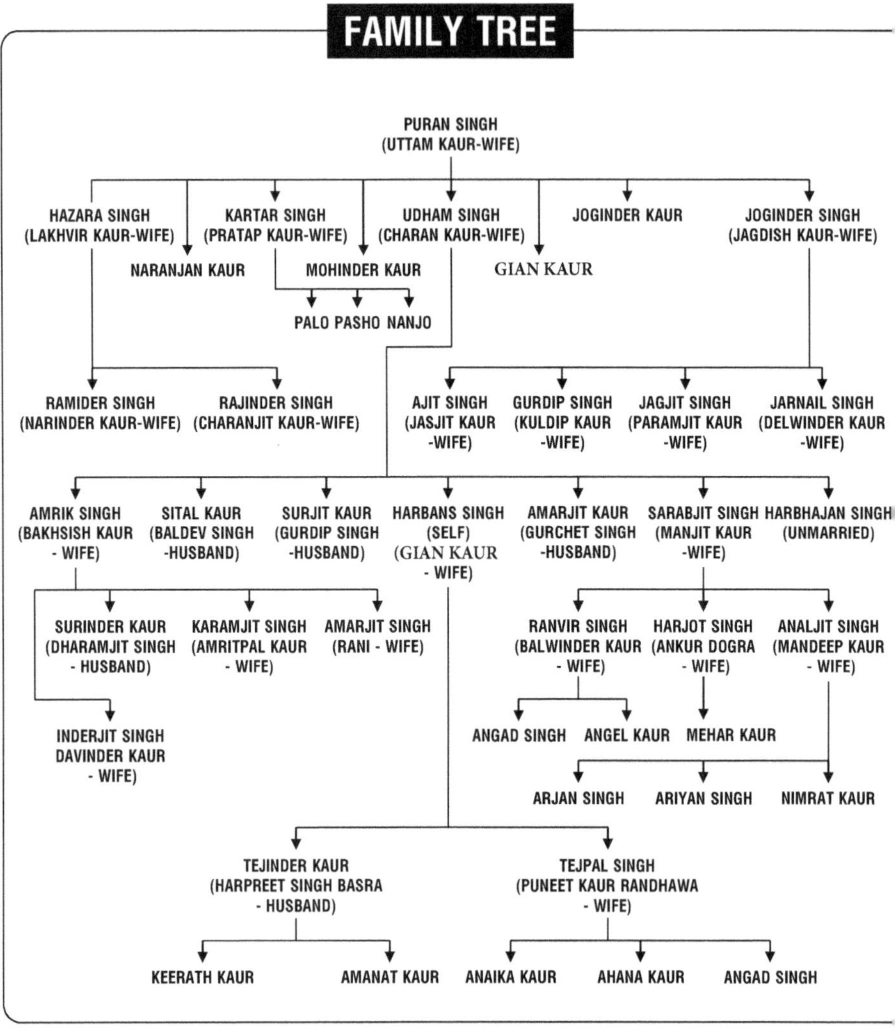

Bapuji was a very well established and famous farmer in our village. My Babaji[4], Shri Puran Singh Sahota, was in the British Army as well and had served in various places in India, including Burma (now known as Myanmar). Having an army background, he had decided long ago that four of his sons would be pursuing different professions (refer to the family tree). His elder son, Shri Hazara Singh, became a doctor. The younger son, Shri Kartar Singh, also known as Tara Singh, became a farmer. After him was Udham Singh, my father, who also became a

---

[4] Grandfather

farmer. The youngest son, Shri Joginder Singh, became a guard in the Indian Railways. Babaji, after his retirement, settled in Garhdiwala and was like a father figure to the whole village. Our village had four more well known families; however, their elders were quite quarrelsome and notorious. Because of his leadership qualities Babaji took a lead role in solving the disputes. And hence, he was made the *mukhiya* (head) of almost seventeen villages around Garhdiwala (which was the only township for those villages). During that period, he came to be known as *Babba ji*. Hence, the name of our family became Babba family.

My Bhuaji used to tell me that I was physically a very weak child. Apparently, I had a frail structure because of which I used to fall very often from a standing posture. Anyway, my bones were strong, so, I did not suffer any fracture. Then came a time when Bhuaji had to join her husband, and so she had to leave for her husband's place, leaving me with my mother, whom I endearingly called Bibiji. Bibiji told me that I was too attached to my Bhuaji and loved her even more than I loved my mother! Once when she left for her in-laws' village, I cried for days together and fell sick because I missed her terribly. Bhuaji's village was about 10 miles away but in those days, the only way to reach her was by foot or by bicycle and we only had a bullock cart but no bicycle. When my fever did not reduce, my father had to walk to her place to bring her home. I was overjoyed on seeing her, but my tears soon replaced this joy as I had missed her so much and apparently hugged her tight, as my mother told me later. Soon after seeing her, my fever started reducing and I became fit within a few days and joined her and my two elder sisters in their games. Before I knew, it was time for me to start my schooling and my Bhuaji also had to go back to her house while I had to stay with my mother and sisters. As told by my mother, it was hard for me to stay away from Bhuaji but I started to understand the situation; my Dadiji[5] was the controlling head of our joint family. I was told that my Dadiji had great respect for all her four daughters-in-law. In fact, she did not interfere in anyone's work or their plans. Instead, she used to help both her farmer sons with farming in the village.

---

[5] Grandmother

2

FRAGMENTS FROM SIMPLER DAYS

Schooling from April 1948 to May 1958

Days of Primary Schooling

My village had four schools—two for boys and two for girls. In fact, my village was almost a town as it had two big bazaars and a police *thana*[6]. There was no co-education system in those days in our village schools. I was taken to Khalsa High School for admission by my senior-most cousin, Mohinder Singh, where I started my schooling in a primary section. I do not have a clear memory of my first two years of school, however, I was told at a later stage that I was quite serious with my studies and in writing my *Fatti*[7]. The *Fatti* had to be poached with yellow mud and after writing the last line, it would have to be washed and dried, to prepare it for the next day's work. Eventually slates replaced our good old *Fatti*. Some were of smooth stones and some of iron material, painted black. On these slates we used to write and practise counting numbers till hundred, learn additions and subtractions. In our third standard, the introduction of multiplication tables took many students by surprise. Every day, our master, Sangat Singh *ji*, used a stick to punish the children deficient in remembering them. With God's grace, I had a good memory, and more so, my sister and cousins made sure that I went to school fully prepared. I remember, I used to tie my turban quite impeccably when I was in fourth standard. In fact, my turban used to be appreciated very often in the school assembly—thanks to my cousins Rajinder Singh and his elder brother, Mohinder Singh. Even my sisters were very particular

---

[6] Police Station
[7] A wooden piece for practicing writing

about my school uniform. I used to arrange my uniform the previous night and was always ready for school on time.

As a small child, I used to be very scared of going out alone, like while going through the deserted path to our fields. So, both my Bibiji and Dadiji used to prepare me to be brave and told me to chant '*Waheguru Waheguru*' on my way to the fields. I sincerely followed that out of fear, or maybe, I had some liking for *Gurbani,* as Bibiji used to recite it every day in the morning while grinding wheat, and sometimes, she would even take me in her lap while chanting. This daily habit of listening to Gurbani must have had its positive effect as I was becoming emotionally stronger each day. Anyway, this fear of loneliness did remain deeply seated in me till I was in fourth standard. I was good in studies and was made the monitor of the class. During that time, an incident took place. One early morning, my mother asked me to go to the fields where labourers were working with my father. This field was one mile away and the path was lonely. I set off and soon started running towards the fields. When I was approximately 100 yards from the fields, I could only see the heads of all the labourers working in the fields. I quickly counted 15 heads and came running to my house as I was getting late for school. As soon as I informed my mother that there were 15 men working in the fields, she started to prepare food for all of them. But, somehow, there was a delay in packing the food in the *tokra*[8] and delivering them to the fields. Because of this delay, my father, in a hot temper, came home and scolded, even abused my mother and sister. Dadiji came to their rescue and told Bapuji that Bibiji got a bit delayed, as she had to prepare food for 15 labourers. Bapuji became even more furious and inquired who had told her that 15 men were working while I had only five with me. I was fortunate to have been away in school at that moment; otherwise, Waheguru knows, what would have happened!

When I came home from school, my mother asked me again, 'How many men were working in our field?' I repeated,'15'. There came one slap on my face, leaving me stunned, but continued to say, 'I counted 15 heads'. She informed me only five were working in our field. There

____

[8] Type of a basket

were 10 more working in an adjoining field for someone else. I then realized my mistake and apologized, joining my hands. A bigger wrath was yet to come from Bapuji. I ran to my Dadiji's lap and begged for help. She somehow managed to work it out for me so that I would not have to come in front of my father on the same day. Bapuji had gone to the northern fields and she told me to head to the eastern fields to collect *chara*[9] for buffaloes and bulls. She also advised me to reach home before him, so that I finish my food and go to sleep early; and that, next day, situation would be different. Sure enough, I got saved as Bapuji only advised me to work more sincerely and honestly and things would eventually work out better and fall in place by itself. I thanked my Waheguru and promised not to do a half-hearted work in future. That day onwards, my outlook and boldness changed to be better. I thanked Dadiji and sought her blessings in the future too.

I was more attached to my Dadiji than my Babaji as he was mostly away on work. I was too young to realize when my grandfather expired as I was only in second standard back then. I do remember having seen a huge gathering of people in our house—all dressed in white and plain clothes—to pay their final respect to him, the mukhiya of 17 villages. May be that was the day of the funeral of my grandfather. As children were not supposed to be around, we were taken away to my maasi's[10] house by my Bhuaji and were made to stay there the whole day.

Days of Middle School

When I got promoted to class five, there was a tea party to celebrate with lots of sweets like *laddus* along with *pakoras*. While on one hand, everyone was overjoyed for my promotion to the next class, both my elder sisters on the other hand were forced to terminate their school from sixth and eighth standards respectively. It all happened due to the pressure of fees and farm work of my father, as it was difficult to arrange ready cash every month in those days. In fact, it was not only about the fee—the extra expenses for uniforms and various activities of the school was also difficult to manage. As a farmer, my father used

---

[9] Fodder
[10] Elder sister of my mother

to get crops twice a year, whereas, our fees and home expenditure was a monthly requirement. Those expenses were managed by buying *daal*[11], masalas and even fodder for buffaloes on credit from our *baniya*[12] in exchange of wheat or maize from us every six months. We also had sugarcane cultivated in our farms with which *gurh*[13] or *shakker*[14] was made through a laborious process once a year. Sometimes, the *baniyas* used to demand *gurh* in exchange of the items they used to give us on credit.

My younger brother, Sarabjit, was only two years younger to me. He had a bit of a stronger built than me when I was his age. We went to the same school and I got promoted to the fifth standard. At that time, there were two permanent workers in our *haveli*[15] to look after all three of our buffaloes and four bulls. I must say that my father was a very proud owner of strong and good-looking bulls in the village. In those days, whenever any boy got married in the village, the bride would be brought to the bridegroom's house by a *gaddi*[16] pulled by our bulls only, as they were the best in the village. I remember, I attended at least 10 marriages where our cart and bulls were used. A pair of bulls used to be called '*Jorhi*'. We had two *Jorhi* of bulls and my father used to be called, 'Good looking and healthy *Jorhian wala Babbaji*'.

---

[11] Lentils
[12] Trader
[13] Jaggery syrup
[14] Brown sugar
[15] House
[16] Cart

After joining 5th standard, I started taking a lot of interest in *Khudo Kundi*—local hockey game where sticks like this were used—

And the balls used to be soft, specially made of cloth and with cross-stitches all around it. There were some boys from our adjoining *mohallas*[17] and the two of us—my cousin Gurdip and I—played *Khudo Kundi* almost everyday and it used to be a match between two teams. We used to keep the same teams for weeks together. I must mention all the names of my fellow players—Avtar, Garmail, Harpal, Sarwan, Dev and Sadhu. We also used to play hide-and-seek from our homes up to the place where all farmers used to thresh their wheat crop—place known as *pirh*[18].

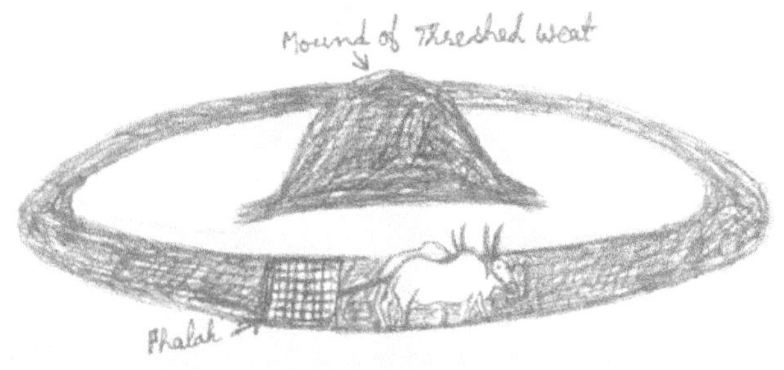

WHEAT   THRESHING   IN   OLDEN DAYS

---

[17] Streets
[18] A hard-surfaced field for manual threshing of wheat with phalah pulled by bulls

For the play of hide-and-seek, all the girls, including my sisters and cousins, and even girls from adjoining *mohallas* used to join after finishing their household obligations. We used to play until 10 o'clock at night. We were a group of 10 to 12 boys and girls every evening for the game. I must mention, in those days there was no discrimination between boys and girls. We were all like brothers and sisters. All the parents were assured of our behaviour towards each other. I must mention the names of the girls in our group as well—Jeeto, Debo, Mindho, Kundo, Sewo, Baksho and many others.

From fifth standard onwards, I also started to take part in school games like basketball and volleyball. Since I was of a lean structure, it took me two years to master my basketball and volleyball game. This is when we also started to study English along with other subjects like Mathematics, Punjabi, Science, History, Geography and religious studies. I remember an interesting incident that took place in this class which taught me to be cautious in such situations. Sadhu and Shinda, both from my village, were playfully trying to break each other's slate during recess. There was a great commotion. Sitting opposite each other, they were hitting the other's slate turn by turn. I happened to see that and went to ask Sadhu to stop as they were damaging their slates. I leaned over Sadhu and told him to stop that idiotic deed. However, Sadhu was determined to hit Shinda's slate, and thus, raised his slate upwards with quite a force. Since I was leaning over him, the edge of his iron slate struck me in my forehead, right in between the eyes. Sadhu pulled his slate and a fountain of blood started flowing from my forehead. I tried to stop the flow with my fingers while crying aloud. Our headmaster, Shri Kartar Singh Bains, was close by. On hearing my cries, he came to the spot. After knowing the whole story, he had beaten Sadhu up with his stick that we used to call *bainth* and had also punished Shinda. I was taken to the school dispensary for treatment and after nursed with first-aid, I was sent home, escorted by two other classmates. After a rest of two days, I was back in school. Sadhu, however, had kept that incident at the back of his mind and secretly even tried to kick me a couple of times despite my sincere attempts to make him realize his and my own mistake. Anyway, he used to consider himself the *dada* of brahmin boys. He neither played any games, nor was he good in studies. Finally, he left the school after class eight. So long he was in school, he went to a different section and so, I had very little to do with him.

My Farming Experience

I was in 8th standard and my younger brother Sarabjit was in 6th. During this time, our househelp, Omi, who was a big help to my father in farming and in looking after the cattle, left our work and went to Bombay to become an actor. He used to act in domestic drama shows in our village and was highly appreciated for his good looks. His absence made it extremely difficult for Bapuji to manage all the work alone. So, he decided to sell one *jorhi*[19], out of the two, of our bulls because he could only utilize one *jorhi* everyday. At this time, I and Sarabjit both became very concerned and reminded my father, 'We have the best of the bulls in the village! We really wish you should not sell the Jorhi!' To this, he asked, 'Will you people ploy the *khet*[20] with me then?' 'Yes!' we exclaimed. He told us to think about this offer again as he reminded,'You have to continue your studies too'. We both replied, 'Never mind, we are prepared to go through this tough time'. For almost one year, our routine was tied up with our father's schedule. Over and above that, we had to attend school, that too everyday on time. After this decision, he used to wake us up at 4 o'clock in the

---

[19] Pair
[20] Fields

morning and put us on a *gadda*[21] and take all four bulls to the *khet* to plough the fields. I remember, the journey to the *khet* generally took about 20 minutes. We used to use those minutes to steal some sleep on the *gadda* and it felt like *amrit*—a blissful pleasure!

Soon after reaching the fields, he used to start ploughing ahead of us and we, turn by turn, followed him with the second Jorhi. Our bulls were very intelligent. They used to follow our father's path very well and that way I used to start first and then Sarabjit, after about an hour, would take his turn. After that, I used to cut *chara* from the nearby field and put it on the *gadda* to be carried home for the cattle.

It is pertinent to define the significance of my school bell. This bell was a thick brass plate of one-foot diameter. It was tied to a tripod and was kept on the roof of my school. It could be heard up to 3 to 4 kilometres easily. One can imagine that in those times this was a tremendous help to keep track of time. Shri Dina Nath ji, our school's peon, would ring it with a hammer one hour before school time as our first warning bell. On hearing the first bell, we used to leave our *khet* on our *gadda,* pulled by one Jorhi of bulls, towards our house. We would reach home, tie the bulls, empty the *gadda* and put *chara* for the bulls in the *khurli*[22]. About half an hour later, the second bell would ring, before which we would wash up, get into our uniform and be ready with our school bags. Our mother used to pack two *paranthas*[23] rolled up. We used to pick that and run to the school while stuffing them into the mouth. Our school was a kilometre away from our house. We used to make it to the school before the third bell, just in time for the morning school prayer. Imagine this happening for almost a year and we were never late to the school, not even for a

---

[21] Cart
[22] Eating pot for the bulls
[23] Flatbread folded with dollops of ghee

day. You will be surprised to know, in spite of our extremely busy routine at home and school, we both would finish our homework immaculately and regularly. I was one of the brilliant students of my class.

In school we had two teachers, Pandits by caste. One was very fair looking and the other had a dark complexion. They were known as *Gorra Pandha* and *Kala Pandha*. Both of them were very sincere and serious about teaching. *Gorra Pandha* used to teach English language to three classes and *Kala Pandha* used to teach Hindi language to the same three classes. Literally the gora and kala colours matched the subjects they were teaching! I am proud to say that both these teachers were very appreciative of my progress in class, especially about my handwriting both in English and Hindi. My notebooks used to be circulated among the other classes as an example to emulate. *Gorra Pandha* was very particular about spellings and English handwriting. We all had to use only GB NIB (fountain pens with nib & ink, we had to refill them often on our own) to write and no other pen was allowed. Besides having a good handwriting, I also used to memorize (*muh jawani yaad karna*) all the spellings very well and was ahead of the class at all times as rote learning was the norm those days.

At home, my mother was very particular that we—all brothers and sisters—recite *Gurbani* in the morning as well as before going to bed. She taught us a short *ardas*[24] which we used to chant every night. Even though our *ardas* was short, our list of demands from Waheguru was very long and it was repeated with ardent faith and conviction every night before going to sleep. We felt protected by Waheguru and whenever I was in any kind of trouble, I prayed to him and invariably got out of the situation. My faith was becoming stronger each day and before commencing any new project or starting on a journey, I would recite my prayers.

One evening, when I was playing football with my friends in my school playground, barefoot. I suddenly saw my family members— my father, mother, elder sisters and younger brother—show up at the

---

[24] Prayer

playground. They told me that in a nearby village a couple of saints had come and they were performing *Akhand Path*[25]. Since they all were going there, I was asked to accompany them too. I, thus, joined them and set course barefoot only. After sometime, it got dark and we had to walk through a narrow path to reach the main road from Garhdiwala to Dasuya. The main road was lined with tall mango trees on both the sides. By then it had become quite dark and we were almost reaching our destination where *Akhand Path* was being recited. There were a lot of different types of tents and the place was illuminated by many kerosene-lanterns. While looking towards that well-lit sight, I could hardly see the road clearly; nevertheless, since I was more excited than others, I was leading everyone. I might have been about 8 to 10 paces ahead of others when I suddenly saw something like a dry branch of a mango tree lying on the road, right in front of me. In my wisdom, I thought I should step over it, break it, pick it up and throw it away from the road. I lifted my right foot and tried to step on top of the presumably dry branch. As I brought my foot down, I heard a loud sound like 'HISSSSS' and sensed a quick movement between my legs. To my horror, it was a snake! On partly seeing and sensing this sound and movement, I jumped forward with a loud cry and warned everyone,'There is a *Dhartiwala Baba* right here!'That's how snakes were referred to in those days. On hearing this commotion, all nearby devotees ran towards me with lanterns in their hands. They spotted that snake and one of them quickly broke a branch from the mango tree and hit it several times until it was dead. Later, we were told that it was a black Cobra, one of the most poisonous snakes, with a massive length of 4 foot. I think, it was out of shock and fear that I kept crying and even ended up having a very high fever that night. My family members and I were extremely thankful to Waheguru for saving me from a sudden possible encounter with death. I could still feel the snake's fluttering breath which sounded like 'HISSSSS' as we returned to our home the next day after the *bhog* ceremony of *Akhand Path*[26].

---

[25] Recitation of Guru Granth Sahib Ji
[26] Completion of recitation of Guru Granth Sahib Ji

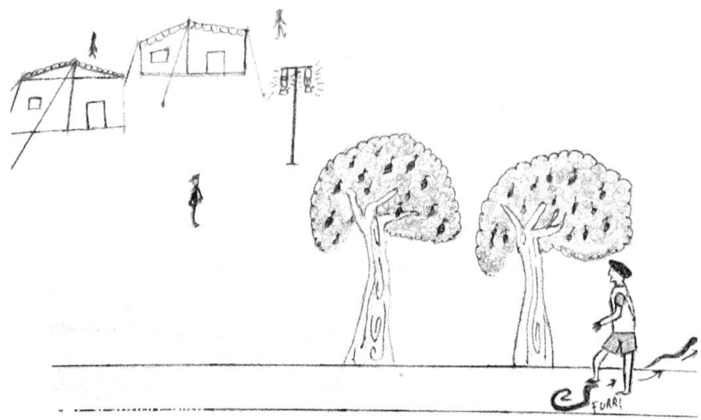
FURR!

3

LOOKING BACK AT THE TEENAGE YEARS

Ipaid equal attention to not only every task given to me but also to my sports. My school had the largest playground in the district of Hoshiarpur. There were two hockey grounds, one football ground, two basketball grounds, two volleyball grounds, one Kabaddi ground and one race track of 440 yards. We also had a lot of spare space for the spectators where our Physical Training classes would be held generally. I am proud to say that my school produced a number of national and international players. The headmaster of our school was very generous and kind to the players as far as their daily diet and preparation for the district tournaments was concerned. But, at the same time, he was very strict and particular about the academics of the players. To attract a greater number of players to play maximum number of games, he had authorized half a *ser*[27] of milk for each player for taking an active part in one game. If a student played four games, he used to get 2*sers* of milk to drink. Headmaster also put a condition that the player must represent the school team in inter-school tournaments. So, these were the standing instructions given to the *halwai*[28] of the canteen in the school. At that time, I was playing three games and was also participating in athletics for the school. The free milk was given only to high school players of classes 9 and 10.

When I was in 7th standard, one more incident gave me another life lesson. One evening, our school seniors wanted to practise a football game but they were running short of one player. They called me and asked me to join them for practise. They knew that I was good

---

[27] A unit of measuring weight
[28] Sweet maker

at football since they had seen me practise with *gendh*[29]. On getting invitation from seniors, I became overconfident and talkative while going near the goal post of the opposite team. I think I was doing that to distract the goalkeeper and one of the full-back players. As luck would have it, I managed to score one goal as I was playing in the position of the centre-forward. After sometime, I attempted the same trick again. This time, one of the full-back players stopped the ball, aimed at me and kicked it very hard. Sure enough, the ball hit straight on my face—forehead and partly on my nose. I immediately went into a spin, fell on the ground and for about a good 15 seconds, I did not know where I was. All my teammates got together and gave me some water to drink. They advised me to leave the game and rest. Anyway, I realized my stupidity and felt ashamed for my mistake. However, I did not leave the game but played the rest of the time very sincerely. At the end of the game, we all had a good laugh at this episode. However, I had learnt my lesson—to never tease or distract the opponent players while playing.

During that period, apart from plucking mangoes by aiming and hitting stones, I also picked a hobby of making kites and flying them. Besides this, I also started making paper darts, which I used to call hawaijahaj[30], and would launch them with my hands while standing on the high roof of my house. And each time, I tried to surpass the previous distance covered by my dart aeroplane. I knew nothing about aerodynamics and had never even heard that word but I used to shape and reshape my aeroplanes in such a fashion that they cover maximum distance while flying and landing on the ground. Designing and flying peculiar new designs of kites and experiment with their stability in the air intrigued me. Flying kites was not a new fixation for me. When I was a little kid, I had designed a paper kite to fly with a thread tied to my finger. I used to run in an open ground with sufficient wind to give a lift to my kite. I used to make the wings of the kite quite flat but at the end of wings, I used to give an upward twist which made the kite quite stable in the air, allowing it to fly at a very steep angle. These raised edges on the kite's wings later on became the winglets on small and bigger

---

[29] Rubber ball of 2-3 inches diameter
[30] Aeroplane

aeroplanes. I am sure, many aerodynamics experts would have done these kinds of experiments for the acceptance of this latest design of aeroplanes. I was totally ignorant but my interest in designing was natural and certainly not attributed to any guidance from the family members. In fact, all of them used to discourage me as I was wasting too many papers and time. My elder sister, Surjit, was always on my side as she saw how thrilled I would be with such activity, and in fact, she was my paper supplier to help me make differently shaped kites. Both of us were 'number one' enemy of all the other members of the family who were our age. Whereas, we both got along very well in all situations and stood by each other in difficult situations and times. Many a times, to save me from our Bibiji's wrath, she would take the blame for my misdeeds.

My parents initially discouraged me as I was wasting too many papers and also because sometimes, I used to pinch and tear papers from the notebooks of my cousins. That action of mine got me into trouble at least two times and my father received those complaints. My father, being my *Guru*, used to play it cool and advise me in his own way in Punjabi language. From his words I felt a deep lovemingled with a sense of caring, understanding and acceptance. He also had very high expectations from me. His support and encouragement were always there for me, may it be sports, studies, hobbies, house work or field work for advancement of agriculture growth. These activities helped in providing me a solid base from which I could grow to my own potential. Whenever I was late in doing my allotted work, he did reprimand me. That, I think, made me efficient and punctual in every sphere. My father used to tell me in Punjabi, '*Jo bhi kam karo, poore dil, dimaag ate rooh naal karo, kam beshak chhote ton chhota howe. Yeh hi kamyabi da raaz hai*'. If I translate that in English, it would be something like this—'Put your heart, mind and soul into even your smallest acts. This is the secret of success'. I always kept my spirits and self-motivation at its highest even amidst extreme discouragement and confusion created by my cousins or friends.

When I was in 7th standard, a very funny incident took place. Our headmaster, Kartar Singh Bains, while taking our English class, called me and asked me to bring a book lying on his table in his office. He said that the title of the book is *Psychology*. I ran to his office and saw only one book lying on his table which I read as ਪਸਾਈਚੋਲੋਜੀ (Psai·cholo·jee). In Punjabi, it meant, 'To lure a girl'. I quickly came back and told my headmaster, 'Sorry sir, there is no such book on the table, but there is one book titled ਪਸਾਈਚੋਲੋਜੀ (Psai·cholo·jee)'. He smiled and said, 'Go, get that book'. I quickly left to bring that book and on my way back, kept thinking, why the hell is he calling this book 'Psychology' (sai·kaa·luh·jee) when the title written on it is ਪਸਾਈਚੋਲੋਜੀ (Psai·cholo·jee)? I handed over that book to headmaster. He at first had a good laugh and then told the entire class how to pronounce 'psychology' correctly as sai kaa luh jee where the letter P is silent. The whole class also had a good laugh at my expense. May be many of them also might have not known the spelling but their gesture put me to shame. Headmaster ordered me to write the spelling of 'psychology' one hundred times and show to him. After this incident, I started mugging up all the spellings, even those with peculiar spellings as English is known to be a funny language with hardly any fixed rules for spelling and pronunciation. By the end of three months, many students of my class used to ask spellings from me as I had finally mastered the art of spellings. The same year, headmaster had organised a spelling competition among four sections of class 7. I scored 100% marks along with Pritam Singh, Sham Sunder, Kewal Singh and Hardyal Singh. My Headmaster gave me a pat on my back and said, 'Very well done'. That had truly encouraged me and I strongly believe that even smallest of gestures by teachers are taken as extremely motivating. And motivation plays a very important role in our life, not only as children but even adults respond very well to it.

With only three months of time left for our term to end, we were getting very busy with our studies. One day, an ex-student of Khalsa High School, who was from a nearby village named Bhanna, came to our school and was introduced as an Indian Air Force Pilot. He had joined Indian Air Force as a pilot and was posted at Adampur *Hawai Adda*[31]. He was a great inspiration for all of us. He once flew his light aircraft over our school and had even performed some *kalawazian*[32] for us. On seeing this, our headmaster gave us 10 minutes of break to watch those *kalawazian*. After watching that, I was really motivated to join IAF and fly like a bird in the sky and perform similar *kalawazian*. Our headmaster informed us about the functioning of Indian Air Force and we learnt a little bit about the aircraft, pilots and aerobatics (kalawazian) that day. He also mentioned that, to join the airforce, one must be good in studies, especially in science and mathematics, and speak English fluently. His words got drilled into my brain like a nail and I knew that my hobby was already somewhat intellectually excellent. I felt an exciting tremor in my whole body. I controlled my emotions and did not mention it to anyone. However, I did mention it to my father one evening. But his reaction somehow was strange and did not favour me. He sternly said, 'Do not daydream; concentrate wholeheartedly on your studies, farming and household work'. Though at first I did not like the answer, but in introspection, I understood that he wanted me to work harder and study well which would eventually enhance my desire of accomplishment. In those days it was difficult to plan ahead because of our limited resources and agricultural environment.

During this time, my cousin Mohinder Singh started a Cinema Talkie in our village. He used to spend a lot of time in making it entertaining to all the villagers, including people from the neighbouring villages. I was given the duty to carry his meals in a tiffin-box in the evenings. I really loved to do that work because, sometimes, Mohinder used to allow me to watch the movie playing in his Cinema Talkie. Carrying his meals

---

[31] Air Force Station
[32] Aerobatics

was my daily routine and I did it with pleasure. Once it so happened, one of his gatekeepers left the job and a movie titled *Shivratri* was to start that day. Mohinder told me to look after the gate and not allow anyone to enter the movie hall without a ticket. I stood at the gate and kept checking all the tickets. I used to cut half of the ticket and hand over the other half to the person entering the so-called hall. Actually, the Talkie had huge tent walls and tarpaulin (hard canvas cloth) cover with plenty of windows and only four gates. For ladies there was a separate enclosure. There was tarpaulin spread on ground for class-two viewers and for class-one there were chairs. I started managing the gate of class-one enclosure daily and it suited Mohinder Singh because he did not have to pay any gatekeeper. Movie *Shivaratri* was airing for 25 days in the movie hall and I saw all the 25 shows of the movie! I really enjoyed that phase until, to my dismay, Mohinder hired another gatekeeper. I had by then even memorized almost all the major dialogues and songs of that movie.

During this period, our morning routine continued and I kept playing hockey, basketball and volleyball in school. Every attendance had to be met by running against time. I used to wish that the day had 28 hours instead of 24 hours. Slowly, this strain started showing on my health. I sometimes felt out of breath while running between my house, *khets* and school. But there was one good thing that happened—I picked up an interest in running which prompted me to go for school athletics. I did try for qualifying trials but since I did not qualify in games and athletics to the school standards; unfortunately I was not selected to join any team for district tournament.

Before our final exams, we used to get 10 to 15 days of study leave. All students were required to stay home and get well prepared for the final examinations of their respective classes. I felt that this time was extremely crucial and beneficial for my preparation, as I wanted to do well. To my fortune, my father started to spare us sufficient time, so that our preparation for final exam did not get affected. However, running from pillar to post was relentless. With Waheguru Ji's grace, my concept of studying and the place and environment for studying was very clear. I wanted no distraction in my room, where I sat on a chair next to the table and always avoided my bed to read or write. We were always given a table and chair each to do our homework as well as final-exam preparations. During the day, I used to go to the nearby field to study under the shade of trees. To make myself comfortable, I used to place my *asana*[33] under a tree and loved to study sitting on it every day. On the day of my first exam, I was well prepared and took the exam quite confidently. Every day, my elder sister, cousins, parents and Dadiji used to ask me how I did in my examination. I had only one typical answer in Punjabi, '*Paper gaddh ditta*'. These words clearly indicated that I had done well in exam. After the exams were over, we again were given a short holiday for leisure to enjoy ourselves. My father, however, had other plans for me. He would load me with work to the brim and I always struggled hard to find time for my games and hobbies. I was allowed to fly kites only in an open field and never on the roof of my house. There had been an accident in our village when a 7-year-old boy lost his life while flying a kite on the roof of his house. In an attempt to get the lift for his kite, he ran backwards and tripped on the edge of the roof (small *banera*). He had fallen, head down, on a concrete area and became unconscious. He was rushed to our town government hospital where he finally had succumbed to his injuries. So, ever since then, no parents ever allowed their children to fly kites on the roof. Bapuji had to warn us only once. When we looked at his stern face, the message sank in like a bolt and we never went for flying kites on the roof. During this vacation, we had a lot of spare time at night before going to sleep, so, this became the time for our bedtime stories when *Dadiji* would narrate stories of our Guru Sahib Ji, starting from our first guru, Guru Nanak Sahib Ji, to Guru Gobind Singh Ji. Nights went by hearing myriad stories from *Dadiji*, punctuated by emotional moments spent together while listening to the *qurbani* (sacrifice) of *Chaar Sahibzadey* (four sons of Shri Guru Gobind Singh Ji). With rapt attention we heard how Guru Gobind Singh Ji prepared Banda Singh Bahadur and sent to Punjab to seek revenge from the then Mughal emperor. These *kathas* (religious stories) were like our history lessons through which we also learnt how Guru Granth Sahib Ji became our last Guru. These *kathas*, despite being orally passed on, were well known amongst almost everyone through the generations. So, all these

---

[33] Quilted cushion

stories are not touched upon or written in this book. However, there are passing references to these stories as examples to emulate when I recite Gurbani or Mool Mantra.

The declaration of our results for the final examination put everyone in a joyous mood as we were all thrilled to get promoted to higher classes. Gurdip, my cousin, joined class 9, I joined class 8 and my brother, Sarabjit, got promoted to class 6.On the day of the results, my two elder sisters were so excited that they bought sweets from the *halwai* in bazaar and distributed them among all the family members. Being a joint family, we were a total of 20 members, excluding my *Chacha ji*[34] and stepbrother, Amrik Singh. While *Chacha ji* was on duty as a railway guard, Amrik was at his station of duty in the Indian Army. I distinctly remember that on that day we all made Dadiji eat at least half *ser* of laddus. The poor old lady was so uncomfortable that she demanded a glass of hot tea to swallow that sweet stuff down her throat. My mother soon hurried to the kitchen to prepare tea for all of us. It was one family feast that we all had thoroughly enjoyed. Whenever we had similar gatherings with the entire family, we used to indulge in a lot of leg pulling which was taken in light spirit by everyone. Since I was very active and always took the lead among cousins, I inevitably would end up making hurried decisions too. I used to be the talk of the town and also the centre of attention in our family I was fortunate enough to have Dadiji around me to always take my side. She knew that I never said a 'no' to anything or any work given to me. When everyone used to be gossiping, lying down on his or her bed at night, someone would ask, 'Harbans, please get me a glass of water from the pitcher' or someone else would demand a blanket or a quilt or a bedsheet. They all relied on me to do the chores. No one ever asked my younger brother or my cousins because they would refuse and say, 'You go and get it, we are not your servant'. Therefore, it always came down to me as I did oblige, offering every one any kind of help. This habit gave me an edge over others, with love and affection of the entire family showered upon me. It gave me an impression of warmth, acceptance and competence. Maybe it is the law of nature that most of us instinctively pattern our lives in a way to please those around us and by this, acquire a sense

---

[34] Uncle

of acceptability. Now I realize that confidence of the family in one can certainly provide a structure for self-discipline and self-reliance, which is a necessary and essential ingredient of adult life. Even our teachers, by showing us a disciplined as well as a creative way of solving problems, also played a very important role in our lives.

I felt that I was fortunate to have been gifted the talent of an artist, beside other things. With good sketching skills, I pencil-sketched Taj Mahal of Agra when I was in class 8. That piece of work had eventually found a frame in my school library for many years to come. My drawing master was highly satisfied with my art skills as I would always secure 90% marks in any type of drawing. I think it was a natural gift by my Waheguru. Apart from that, I also had a very sharp memory. In my 9th standard, during speeches or school talks, I used to easily memorize 15 to 20 pages and speak flawlessly without referring to any paper, but of course, it was all in Punjabi language in those days.

With the advancement of the classes, the responsibilities kept on increasing. I was in 8th, my younger brother in 6th and younger sister was in 5th class. The burden of uniforms, other clothing, pocket money and above all, school fees, started to weigh down upon my father. As it is a well-known fact that farmers are rich in only *Harhi*[35] and *Sauni*[36]. The ripe crops like wheat, maize, lentils and *gurh*, made out of sugarcane juice, were available for our consumption only twice a year, which were stored for the whole year. But day-to-day expenses started to seem like a monster eating away all our bread. During this time, my father thought of a scheme to make some extra money by using one of our *jorhi* of bulls and cart to deliver load for some *baniyas* and also carry wood for saw mills. This brought us some ready cash every now and then. My duty on most of the Sundays and holidays was to find out where to get load from and then do the needful. This way, we managed our school fees and some other day-to-day expenditure, too. It was a very lofty task and sometimes it got awfuly tiring and boring as well. However, what constantly kept me motivated was an urge to help my father, who always worked tirelessly for days and nights for his entire family. Here I must mention, the unconditional

---

[35] Harvest of wheat
[36] Harvest of maize and sugarcane

love that I received from my grandmother, mother, aunts and cousins, and above all, from my own brothers and sisters, always motivated me and prepared me to give my best. I also had a charitable attitude, which, inspired me to always help others. My purpose was to go all out while extending a helping hand. I did not limit this to only my own family, but to all my neighbours, villagers and also to anyone in need. I never cared to ask anyone's caste as was the norm those days while offering my unconditional help. This instilled a feeling of love for humanity as a whole.

4

GAMES I GREW UP PLAYING

I cannot not mention the rural games of Punjab, which I played while growing up. With keen interest and a natural precision, I earned a good name as a scorer in *Khudo Kundi*, football, *Gulli Danda*, *Pithhoo Garam* (also known as *Pithhoo Kaem*) and *Annar Choochi*.

Pithhoo-Garam; Source: Google

This game is also an exclusive part of the culture of Punjab. The game refreshes the charming memories of one's childhood and it takes one back to the golden period of his/her life. There is a big trend of this game in the villages of Punjab. The game does not require any special equipment except for a rubber ball and five–six flat disc stones. The importance of the game is that it generates a lot of team spirit and co-ordination among the young children.

> *Life must be lived with love and humour,*
> *Love to understand and humour to endure.*

Let me tell you what the game of *Annar Choochi* is. We used to put one person in the middle and place a piece of wood on the ground between his legs. He was to guard that wooden piece while others around would try to distract him. One would have to pick the wooden piece in the meantime, without being touched by the centre man. If the centre man touched the person before he picked up the piece, he would have to shift to the centre, and likewise, all of us took turns and laughed like crazy, happy children. Hours would breeze through, as we would be engrossed in playing this game.

There was another game, which we used to play very often. This game is known as *Bara Tehni* (twelve stones). This game was most probably derived from Chinese checkers and it was quite famous in Punjab. To play this game, two players used twelve differently shaped or coloured stones on both sides. It could go on for hours together and was very good in improving one's memory and retention power. Though it was a time-consuming game, it would help in the overall growth of the young kids if played once in a while. The one who would collect the maximum *tehnis* or *geetis* (stones) would be considered the winner.

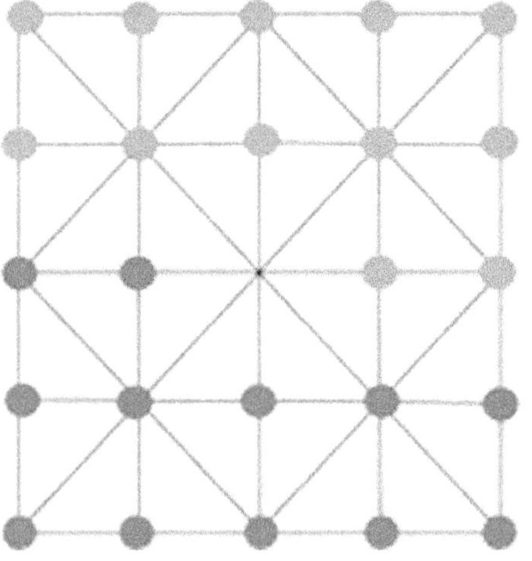

Gulli Danda, also known as *Gilli Danda*, is a familiar game in North India.

Gilli Danda is played with two equipments—a *danda*, a long wooden stick, and *gilli*, a small oval-shaped piece of wood. It is played with 4 or more players of even numbers and can even go up to100 players.

Standing in a small circle, the player balances the *gilli* on a stone in an inclined manner (some what like a see-saw), with one end of the *gilli* touching the ground while the other end is in the air. The player then uses the *danda* to hit the *gilli* at the raised end, which flips it into the air. While it is in the air, the player strikes the *gilli*, hitting it as hard as possible. Having struck the *gilli*, the player is required to run and touch a pre-agreed point outside the circle before an opponent retrieves the gilli. There are no specific dimensions of gilli danda and it does not have a limited number of players.

The *gilli* becomes airborne after it is struck. If a fielder from the opposing team catches the *gilli*, the striker is out. If the *gilli* lands on the ground, the fielder closest to the *gilli* has one chance to hit the *danda* (which has to be placed on top of the circle used) with a throw

(similar to a run-out in cricket). If the fielder is successful, the striker is out; if not, the striker scores one point and gets another opportunity to strike. The team (or individual) with the most points wins the game. If the striker fails to hit the *gilli* in three tries, the striker is out (similar to a strikeout in baseball). After the *gilli* has been struck, the opposing players need to return to the circle or, in the best case, catch it in mid-air without it hitting the ground—this was believed to have later evolved into a caught-out in cricket and baseball.

Somehow, I had very good aim and used to hit the *danda* from quite a distance. I was regarded as a good *Gilli Danda* player. But my team had to pay the price by giving one extra player to the opposite team. My smart cousin, Gurdip, dearly known as Deeka, who was one year senior to me, devised this compensating system. My uncle, his dad, was in the Indian Railways and so got frequently transferred to various new cities in India. Since his family accompanied him, Gurdip had a good exposure to good schooling. But now that his family was back in the village, he joined my school in 5th standard. At that time, I was in the 4th standard. With his manipulative attitude, he used to decide the teams in almost all the games that we played. For that reason, we used to call him *Chanakya*[37]. My aim being excellent, I used to remain the focal point in every game. I often wondered how I got an excellent aim and shooting precision as a gift from my Waheguru. In introspection, I think my excellent aiming skills came from plucking the mangoes from the trees by hitting stones and small sticks at the ripe mangoes.

We had three mango orchards for the entire family. My father used to sell the mangoes from two bigger orchards and distribute the money among his brothers. And the third orchard with 30 mango trees was kept for the whole family to cherish. We used to eagerly wait for the mango season because it used to be a lot of fun in collecting and

---

[37] Chanakya was an ancient Indian teacher, philosopher, economist, jurist and royal advisor. He is traditionally identified as Kautilya or Vishnugupta, who authored the ancient Indian political treatise, the Arthashastra, a text dated to roughly between the 2nd century BCE and the 3rd century CE. As such, he is considered the pioneer of the field of political science and economics in India, and his work is thought of as an important precursor to classical economics. Chanakya assisted the first Mauryan emperor Chandragupta in his rise to power. He is widely credited for having played an important role in the establishment of the Maurya Empire. Chanakya served as the chief advisor to both emperors Chandragupta and his son Bindusara.

relishing the fruits. Our relatives who did not have mango orchards of their own in their villages used to visit us to enjoy the ripe fruits. Interestingly, instead of plucking the mangoes and bringing them home for our guests, we used to take the guests to the orchard and pluck fresh mangoes and offer them right there. I improved my aiming skills by procuring a ripe mango in my first attempt itself. Hence, in a single hit, I would get one mango. May be it was the result of years of practise during many mango seasons since my childhood. But my excellent aim used to impress all our relatives. Even my brothers and sisters would ask me to get fruits for them too. This game may seem easy and funny but was full of danger because one had to keep a track of the stone too. Once, I threw a fairly big stone at a ripe mango and had managed to get it with a single shot. I quickly ran to catch the mango before it hits the ground, totally forgetting about the stone, which took a little extra time to travel through the branches. Sure enough, I managed to earn the mango along with a blow of the stone on my head. Luckily, it didn't need stitches but there was a big lump on my head, which kept hurting for almost a week.

I must tell you about one more game—*our* football. Though it was called football, it wasn't like the proper one. Here, we played with a rubber ball or a tennis ball. This ball was known as *gendh*. All rules of football were the same—only kicking the ball was allowed but goalkeeper could use hands to catch the ball. I had mastered this game quite well. We generally played football in a hockey field which was 100 yards long and 50 yards wide with goalposts only 10 feet apart. I was able to kick the ball from the middle of the field and score a goal, but at times, the goalkeeper would block and save the goal. Once, all my friends had organised a very interesting competition. Four of us were nominated and selected by other friends to take part in the event. One senior was appointed as a referee and others were to assist him. In this event, we all were to kick 10 balls each into the hockey goalpost from the middle line of the field. My friends who were participating were very excited and seemed to be highly confident in putting all ten balls into the goal post. I was always confident in this game but that day, seeing their confidence, my confidence wavered a bit and nervousness surged through me as my legs started shaking. However, what saved my day was that I was the last participant. The first one scored 3 goals, the second one secured 5 and the third one had 2 goals only. Then, as my turn came, I prayed to Waheguru to help me get at least 6 balls into the goalpost. To my surprise, I felt, with every kick, some godly power taking the ball straight to the goalpost. I managed to score 7 goals! My friends were screaming on top of their voices, cheering for me since the moment I went past 4 goals. I was absolutely thrilled to win this event, so, we all headed to the school tuck shop for a treat. I had spent a total of Rs.10 that day and in those days this amount was a huge sum. This was all the pocket money I had saved over three months that was kept with the tuck shopkeeper. Anyway, to become an uncrowned king, some price had to be paid!

All those native (desi) games were not new to us. Young boys and girls for generations have been playing those games. Somehow, these games became a passion for all of us. We had fun playing together. Every day was allotted with its share of fun that drove us crazy and motivated us for healthy competition, taught us to take loss lightly by laughing at each other. It, in general, taught us to embrace winning, losing, exercising, developing early social skills and learning many of life's lessons. Our elders always told us that fun and games must go together . So, they cannot be separated and are enjoyed at the same time. At times, there were so many innovative approaches to simple games to turn them into memorable fun. There were so many fantastic lessons I had learnt from them that I carried even to my adulthood.

Now a days, kids do not have enough time for those native games. The TV shows and mobile games take away their valuable time, which they could have utilized to develop personal skills and hone natural flare for games and competitive spirit. In our times, it seemed like we had much more time to spare than what the kids have today. In fact, the youth in our times enjoyed a lifestyle less structured, with more time in their hands. I personally feel that my involvement in those native games helped me in building a strong personality that certainly led to my personal success.

During the session of class 8, I got selected in the school's volleyball team. However, I was made ball pusher (playing near the net) for the smasher since I was shorter than the other players in the team. There was a boy named Jagtar Singh from the village Dhoot Kalan; he was our smasher. He had a very good height and could jump quite high to smash the ball on the opponent side. With this selection, I was entitled to half *ser* of free milk everyday from the school. I stopped carrying my heavy lunch from home, and instead, took a few snacks to enjoy with the milk from the school's tuck shop. My mother always insisted us to drink milk daily in the evening too to prepare us for heavy, extensive agricultural work. In the annual district tournaments, my school participated in games like kabaddi, hockey, basketball, volleyball and athletics. One boy of my village named Kewal Singh, intimately known as Keba, was very good in disc-throw. He represented our school and won the district shield for our school. That year, my school won district inter-school tournament in kabaddi, volleyball, basketball, and hockey as well as in disc-throw. When all the trophies came to our school, our headmaster declared one day holiday for the entire school in celebration. Extremely thrilled, we all headed home in sky-high spirits. This holiday was declared immediately after the first period of our school so our teachers did not even had a chance to load us with homework. As the bell rang, the students were already out of the school gate in seconds. No homework meant more time to play; then we also had our game of hide-and-seek till midnight. While hiding, we would end up disturbing everyone in the village because we used to hide in different houses. Various shortcuts were taken in attempts to hide by running and climbing onto the roofs of the adjoining houses. This special modus operandi was far beyond anyone's comprehension!

5

SOME THINGS MUNDANE
AND SOMETHING MARVELLOUS

After the district inter-school tournament was over, the seriousness of studies began to loom in the air. All teachers made us pull up our socks and the momentum picked up for our studies; and with momentum came plenty of homework. With constant engagement in helping my father with farm work and my usual play hours, I was so busy that the days seemed to be passing by quickly, like a dream. Talking of dreams, I remember having many interesting dreams at night. In my dreams, I would be running some distance until I get airborne, but not too high. I was able to visit places near my village. This used to happen almost every night. Once, I told my Dadiji about this and she said, 'you keep running around too much during the day and you want to complete every work in a hurry. That's why you fly like a bird and reach places faster in your dream. Just don't worry'. But these dreams never stopped, not even after my school got over and I do get them once in a while even now. I won't deny, but I really enjoyed these series of dreams.

Soon the time came when we were given 15 to 20 days of study leave before the final examination of another year. It was the same routine—hours of preparation, revising each subject everyday beneath the shady trees in the open field nearby. Along with my textbooks and notebooks, I also used to pack my lunch, *lassi*[38] and water. I had devised a meticulous method of studying—an hour allotted to each subject with breaks of 5 to 10 minutes in between starting another subject.

---

[38] Sweet buttermilk

It was just another day when I was sitting in my usual spot, under the tree when something extraordinary happened. Around noon, all of a sudden, a flying object caught my attention. It was landing in a field about 500 yards away from me. I remember that it was the month of March of 1956. I got up and ran towards that object which had lights flashing from it and was standing on three legs. As I was running towards that object, I saw two creatures, short in stature come out and go under it. When I was only 50 yards away, I saw those two creatures getting into the object through a ladder, which was in the opposite direction to me. Suddenly, the lights brightened, releasing fire and thick smoke, and within seconds, the object went up in the air and moved northwards and picked up speed beyond my comprehension. Soon it disappeared into the sky. I went over to that spot and saw three marks, almost the size of an elephant's footprint. It was the day I sighted a UFO!

There was also a spot in the middle of three-foot prints, which was completely scorched. I waited at that spot and looked around for someone else who might have been nearby to witness what I just witnessed. As it was around noon, there was no one in the vicinity as far as I could see. I kept wondering and thinking what this object could have possibly been. I remembered that once our headmaster had mentioned to us in a class about flying saucers. Approximately half an hour later, when I saw two men going towards my village, I ran up to them and asked them to check the ground and see the marks where the flying object had landed. They came with me and saw the spot. I told them the complete episode. However, not only were they unconvinced, they even questioned me, what was I doing there! I told them how I was studying about 500 yards away when it landed and how I ran to see everything. They asked me to take them to the spot where I was studying under the tree. My books were still lying there. After reaching that spot, they looked towards the spot of landing and concluded, '*Yeh ladka parh parh ke pagal ho gaya hai*'. It meant that too much of studying had turned me mad. They had a good laugh and then headed towards my village. Exasperated by their reactions, my head spun in annoyance because they did not believe what I had just witnessed. I picked up my books and reached home, hoping my family would take me seriously. Once I started narrating the same incident to my cousin brothers, they all broke into peals of laughter and completely disbelieved me. Anyway, I did not get discouraged and on the next day, on meeting my headmaster, I narrated the complete episode. After listening to me very patiently, even he remarked, 'Harbans, it cannot happen like that. These objects do not land on ground. Don't mention it to anyone else; people will call you a mad boy'. On hearing this from him, I was shocked and surprised. It took me a couple of months to reconcile and forget the sighting of the flying saucer landing on ground in spite of the physical indications on ground. Even today, I feel fortunate to have sighted a UFO, which is something so rare to experience.

I became a member of the school's hockey and basketball teams during class 8. Even while the preparations for final exams were in full swing, Deeka, my friends and I managed to practise both the games alternatively. Deeka was a mainstream player of our school and so he took a lot of interest to teach Sarabjit and me how to tackle and go past the opponent in a faster technique. He also helped us in imbibing a solid team spirit. He was incredibly focused but, to win a game, he was ready to go to any length. He would not hesitate to hit the hockey ball on the legs of the opponent or even gesticulate to hit, only to scare him and get his path cleared for scoring a goal. He had to win by hook or by crook. We all were very supportive of that and never took offence in his behaviour or rashness.

Another very interesting incident occurred during my tenure of class 8. Just before my final exams, one day, some people from a nearby village had come to my school and called for me. One of my teachers had known them so he came to inform this to me. They were sitting in the school tuck shop. They called me inside the shop and gave me plenty of sweets to eat (even my favourite, barfi) and kept discussing something among themselves. I thought they were friends of my father, that is why they were treating me like a special guest. Before they departed, one of them took out a one-rupee note and handed it over to me. I wasn't even told which village they had come from. They also instructed me to let my father know about this and left the tuck shop on a happy note, asking me to get back to my class. I must have spent about 15 minutes with them. I remember, one of them had asked me about my plans after class10. To that I had promptly answered that I would join a service—army or civil to earn some money to support my parents and siblings. I was indeed very happy to have a one-rupee note in hand, all to myself! I immediately went to Beant Singh's bicycle shop and booked a cycle on rent to paddle everyday during recess, which generally was for half an hour, at the cost of one anna. I gave that one rupee to Beant Singh and spent one anna from it on the same day. After the school hours, we went for hockey practise. Soon after practise, I ran home, dropped my school bag and ran to fetch fodder for buffaloes from a nearby field. At night, while sitting for dinner, I excitedly narrated to my parents and Dadiji how the men had come to visit me and had handed me one rupee. When my father enquired about the rupee, I said, 'I have given it to Beant Singh to rent a cycle during recess everyday for the next 16 days. Today was my first day!'My grandmother asked for the names of those people and their village. I told her I knew nothing. That seemed to vex them even more. I received one stern Punjabi *gali* (abuse) from my father and then my mother went on to explain how those people had slyly established *thakka*[39] of their daughter with me. The moment I heard that, the earth beneath my feet seemed to slip away as anger and frustration surged through me. Now the real problem that stood ahead of us was to find those people, so that my father could return their rupee. My marriage was out of question because my immediate elder sister was yet to be married. I couldn't even recall the name of the teacher who had called me and sent me to the tuckshop. Meanwhile, everyone at home racked his brain with one guess after another but reached no concrete result. With no access to telephones in those days, all messages used to be delivered through friends and acquaintances. Hence, the lull and suspense followed for three more days. Every night during those days

---

[39] Half engagement in matrimony

at dinner, I was bombarded with questions from everyone in the family, inquiring about those men. Finally, on the fourth day, I stumbled upon that teacher and begged him for the name of those people. Even though he was unsure, he remembered the name of the village they came from. As soon as the bell for recess rang, I ran home and told the name of the village to my mother and Dadiji. Bapuji went to that village and met their *lumberdar*[40] and inquired why had someone from his village done such an act. To my father's surprise, the *lumberdar* owned the responsibility and told my father that he, along with his two younger brothers, had come to me since he was keen for the *rishta* of his daughter. My father then explained to him that it was not possible because I wanted to study further and stand on my own feet before getting married. With great difficulty and further convincing, my father returned him his one rupee. This is how this chapter of getting me married got closed, for the time being at least.

Now I couldn't ride a bicycle, as I had no money to pay the shopkeeper. But somehow, things worked in my favour as Mr Beant Singh's younger brother, Surjit Singh, familiar as Jeet, was studying in my class, but in section D. Our friendship, despite our different sections, and Beant's intimacy with my eldest cousin Mohinder 'Cinemawala', had earned me his favour; so, he would always keep a bicycle ready for me to ride for one anna during recess. His shop and house, which had a backyard, were both located just opposite our school's main gate. Even the school tuck shop was right next to our school gate. Both these facilities were located at very convenient places—just within our reach! Fortunately, both the owners, of the bicycle shop and tuck shop, were affectionate, sympathetic and helpful to me. Even I used to pay them due respect and never argued with them on any issue. We shared mutual faith in each other.

High School Days

Another year passed—all my friends and I were promoted to higher classes. Class 9 brought with it a sudden increase of load in studies along with an additional load of farming and household work. Now, I definitely wished that a day would have 28 hours. With just 24 hours in a day, the whole work weighed heavy as a huge rock. When I lacked

---

[40] Head of the village

in any household work, Dadiji used to take my side and save me every time from the fury and punishment of my parents. My sister, Surjit, who had left studies after her 8th standard, was always sympathetic towards me and protected me from others. But my elder sister, Sital Kaur, despite leaving studies after 6th class, was very strict and a tough disciplinarian, calling a spade, a spade.

In our school, since the subjects of mathematics and science were all taught in Punjabi, all the textbooks were printed accordingly in Punjabi. But some of us—Pritam, Kewal and I—got together and demanded from our headmaster for Science and Maths to be taught in English. After several discussions with the teachers old and new, including my cousin, Rajinder Singh Sahota, who was our new science teacher, the decision taken was that only section A would get to study Science and Math in English. There were 45 students in one section. The other three sections B, C and D would continue to study both these subjects in Punjabi. Each class in our school had four sections that were generally divided as per the grades of the students. The students, however, were not told about this classification to avoid superiority or inferiority complex amongst themselves.

From thereon began my study of Science and Maths in English, which certainly improved my spoken-English skills to a great extent too. At this point, I left playing volleyball and concentrated mostly on basketball as the captain of my team. Since I was in the league as captain of my basketball team, I became a member of the school's number one hockey team as well. This meant half a *ser* more milk from school! That very year, I took up running and started practising for 100 yards, 440 yards and 880 yards races also. This again authorized me to have another half a *ser* of free milk from school. So now, I was entitled to one and half *ser* of free milk in a day. A maximum of two *ser* of free milk was permitted even if someone played more than four games. Tuck shopkeeper was told by some players to provide other sweets and snacks in lieu of the milk to which the tuck shopkeeper had agreed. He was very flexible and helpful to all the players.

During this period in class 9, I learnt to be mentally tougher and evolve to a superior level by shunning stereotypical behaviour with creative use of intelligence. All teachers started to demand the students to shine in their respective subjects. Master Dev Raj, our Maths teacher, master Thakur Singh, our History and Geography teacher, master Harcharan Singh, our English teacher, and master Rajinder Singh, our Science teacher, were all geniuses who kept us motivated with positive impressions of perfect teaching. I started burning my midnight oil a bit longer and managed to secure 'A' grades in all subjects but I was still behind Kewal and Pritam who had secured A+. I had to be satisfied with my grades since not only had I additional agricultural work to attend to, but to earn my school fees, I also had to cart loads at odd times. I thought to myself—both of them were not active members of NCC or any sports and games so they could devote more time to their studies. I felt much better about myself as I was able to juggle many chores at the same time. My circumstances and surroundings did compel me to change, but something kept me from changing. I liked to control things, I liked to win and take things or situations to the edge. A life spent defensively, criticizing others and brooding over the past was a sheer waste of life to me. I would rather spend my time meditating, helping my parents, sisters, brothers and cousins than whiling away time with gossipers. This way I was forming my own philosophy of life just the way I wanted to live it.

Kanchhe/ Marbles

There were a few things, which my father was very strict about—playing with cards and marbles. With his wisdom, he thought that these games were for gamblers and people who just wanted to waste their time and do nothing constructive. Anyway, we found those games quite interesting and did not bother about the consequences. Once, my father caught my younger brother and me as we were playing marbles with some boys. One slap each was enough to teach us a lesson for not obeying him. The next time we got caught for not listening to him was for playing cards in spite of him warning us. There is a popular game of cards in Punjab, called '*Bhabi*'. We all cousins had pooled money and purchased two packs of cards without the knowledge of our elders. We all used to play one odd game of 'Bhabi' while keeping one eye at our Haveli gate every second. As soon as we would see our father, we would hide the cards and pick up books, pretending to read our lessons aloud. On seeing us engrossed in our books, he used to feel quite appeased, as he was very particular about our education. He might have noticed us doing that trick twice or thrice and soon smelt a rat. One day, he tricked us and came home early, heading straight to the place where we all were sitting in a circle. Panic-stricken, my cousin, Nanjo, couldn't manage to hide all her cards and my father saw one of them. Now Nanjo got the first slap, followed by my sister, younger brother and me. After that, he made us hold our ears and run around in our courtyard for almost 15 minutes. Further more, he took away all the cards and burnt them down. He warned us of dire consequences if he ever saw us playing cards again. I must say, my father's action was detested by all of us at that point, but later we realized in introspection that it saved us time and money, giving us extra time to utilize for constructive habits and help around the house. But my father never objected to our outdoor games as long as we did not neglect our homework, household chores and agricultural work. With years of wisdom, he was probably aware of the fact that outdoor games were good for our physical and mental development.

6

PREPARATION FOR DISTRICT
INTER-SCHOOL TOURNAMENT

Besides being the captain of our basketball team, I was also elected as the vice-captain of our hockey team, with Deeka as its captain. After practising these games regularly for almost six months, we proceeded to participate for the inter-school tournament held between all the schools in district Hoshiarpur. We were all well prepared to take part in the tournament. I was trained for long throw baskets. One of my cousins, Chanan Singh Sahota, who was Punjab state-level basketball player, made us practise even in the moonlit nights. I trained my team under the guidance of Chanan Singh. One of our physical training masters, Mr Joginder Singh, dearly known as Jindoo, also put in all his efforts and felt that the team was well prepared for the tournament. Our kabaddi team also was not far behind. Even our hockey team, under the guidance of master, Gandha Singh, was ready for the tournament.

During those months of vigorous training, we happened to chance upon many PT masters, coaching for particular games. While some were passive and indifferent, only enjoying their time with no sense of thrill or motivation, there were some others who were aggressive and reminded all of us about the famous Second World War leader, General George Patton, yelling orders at his troops before going into the battle. Our PT master, Gandha Singh, was someone like that. He, too, before any game, would bombard his orders and rules of the game, yelling like a General. His voice and physique were good enough to scare anyone on the playground. No one dared to disobey his orders.

Finally, the much-awaited day of the tournament had arrived. The games were to be played in a knockout system. Our first basketball match was against Pajjodeota Khalsa High School, and we were quite confident to win as that school had never won a basketball match earlier in any of the tournaments. To our surprise, Pajjodeota team started the game in a very organised manner and scored their 1st basket within a minute. We tried to equalize the score but our moves looked quite inferior to theirs. They defended their poles in a very strategized manner, marking me—being a top scorer—by two players. They just wouldn't let me get the ball. We lost this match awfully and got knocked out of the tournament. I, being the captain of the team, was put to shame. That year, Pajjodeota Khalsa High School won the basketball district trophy. My school won the kabaddi trophy and we got a second position in hockey. We were far behind the other schools in athletics as well. On returning to our school after about 10 days, it was the time to analyse our mistakes and figure out how we had lost the basketball match to a school, which had never won this game earlier. With great difficulty, we found out that this year, Pajjodeota's basketball team was trained by a Defence services' coach whom their headmaster had hired to train them. It took almost six months for us to find out the name and address of that coach. After the shameful defeat in the basketball game, I as the captain kept fretting until I found the same coach who had trained the winning team. I wanted him to train us for the next year's tournament. I requested the coach to meet our headmaster and physical training master, Mr Jindoo, with whom I had discussed the matter thoroughly. My colleagues were also briefed about this development.

Our school session was nearing the end of the academic year—it was time for our study leave. I followed the same pattern of studying by myself under the tree in the fields. Every day, I used to finish my household and agricultural chores—supply fodder to the buffaloes, accompany father to the fields for ploughing and bring the bullock cart back to the house—and then packed a light lunch with a full bottle of *lassi*. Quite often, while studying on the small mattress under the tree, my mind would wander off to the skies, searching for that flying object known as flying saucer. I also prayed to God to give me one more chance to see the same thing again on earth, just to prove my point. Anyway, that did not happen and

I had other things to worry about. My daily routine continued for quite some time until my father gave me a break from waking up at 4 am to accompany him for ploughing. This left me with more time to revise all the subjects one by one every day and would enhance my sequential thinking and help me in my essential accomplishments.

And finally came the time for our school finals. With Waheguru's grace and my hard work, I was quite confident to do well in the exam. I had to live up to the expectations of my family. Therefore, it was imperative to be grateful and confident, especially when Dadiji would show concern and ask me, '*Imtihana di tyari ho gayi?*' (Are you ready for your exams?) She used to heave a sigh of relief when I would confidently assure her and then she would exclaim, '*Shabash!*' (Very good) and that *ashirvad* (blessing) from her was a priceless gift. Many a times, she used to place her hand on my head and bless me. I owe a great deal of my success in life to my Dadiji. One more thing peculiar to her was that she always held one long *danda*[41] in her hand. She was an incredibly brave lady and once she had even warded off thieves who had entered our *Haweli* to steal our buffaloes and bulls. Usually, she would take nap during the day and remained awake at night. While we were in deep slumber, she would walk to and fro between our house and *Haweli*. With this practice, she had actually managed to scare away the thieves, twice!

During the preparation for my exams, I used to try different methods of studying. We used to have a huge dining table with six chairs. I planned and bought a huge

---

[41] Walking stick, something like a *khoonta* which was used by *bhangra* groups in the village

Kerosene lamp so that we cousins could study together at night. We were a total of six—Deeka, Gurmail, Harpal, Jagjit, Sarabjit and I—studying together. This arrangement did not work very well for too long though. As soon as one passed a trivial remark, all of us would start laughing. Our parents did not like this idea and we were immediately separated into three groups. Harpal and I were put together as we were classmates. Gurdip and Gurmail would sit together and Jagjit and Sarabjit were to study in the third group. Thus, continued our study-time at night in such groups. But during the day, we were all on our own and studied separately at different places.

All of us were well prepared so we all got remarkable results and got promoted to higher classes. Gurdip and Gurmail cleared their 10th, Harpal and I cleared 9th and Jagjit and Sarabjit cleared their 7th standard. My father realized our increased academic pressure in higher classes and decided to finally sell off one *jorhi* of bulls, much against our wishes and liking. My younger brother and I wept for many days, that's when Dadiji would take us in her arms and console by convincing us that our father was right in his decision. She explained how it would be difficult for us to devote time to farming now that we were in higher classes and that our father feared that we might fail in our exams if we continued farming. She especially hinted at me and said, 'Pass your 10th class and then help your father in doing a little mechanized farming'. She always uttered an age-old saying, '*Uttam kheti, madham vapaar and nikhidh chakari*'.(meaning highest profession is farming, then comes business and then the lowest is service according to the notions at that time). Basically, she attempted to persuade me to remain in the house and help my father in farming after my 10th.

Eventually, studies began to pick a pace and time started to run out. Even the annual sports were coming closer so preparations had begun. We started to concentrate harder on studies to be ready to perform well in our finals. I remember that I used to spend at least 10 to 15 minutes sitting quietly by myself on my bed before going to sleep. I used to pray to Waheguru for my well being, health and studies, to get better marks in assessments. I don't remember exactly when had I started to meditate, and to be honest, I did not know anything about meditation at that time. I used to see my mother praying every night while sitting on her bed with folded hands and say, '*Hey Waheguru, sabh nu tandrusti bakshna, sabh de sir te mehar bharya hath rakhna, Sat Naam Waheguru*' (asking God to bless all with good health and happiness). She used to religiously pray every night before going to sleep. I think I started initially by imitating her and eventually got pulled into meditation. Though at that time I did not know much about meditation, I continued with my prayers with closed eyes.

During our study break in 10th, my cousin Ajit Singh, who was staying in a hostel and was studying for an Overseer's Course, came to our village. I told him about my difficulties in Maths and so he started to coach me and help me memorize some important mathematic formulae. With his support, I started to shine in Maths class and even began to score around 80% in the monthly and quarterly exams.

Meanwhile, practise for hockey, basketball and athletics were also going on in full swing. I had more time now as my household and agricultural work had reduced a considerable amount—all due to my father's visionary thinking. As the district inter-school tournament came closer, I started to play matches withsome ex-students of our school and senior teams from other villages. I also stepped up my running practise for 440 yards and 880 yards. One day, our PT master made the entire hockey, football and basketball players stand in a line and asked us to race a run of 100 yards. To my surprise, I left all the players far behind and finished the race within excellent time as per our PT master. Next day, my headmaster called me to his office and told me to take part in 100 yards race as well. The same day, he increased the quantity of milk by half a *ser* for me as an incentive and to supplement my diet. Now I started getting a total of two *ser* of milk every day from my tuck shop. Also, during my running practise, which used to be early in the morning, I would run one and a half mile out of my house and come back the same distance. When I used to return home after my run, my mother would give me one big glass of hot milk with a dollop of desi ghee in it. Because of having so much milk at home and also at school tuck-shop, I was called a 'Doodhadhari'. It means a person who lives on milk only.

Our studies and games progressed simultaneously. Our basketball coach, Shri Satnam Singh, had also arrived and so began the daily coaching sessions. I now realized that Mohan and I were good players but we were playing a kind of selfish game everytime. I think this was due to the fact that we wanted to prove who scored more baskets in the game. This was a major drawback in both of us, thus, affecting our team's performance. Once, the coach pointed this out and put us on the right track of coordinated moves. Soon, we picked up the momentum of the game in a very sporting manner and the whole team became a homogenous unit of five musketeers and sharpshooters. There was no dearth of under-baskets, long throws had automatically reduced and so had the missed baskets. This year, Mohan Singh was made the captain of the basketball team and I was made the captain of the hockey team. Mr Karam Singh of Jia Sahota village did a wonderful job in guiding and coaching us in hockey. I was playing as a centre forward as I had a good control of stick-work and was a fast runner too. My control over the whole team was very beneficial to the team. They were also pinning a lot of hopes on me for this reason. My headmaster and PT master were very happy and confident that my team would certainly win the district trophy this time.

We played plenty of friendly matches and won almost all of them because there was certain amount of hunger to win the matches. Somehow, I concentrated on teamwork and played the ball well during the game to show the opponents that we possessed superior skills. Our confidence level during the game used to be far superior to the other teams.

Just ten days before our District Inter-School Tournament, while playing a friendly match, I seriously injured my right foot while taking a short corner hit. The hockey stick of Mr Santokh Singh, a senior player, had scraped my right big toe and the skin peeled off; exposing the bone and it started bleeding profusely. I was immediately given the first-aid and sent for an X-Ray; I had to be taken to Hoshiarpur, which was 25 km away. I was taken by normal passenger bus as there was no ambulance in those days. Fortunately, the X-Ray of the foot revealed no fracture but the wound was very deep. The whole of my school felt a major jolt in their sports aspirations because of my injury, as I was one of the best sportsman of my school. Not only was I the captain of the hockey team and a very good basketball player, groomed well by the coach, but I was also taking part in three races—100 yards sprint, 440 yards straight-run and 880 yards relay. Everyone in school was praying for my recovery. My mother and Dadiji prayed to Waheguru every day religiously as they were concerned about me. Finally, I became somewhat fit to play both the major games but on a condition: I had to play barefoot. Athletics was out of the question, as my injured foot could not take my weight while running fast. This setback demoralized me to a great extent as I cried almost every evening and prayed to Waheguru for my speedy recovery. However, as luck would have it, we lost hockey match in the semi-final. But we won basketball match with great laurels by defeating all the teams, including Pajjodeota. Since Mohan was the captain of the basketball team, being my very good friend, we kept celebrating the winning of a trophy for the school for the whole week. This sort of celebration carried on from school tuck shop to his house and from there it reached my house. Our parents were also very happy and supportive of our motivational and talented mentors.

By this time, I decided to pair with Pritam Singh of my village to prepare for our final exams of 10th class—Matriculation. Pritam was brilliant in Maths and I wanted to take advantage of that. He used to score a 100% in all the tests, whereas, I did not cross 80%. This time, however, I was determined to get a 100% in Maths in my finals. We chose his old house, which had two floors (chaubara), to study peacefully. It was quite near his new house in the east of town Chardah Passa, (eastern side) while our house was on the other side of the village in the western side, Lenhda Passa. After a couple of days, I started joining him for studies at night and spent many nights at his *chaubara*. Every night, after having an early dinner, I would leave for his place. While we would be studying, Pritam's mother would bring hot milk for both of us to drink. Despite my attempts to tell her that I have milk daily at about 4:30 pm, she would still insist and not listen to me. She would say, 'If I had two sons, do you think one would go without milk?' She was a very generous and affectionate lady. She trusted our hard work and knew that we were determined to study well. I certainly did not let her down and scored 145 marks out of 150 marks (96.70%) in Maths in the final exam. She was very proud of her son Pritam who scored a perfect 150 out of 150 (100%). My parents were also very proud of my achievement and we were extremely grateful to Pritam and his mother for all the help they had extended to me.

I must also mention how grateful I was to our Math teacher, Shri Dev Raj, for all the help he had bestowed upon us. His house was on the way to Pritam's house so I took maximum advantage of that situation and learnt many formulae and problem-solving skills from him too. He, unfortunately, has expired and is resting peacefully in heaven since long; I offer my respect and gratitude to him.

Our Matriculation exams were over by 20th April 1958, and the results were finally declared by the end of May 1958. I passed my exam in first division with 560 out of a total of 750 marks. Pritam too passed in 1st division but secured much higher marks than I had. I think he obtained a total of 592 marks. Hardyal obtained 610 and Kewal obtained 640 marks. Hats off to all three of them for their remarkable performances. As I have mentioned earlier, I was satisfied with my result because I had two major games to my credit, whereas, none of them played any school games. However, Pritam was very good in kabaddi but only played for the junior team of our village. I was also a member of the same team. Pritam and I played very well and won many of the junior tournaments. After passing out, Pritam joined Government College at Hoshiarpur. Later, I heard that he played great kabaddi for his college team too. I remember that while going for kabaddi to the opponent's side, many a times, he used to jump over the opponent and complete the point for his team with ease. Opponents were generally scared of him, so, he had an edge over every one. He pursued FSc from the same college, BVSc from Hissar and finally MVSc and PhD (veterinary pathology) from Ludhiana. He became a veterinary doctor and after some years of service in India, he migrated to the UK and then eventually to USA. I used to contact him occasionally.

Let me now tell you about my kabaddi experiences. In the village tournaments, we used to be selected to play as per our weight. Pritam and I chose the 95 lbs weight-team. Both of us had to put in a lot of effort every time to come into this range of weight. He was a slightly chubby so had to lose some weight and I was overweight because my bones were heavy. From nearly a week before the tournament and also on the day of measurement, we used to eat very little and run at 4 AM in the morning and sweat profusely only to lose weight to get into 95-lbs-category. Finally, having been able to enter the team after the measurement procedure, we began to hog on eggs, eating at least10 to 12 per day. Our kabaddi team was well known among all the villages around Garhdiwala.

After passing Matriculation exams and obtaining a good result, my mind was fixed upon higher studies or on getting a job to support my family. But there was something else cooking in the minds of my Bapuji, Bibiji and Dadiji—they were planning my marriage, so that I get settled in the village and help my father in mechanised farming. When I was in class 9, my cousin Mohinder had one tube well installed to help my father in irrigation of fields in order to get more output from our crops. It was a big help since it was the only tubewell in the vicinity of our village, Garhdiwala. There was no electricity in our village those days so the tubewell was running on diesel engine known as Salavia. It gave us excellent service for almost three years. In the year 1958, the village agricultural land consolidation had commenced. My uncles opted for division of land before consolidation. Due to this division, our major portion did not come around our tubewell. Someone else's major portion fell there and so our tubewell got allotted to that person who was no where near us as far as agriculture work and produce was concerned. This came as an unpleasant shock to Bapuji. To add to this, even I did not agree for marriage and asked my maternal uncle, Shri Charan Singh, who was a Punjabi master in a DAV High School, Balagran near Dasuya, to convince my parents. He spoke to my parents and Dadiji and told them, 'Harbans passed his matriculation with very good marks and he must study further and do his B.sc to become a teacher in Khalsa High School, Garhdiwala'. My father accepted the advice of my Mama Ji ,Charan Singh, as he was a respected teacher at his school. In fact, my entire family had high regards for him. Finally, I got saved from this situation with my Mama ji's help.

7

COLLEGE AND ITS MANY FACETS

I had about two more months of time in hand before the admissions began for college. To my fortune, I came to know that principals of various colleges from nearby places like Hoshiarpur and TandaUrmar were pulling strings to get me to join their respective colleges. It was all happening because of my sports background and good marks in Science subjects. Finally, Shri Rala Ram, principal of DAV College, Hoshiarpur, succeeded to get me an admission with the help of Chaudhary Pritam Singh, who apart from being a very famous landlord, was also president of the committee of village Garhdiwala. They spoke to my father and lured him with promises to completely exempt my fees and partially pay my hostel expenditure. They also insisted me to join F.sc and play for the college games—hockey and basketball. My father and Uncle Pritam Singh both discussed this offer and promises made by Shri Rala Ram Ji with me and convinced me that this was good for me. I, on the other hand, was inclined to join Government College at TandaUrmar. The principal of that college had also made an offer to exempt three-fourth of my tuition fees and some of the hostel expenditure as well. If I chose to stay in Hoshiarpur, I could stay at my aunt's house (Mrs Mohinder Kaur, my father's elder sister) while I also had an option to stay at another aunt's house (Mrs Gian Kaur, my father's younger sister) in village Dhadiala if I stayed in TandaUrmar, Another added advantage was that two of my cousins, Tarsem Singh and Gurdip Singh, were studying in the same college. Anyway, the phrase 'exemption of full fees seemed to be far more appealing to our financial condition at that time, so, a unanimous decision was taken for me to join DAV College, Hoshiarpur, and stay at the hostel there. I joined the college in July 1958. I also met principal

Rala Ram Ji for a letter of exemption of fees and hostel expenditure. Even though he had issued the letter of exemption of college fees, he refrained from issuing the letter for exemption of hostel expenditure. In fact, he said that two exemptions could not be given to one student. This was quite contrary to what was promised to Uncle Pritam Singh and Bapuji. I was very upset but nothing could be done at that point as I had already signed the bond for playing the university tournament, coming up in November–December 1958.

The studies had started in full swing and so did the practice for the major games. I became so busy that it started to reflect on my health. I did not get healthy food like milk, butter, desi ghee or even sufficient fruits in the hostel. It had become a situation of survival-of-the-fittest and I kept grabbing whatever looked a bit healthy to eat. This continued for about three months and then I was given a bill of Rs. 200. I was told by the hostel in-charge that the principal had exempted only half of my hostel expenditure. It was a shock for me as it was very difficult to pay even a rupee extra anywhere as my tuck shop bill was approximately Rs. 100 per month. To get this much of money from home was impossible for me. I tried to get some support from my aunt in Hoshiarpur and spent the next six months in her house and attended my college and games from there. About this time, an incident took place, which was an eye opener for me. My aunt forced me to go and visit my elder stepbrother, Amrik Singh. He was in the army and was posted in Amritsar at that time. She told me, 'Go to him and request him to support your studies financially'. Since my PT shoes were torn from the sides, she also told me to ask for a pair of PT shoes from him. I mustered the courage and went to Amritsar by bus and spent one night with my brother. I spoke to him about aiding my college expenditure and asked him to keep a record of all the money he would spend on me so that I could return him later. I promised to return each rupee to him after I should get a job. He, however, flatly refused on my face. I was thankful that at least he gave me food to eat during my stay with him. I think, in the long run, this incident helped me strengthen my determination and courage to stand on my own feet as soon as possible without anyone's help. I told this story only to my aunt and did not mention any of this to my parents. During this time, one of my cousins, Tarsem Singh, had completed his F.sc (Faculty of Science) and had joined the Indian Air Force. He was getting only Rs.50 per month as a salary during his training period, yet he promised to help me and extend support for my studies by sending me Rs. 20 to 30 per month for the next eight months. I will forever be indebted to him for his support. I did return his money later but I can never return his kind gesture and timely support.

I played for the college teams in hockey and basketball, but unfortunately, both our teams lost in the semi-finals against Government College of Hoshiarpur.

I did not even do well in my exams. The result was shocking, shameful and not worth mentioning to my parents, who had very high hopes from me.

After this, I finally took a decision to change my college from DAV College, Hoshiarpur to Government College, TandaUrmar, after three months. The principal of Government College wanted me to play for his college and promised to charge only half the fees till I completed my F.sc. I had cleared my first year of F.sc but the second year of F.sc was turning out to be awfully tough for me due to my sports activities as I had to travel to attend tournaments. Let me tell you all an amusing incident that took place during my stay in the college. As part of college annual celebrations, our college hosted cultural programmes like short skits and bhangra performance along with some rural games like kabaddi and a very interesting donkey race. I wanted to participate in the donkey race. But the problem was to arrange for a donkey, as we had to do it ourselves. First of all, I'll tell you why I decided to take part in the donkey race. There was a *basti*[42] across the street in our village and they had many donkeys, which they used for carrying loads. Some of these donkeys used to wander and get into our fields. Sarabjit and I used to catch those donkeys and chase them away and then take rides on them. There were many times when we even had very nasty falls from the donkeys. Anyway, over a period of time, I became an expert in riding a donkey. If the donkey rode very fast, I used to latch on to the neck of the donkey to prevent a fall. That is why; I dared to

---

[42] Hutment area

take part in this race. Since, it was a problem getting a readily available donkey, we had to search near the Government College inTandaUrmar and hire the donkey for the race. Luckily, we found a dhobi who had two donkeys. I requested him to give us a donkey on rent for our race of 10 minutes for Rs. 5 only. It was a steep amount for me to pay in those days, but at the same time, for the requirement of participation in the race, I paid the amount to that dhobi. With great difficulty I had to drag the donkey up to the spot of the race as the donkey refused to budge from dhobi's house. It appeared that others taking part in the race had brought donkeys from their own villages. For my friends and me it was a herculean task to make the donkey stay and prepare it for the race. Within another 20 minutes, the race was announced and the participants were asked to get ready to ride the donkeys. Friends of other participants were there to beat the donkeys to run faster. As the whistle blew for the race to begin, my donkey started running as fast as it could, surprising everyone and horrifying me when it did not stop even at the finishing line. In spite of my best efforts, it kept running and headed straight for a gate which had only one round pole, just about a foot higher than the donkey's height. Sensing the donkey would not stop and go under the pole at a great speed, I quickly latched onto the neck of the donkey and held on very tightly to avoid hitting the pole at the gate and falling from the donkey. In both the situations, sitting straight or falling from the donkey would have resulted in serious injury to me. Finally, the donkey stopped only after reaching its owner's house. The dhobi was very pleased that I returned his donkey as promised. But at the site of the race, there was a commotion as everyone started to wonder where the boy who stood first was. They were looking for me all over the place; meanwhile, I was on my way back, running towards the spot of the race. I wasn't even pleased to win the race that day, as I was only thankful to Waheguru for saving my life. I could have either hit the pole or fallen from the donkey and fractured my ribs or neck.

As soon as the organisers saw me running towards the *dais* (stage), there were cheers and claps in galore. Perforce, I had to laugh along with my friends and others, as I was just too shocked and relieved to be alive. Later, when I told them how I won the race, we all had a great laugh about it. It was all because the donkey, by chance, was facing towards his owner's house at the start of the race and that was why it had started to run so fast to reach back home. I narrated the whole incident to them and how dangerously I got saved. I humbly accepted my trophy and kept narrating the same story again and again. It had become a joke and over a period of time, I took pride and amusement in the whole episode.

8

SHARE OF MY WISDOM

I have been only talking about my failures and successes so far. With my years of experience and wisdom, I must put down the lessons, which the parents must follow to make their children strong and provide them an opportunity to do well in studies and games. First of all, about studies, I will put down some of the practices, which I followed to improve my study habits. During my school and college days, I was not aware of the simple steps that I had taken to discipline my life. But the results, which I achieved from those simple steps, were certainly out of proportion. I would like to share those practices for the benefit of young students. When parents expect good grades, I think, they too have a significant role to play in the schooling or college education of their children. They have to allot sufficient time to both studies and play for children, who must learn to manage time properly and have healthy study habits. Going to class and following the instructions or taking notes are not enough to stand first in class, but it's how you prepare for the next day's class that makes a lot of difference. Self-study after the lesson is over helps one to analyse how much one has retained and remembered. You may call it regular homework or healthy study habits. Let me explain the habits to you:

1) **Choose a Single Place to Study:** In the present-day world, research has shown that when the mind is directed to a specific task in a specific place, over a period of time, it becomes easier to get into the same frame of mind. Find a quiet place where there is no interference or disturbance. I chose a tree in a field near my village. It was very safe from any wild animals. Parents should always keep a watch that children are kept away from places where they can engage in other activities such as bedroom, a cafeteria or canteen

or a recreational area where there is a distraction. For example, if they study in their bedrooms—where they sleep—they may feel drowsy, which would hinder their studies.

2) **Juggle between Subjects or Topics:** Studying one subject again and again for hours at a stretch can be very monotonous and may even harm the student in the long run. When similar topic is studied consecutively, the topic can seem jumbled. For example, studying Chemistry and Algebra one after the other would leave your child confused with numbers and formulae. Instead, they should split up similar topics. One may add English in between Chemistry and Algebra to avoid boredom. Doing so will not only help in keeping subject interesting, but will also shift the information from your child's short-term memory into long-term memory. Retention will be much better.

3) **Take Regular Breaks:** It is very important for the students to take a break during their study routine. Even a ten-minute break after every hour can make a huge difference. During the break, one should get up, stretch, get a snack or use the bathroom. Regular breaks also help the information to reach long-term memory faster.

4) **Get Good Sleep:** One must have a good and sound sleep at night. An early dinner also helps. Eat your food by 7 PM in the evening, so that by the time you go to bed, your food will be digested and you will have a nice, restful sleep.

5) **Eat Healthy Snacks:** It is important for your children to keep their mind sharp and their energy charged when they're sitting for a study session. An easy way to do this is to eat healthy snacks. Bananas or apples dipped in peanut butter gives energy, fills the stomach and provides a lot of protein to keep you going. Almonds and other nuts are heart-healthy fats and proteins that will keep the child alert. Fresh fruits are also an excellent way to fill the stomach and keep the mind attentive while providing them with nutrients and energy to keep their mind on track. If there's nothing else, the good old *desi ghee ka parantha* with any vegetable is also a great snack. Students must carry hot milk in a flask and any food that will keep you alert and healthy. If parents and students follow

these simple ways and steps, both will benefit for years to come, students will have better grades and will be healthier. Parents will certainly be proud of the achievements of their children. The environment in which I studied has gone through a huge change. These days, almost all parents are educated and are technologically savvy. In our times, going to a library was considered a punishment for the students. These days' children like to spend more time in libraries, go through the books and magazines for widening their knowledge. I would like to give some more tips to the parents and our young readers. Remember when you first learnt how to read, a whole new world just opened up suddenly? You could learn about anything—from your favourite animals to foreign cultures, from sports to news events of the past. Reading is a great habit and I have some tips to inculcate this essential habit.

i) **Start at just the right place and time:** Pick a book that your child is comfortable in reading. Selecting books based on children's ability and interest helps them strengthen current reading skills and progress smoothly to the harder material.

ii) **Child wants to see the same book:** Don't be surprised or get put off if your child wants to read the same book over and over again. Books that have recognizable, loved characters make the story-experience more enjoyable and full of mirth for new readers.

iii) **Introduce new vocabulary:** Look for a book that covers a variety of new words that will help your child build his vocabulary. Children can learn new ways to express themselves by building a strong vocabulary. Be sure to use those new words throughout the day.

iv) **Understand the story:** Books that are based on real life experiences that the reader can relate to—such as the first day of school, sharing things, good team spirit and sportsmanship—and by trying new things to enhance the enjoyment of reading.

v) **Develop a reading routine:** Busy schedules can be disruptive to daily routines, but finding 20 minutes each day for special time to read together can develop the strong reading skills. Whether it's after lunch or just before bedtime, story time can be one of the most enjoyable moments in a day.

vi) Have book talks: Discuss your child's favourite part of the story, then have him/her draw a picture and recall the story. These observations and activities will help the new readers to understand the story and develop the skills necessary to become a good and inquisitive reader.

We all are in computer age and our busy schedules and social gatherings keep us so busy that we leave younger children deprived of their playful, enjoyable and habit-forming time. If we spend at least 20 minutes with a child or children on everyday basis before they go to bed, it will pay great dividends and children will pick up good reading habits too. The joy of childhood is getting lost in our busy, fast-paced world. Our children are growing up learning that only a programmed, good oriented activity is worth doing. The joy and the fun in the early age, playing innovative games or native games are getting lost among our children. I am now involved in bringing up my three grandchildren and the grandson is the youngest. I once asked him to play with me and have some fun. He questioned me, 'Dadaji, you are saying "fun fun", but what is fun?' It hit me hard and I had to look into a dictionary for the meaning of fun—something that provides mirth or amusement. A picnic, for example, would be fun. After getting the meaning from dictionary, I could convince him about what is fun. While playing football, I kept reminding him what is the fun in the game. Winning or losing has no importance. Enjoyment and laughing at your mistakes or opponent's mistakes of playing the game also was included in all the fun. Actually, I think that fun is a relative term and its meaning is different for individual children of different ages as per their perceptions.

Children at an early age learn to live and cope with winning and losing situations; that is where the fun lies. Fun is a critical part of children's games and their individual motivation. Every kid is 'I'-focused, that is, self-centred. Games help to change their focus from 'I' to 'we' which is a very essential ingredient of team spirit and team work. In fact, 'we' attitude slowly becomes a part of life and the individual becomes a solid brick of the block, thereby, always having a supportive attitude and co-operative attributes. Games teach the kids cohesiveness, a good working relation and respect for each other's ability to co-operate and communicate. Parents can also have a great influence by finding positive skills and traits in their own kids and reinforce them. Actually, when we as parents play with kids, we are enhancing their confidence. We must praise positive performance and tactfully criticize their weaknesses. All kids need positive praises and pats on the back, as they may feel disgusted with harsh critical debriefing of their game or fun play. My advice to all parents—have a small cut on your pleasures and take time to play with your kids. If possible, slow down your life. I am sure; the pleasure of seeing your kids grow with you will certainly add a couple of years more to your life. You must know that kids are growing up quicker than you know. They will be gone before you say 'Jack Robinson'. Time is now for love, love and play, before it is too late. I have reminded all parents about kid's games of yesteryears compared to organised sports of today along with the methods to positively prepare and motivate kids and sow seeds of positive team spirit. This happiness of togetherness will certainly promote their physical and mental health too.

Don't live in the past, don't dream of the future, but concentrate on the present.

9

JOINING THE INDIAN AIR FORCE

The chapters of my childhood, farming, school and college life then advanced to my Air Force Recruitment. I was studying in 2nd year of F.Sc in Government College, Tanda Urmar. Our college hockey team went to Ambala Cantonment to play with the teams of some clubs, schools and colleges. This was our preparation for the Inter-University Tournament, which was to take place in Jalandhar after about three months. All the hockey players were staying in a *sarai*[43] in Ambala Cantt. Our last match was over at about 9 AM and so my teammates had decided to return to the sarai and leave on the same day for TandaUrmar. While leaving from the hockey ground of a school, I missed the bus because the principal of that higher secondary school was very impressed with my game and held me back for a cup of tea with him. Since other players had gone back, I dared to walk and run the 3-kilometre-distance up to sarai. While walking through a shortcut, I happened to see the Air Force Recruitment Centre in Ambala Cantt. I noticed that there was a long queue of boys and I read a notice on the board which said that there was recruitment going on for certain trades in the Air Force. I asked one of the boys what was he doing there and why was there such a long queue. The boy explained that all the people in the line were waiting for the recruiting officer to come out of his office and visually select the capable boys and take them in for a written test of English, Maths, etc. He also told me that one had to be a Matriculate in Science and Maths to go in for the recruitment. His words passed through my head like a tremor and I boasted in front of him of my Matriculation with Science and Maths subjects in high 1st division. That boy told me that I could try my luck too. I immediately

---

[43] Inn

joined that queue and waited for the recruiting officer to come out. A little while later, there came an Air Force Officer, about 6 feet, 2 to 3 inches tall, in a very impressive uniform. He also had a flyer's badge and some ribbons above his left pocket. I couldn't understand his rank. Anyway, he came right in front and introduced himself as Squadron Leader Hazara Singh, the Recruiting Officer. Immediately, he walked to the boy 1st in the line, which happened to be on the opposite side of where I was standing. Now, a lot of silly thoughts swirled through my mind but I was controlling my nerves. As the Recruiting Officer came to the 6th boy from me in the row, I could hear his questions. This gave me the added advantage and I kept preparing my answers to those questions. I started feeling confident of myself. When the Recruiting Officer came in front of me, he laughed and said loudly, '*Sardarji bharti hon aye ho ya hockey khelney?*' (Have you come for the recruitment or to play hockey?) This was befitting because I was in a player's uniform and I had a hockey stick in my hand. I quickly wished him a good morning and started the conversation in English. I explained why I was in a uniform and that when I saw the recruitment notice, I got tempted to join IAF.

He then asked me, 'Why do you want to join the IAF?'

'I wish to earn some money to help my father who is a farmer in a village and has the burden of fees for three school-going children on his head'. I further continued, 'While doing my duty, I will also be serving my country'.

'What is your qualification? He enquired.

'Currently, I'm studying F.sc in 2nd year after my Matriculation with Science and Maths subjects. In matriculation, I obtained a high 1st division' I replied.

He then asked," show me the matriculation certificate". I replied, "I did not come prepared for the recruitment. It will take at least one week for me to come back with certificates".

I don't know what was going on in his mind; he thought for a while and said, 'you can appear for the tests and practical examination. If you are selected, you will not be given joining instructions until you show your original certificates to me personally by then'. After this, he called for one sergeant and asked him to take me for the tests. The very first day, there were two very simple tests and the second day, two practical tests. On the third day, I was sent for a medical check-up. By now, the money, which I had with me, was almost exhausted. My food, stay and bus fare to my hometown were pinching on my pocket. In the morning, at 8AM, I reported to the Medical Inspection Room of Air Force Station, Ambala. There were five boys—all new recruits. I was number 3 in the roll call. When my turn came for medical, I was called into the doctor's room; he was an officer of Flt Lt Rank. Doctor checked me with stethoscope and felt very happy with my health. Thereafter, he checked my eyes and ears. After checking my ears, he told me that there is excessive wax in my ears; I should get it cleaned from some civil doctor and report again the next day. I was not happy with this prescription as I was running short of money. Anyway, I had to abide by the order of the doctor so, wishing and thanking him, I came out of his office. I walked straight to the Cantt. bazaar and found a doctor who would clean my ears and requested him to charge me less money as I had very limited cash. My stay was extended by one more night and with the payment of my room rent, I was short of money for my bus fare to my hometown. The next day, I reported to the Air Force MI Room. I walked all the way; the distance was approximately 3km from my place of stay. I was called in by the same doctor and made to sit for ear inspection. The doctor was not happy with the cleanliness of my ears and again asked me to go back to the same civil doctor and get the ears cleaned thoroughly and ordered me to report the next day. This time, I could not hold myself and spoke to the IAF doctor in English and requested him, 'If you can, why not clean my ears yourself?' And in the same breath, I told him my story of arrival in Ambala to play hockey for the college and then my abrupt decision to stay back for the IAF *bharti*[44].

'I have no money to pay to the civilian doctor or even for the stay of one more night. If you cannot help me, Sir, you should reject me, let me go home. I don't want to beg for money'.

---

[44] Admission/ Recruitment

I think my frankness made him think for some time. He asked me to wait outside his office. Now, while waiting outside, a lot of thoughts—fearing rejection—flashed through my mind, making me shaky. As an after thought, I believe, a Punjabi movie could have been made on these few dramatic moments, reflecting the feelings and speculations that I was going through at that point of time. After about half an hour, the doctor inside his office called me. I was fully prepared to pack up and go home with a rejection letter in hand. But I found a unique smile on doctor's face; he told me that he would clean my ears and that he was not rejecting me medically. He took a syringe and some water and cleaned my ears. He showed me the muck, which came out of my ears. That was a shock to me! In fact, even the medicine which the civilian doctor had used, had remained inside my ears. Anyway, I was happy that the IAF doctor listened to my plea and agreed to help. He signed my medical papers and gave me a letter to be handed over to the IAF station orderly room. At that time, I only knew that it was Air Force Station, Ambala. Rest of the air force and its terminology was totally unknown to me.

In my excitement I quickly ran to the orderly room and reported to a Sergeant, who guided me to the correct window. I submitted that letter, given to me by the IAF doctor, to the person sitting inside. He opened the letter and said, 'You are selected and allotted Instrument Repairs Trade". He also informed, 'One batch is leaving for a training centre tomorrow and you should join that batch.' I went on to asked him, 'When is the next batch leaving?' 'There's another batch after four days', he replied. I requested him to send me for that batch as it would then allow me to meet my family before leaving for the training finally.

He agreed and said; 'Report back to me within three days, as on the 4th day, the batch will be leaving from Ambala Cantt Railway Station at about 2 PM'. All trainees had to collect their warrants and some journey allowance well before the departure of the train. He also informed, 'Your training is at No. 2 GTS (Ground Training School) at Tambaram in Madras[45].' Curiously, I inquired, 'How will I be allowed to come to the same office without a letter?' So then he handed over one letter

---

[45] Now known as Chennai

with blanks filled in and the date and time was given to report back. I took that letter and left for the *sarai* where I was staying. I packed up my baggage and counted my money, which was less than the bus fare to my village. I also had to change the bus at Hoshiarpur before reaching my village Garhdiwala. I thought of at least reaching Hoshiarpur the same day and see if I could meet some known person to borrow some money to reach home.

I walked from Sarai to Ambala Cantt bus stop, which was about a kilometre from *sarai*. Before buying the bus ticket for Hoshiarpur, I went outside towards the GT Road when I saw a truck parked by the roadside and noticed a Sardar Ji sitting on the driver's seat. I got an idea of asking him for a lift. I picked up some courage and approached that gentleman and told him that I didn't have bus fare with me to reach my hometown, Garhdiwala, in district Hoshiarpur. If he could take me upto some distance or up to Ludhiana, I would be able to reach my hometown. That gentleman took pity on me and asked me to jump in behind the driver's seat. Once I got inside the truck, that gentleman told me that his name was Jarnail Singh and he was from village Mahilpur in district Hoshiarpur. He was going to Pathankot via Mahilpur, Hoshiarpur and Dasuya. I felt so relieved and thanked Waheguru incessantly. He and his cleaner were buying lunch for themselves. In a few minutes, the cleaner named Tarsem Singh came in with packed lunch. They happily shared their lunch with me. I agreed hesitantly, though from inside I was very happy and was thankful to God almighty. Jarnail Singh gave me half a tandoori roti and some *aloo gobhi sabji* (vegetable). After having that, I took out my water-bottle and drank some water. That was a great relief, as I did not have to spend on anything. Within about half an hour, they set course for Ludhiana, Phagwara and Hoshiarpur. It was about 3 PM in the afternoon when we left Ambala and reached Mahilpur at about 10:30 at night. I think they stopped on the way for a cup of tea. As I was sleeping, they did not wake me up. While Jarnail Singh parked the truck near the bus stop at Mahilpur and went to his house, the cleaner, Tarsem Singh, stayed in the truck with me. Jarnail Singh came back at about 4 AM in the morning and embarked on the journey to Pathankot. We reached my village Garhdiwala, which was on the main road from Hoshiarpur to Dasuya, at about 7 AM in the morning. There were 30 odd *chows*[46] to be crossed from Mahilpur to Garhdiwala. The truck was moving at a slow speed. As we reached my village, Jarnail Singh stopped the truck at the bus stop. After getting down from the truck, I requested Jarnail Singh and Tarsem Singh to come to my house and have *nashta, lassi panni* or *chai*[47], but both declined and showed the urgency to reach Pathankot for loading the truck for return journey. During our journey, I had told them that I was selected as Aircraftman II with Instrument Repair Trade and within three days, I was to leave from Ambala Cantt for my training. Both of them wished me good luck. I was so thankful that I wanted to touch Jarnail Singh's feet but instead, he took me in his arms and hugged me. He said, 'you will become an Air Force *sahib* (Officer). Pray to God and do your duty well'. With these affectionate words and feelings from a complete stranger, my eyes welled up and I had no words to thank him with. I stood by the side of the truck till they moved for their onward journey and waved goodbye with both hands in much gratitude.

I picked up my baggage and hurried home to break the news. When I reached home, Bibiji, Dadiji, my younger sister and youngest brother were all at home and I paid my respect and love to them. I did not say anything about my recruitment to the IAF and waited for Bapuji to reach home. I kept talking about my hockey trip to Ambala Cantt. Bapuji came home at about 2 in the afternoon after finishing his work in the fields. As I greeted him, he was happy to see me back at home. He was planning some farming work together with me the next day. I went along with him and started massaging his legs and feet while he laid on his bed for some rest in our *deorhi*[48]. I started to talk about my hockey game and also mentioned, if I get some job, it would be a great help to our family. He had a very cold response to my suggestion and started discussing his plan of expanding farming and asked me to quit studies as I was spending more time in the college and used to come home only on Sundays. I once again mentioned that my cousins

---

[46] Rivulets
[47] Breakfast and tea
[48] Big hall

Tarsem and Gurdip have joined the Air Force sometime back and are very happy. If I can also join Air Force, it would be a great help to him. This time he asked, 'How is this possible?' I found this to be the right opportunity to inform him that I had already managed to join the IAF as Instrument Repairer and was required to leave the next day for Ambala Cantt for my training. As soon as he heard this, Bapuji jumped out of the bed and became angry with me and said, 'Why do you want to leave home? We have a lot of plans for you and for upgrading our farming too'. Anyway, I told him that nothing could be done as I had already signed a bond to join the IAF and I had to reach Ambala Cantt by the next evening so that on the third day, I could leave on time by train for Tambaram from Ambala Cantt. He asked me if I had informed others at home. 'No, I wanted to inform you first', I replied. He went inside and told my Dadiji and Bibiji about my *bharti* in the Air Force. Both the ladies started crying and started convincing me about how bad a *naukri* was.

My Dadiji repeated her old saying again and again, '*Uttam kheti* (farming), *madham vapaar* (business), and *nikhidh chakri* (Service)'. It meant that farming was the best, followed by business, leaving service to be the last in order.

I sat quietly on a *charpai* (bed) and kept listening to them. After about 10 to 15 minutes, I told them, 'I have to leave tomorrow and go to Ambala Cantt, and from there I have to leave for Tambaram (Madras).'

This added more fuel to the fire and they continued crying. After seeing them cry, my younger brother and sister also started crying. Looking at that scene, even I couldn't hold back my tears. On hearing this commotion, my other cousins and neighbours hurried to our house. Initially, they were worried but on hearing about my job, all were very happy and started laughing. But my mother and Dadiji did not stop shedding their tears.

Then I requested Bibiji, 'please pull out one small suitcase and pack up my clothes".

With this diversion of attention, she became a bit quiet and started searching for a small suitcase.

However, Dadiji kept probing, 'Who would help your father in farming and how could he expand his farming work in your absence?'

I tried to convince her, 'I will be earning some money for two of my younger brothers and one younger sister to get them educated to stand on their own feet. I will pay their fees and my father will have less burden of managing cash every month.'

This way, my father could continue farming with ease. Sarabjit, my immediate younger brother, could continue to help Bapuji as long as he was in school/college. But Dadiji loved me too much to let me go away.

I somehow managed to coax her, 'My going for this training cannot be cancelled as I had already signed a bond.'

My grandmother loved me the most and I too used to take care of her a lot. Whenever I used to be depressed, she would tell me stories of Guru Gobind Singh Ji and his *Chaar Sahibzadey*. Maybe it was a shock for her or she felt a little uneasy, wondering who would take so much care of her as I did. By then, it was evening and there was a *mela* (gathering of well-wishers) of people in our house. All the neighbours came to know of my selection in the IAF. One of my cousins, Mr Chanchal Singh, brought some *sharab*[49] and wanted to celebrate. He was very well known for drinking almost every evening but no one in my family touched liquor at all. That evening, he forced me to taste. I think I took two pegs of that and got drunk. I started to shout and speak loudly in English. Everyone around me told me to speak softly, sit down and relax. I don't remember what had happened thereafter. The next day, I got up with a terrible headache and felt like throwing up. I was to pack my clothes but I couldn't lift up my head from the pillow. Everyone at home cursed Mr Chanchal Singh for putting me in such a condition. Finally, I admitted that it was my fault as I had agreed with Chanchal to celebrate in that manner.

I packed my clothes with a great difficulty and got ready to leave for Dasuya railway station to take the train to Ambala Cantt. My father accompanied me up to Jalandhar Railway station. He returned from there by bus. Our train was at Jalandhar railway station for about 20

---

[49] Desi liquor

minutes. While parting, both of us hugged each other and cried aloud, as that was the first time I was going so far away and for such a long period. We both were going to miss each other immensely. My train whistled and the steam started to emit. I got into the train and stood at the doorway, waving to Bapuji as long as I could see him. He reached home by midnight as I was told later. There were no mobile phones in those days; the only telephone was in the post office and phone calls were quite expensive. My train reached Ambala Cantt Railway Station at about 4 AM. It was summertime and the weather was very pleasant. I was required to report to the air force station orderly room at 8 AM on that day. I spent my time at the railway station and had breakfast of *cholle*, *puri* and *chai*. As soon as it was time for me to leave, I took a cycle rickshaw and set course for the AF orderly room. I had the letter, which was given to me at the orderly room, with me. This letter was a permit to reach the concerned window. As I was off loading my suitcase from the rickshaw, I saw two more boys coming to the same window. Within a few minutes, three more boys reached there. We all stood in a queue and waited to be called by someone in the window. For all six of us, a party warrant was prepared and we were given Rs. 25 each for the journey as journey allowance. All travel instructions were given and Mr Kuldip Singh Lubana was made in-charge of the party. All of us introduced ourselves. One Corporal was detailed to go to Ambala Cantt Railway Station to exchange our warrant for the tickets and hand it over to Mr Kuldip Singh. He was also given one big, sealed envelope, containing some official documents addressed to Air Force Station, Tambaram (GTS).

Departure for Tambaram for Technical Training in the IAF

The journey commenced on time and during the course of travel, our acquaintance with each other developed further. We were a group of six, travelling together. Kuldip and I somehow got along and became friends instantly. We exchanged our views on various subjects. In fact, like me, he was also studying in F.sc 2nd year before his recruitment. We had similar qualifications and our views on life matched too. After travelling for two days, we finally reached Chennai. On reaching the railway station, one of us went to RTO's office to check if there was any vehicle to Air Force Station, Tambaram. The RTO informed us that we would have to wait for the Air Force Recreation Run (one three tonner vehicle). He told us to keep an eye outside, as the vehicle should be arriving within an hour. Since there was time, we kept our luggage at one place and made one of us in-charge of it. The rest of us started strolling on the platform. Kuldip and I were together when we happened to see a couple—the man was of darker complexion and the lady was of fair-skinned and looked like a Punjabi lady. When we were crossing them, both of us commented at the same time, 'Look, the guy looks like a Madrasi, whereas, his wife looks like a Punjabi'. This remark was so loud that even the couple had heard it. They threw us a dirty glance and carried on their way. It was our way of having some fun as we were feeling like grown ups that were going to be trainees in IAF.

After some time, we were informed that the Air Force vehicle had come. We all picked up our luggage and ran towards the vehicle. The driver of the vehicle was a man in uniform, his rank had two stripes and he asked about the trainees and then introduced himself as Corporal and MTD of the vehicle. His service jargon was beyond our understanding but the Air Force Station was the only thing that we understood. As we reached the main entry gate of Air Force Station, Tambaram, we were very thrilled to see a new place and, more so, our training centre. As our vehicle reached the centre, the MTD got down and handed over our letters which we had brought from the Air Force Station, Ambala, to someone sitting at the window. He also enquired about our billet (barrack) number from that gentleman. The MTD took us to one billet and dropped us there. We saw the billet—it was half-empty and the occupants were also trainees who had arrived a day before us. All of them had one bed and one small cupboard to themselves; the rest of the room had only twelve *charpais*[50] and cupboards. One trainee came out and asked us to occupy one bed each and leave the rest of the beds for the other trainees arriving late at night. This trainee was Mr Yadav, who was the in-charge of all of us. He made us stand in a line outside the billet and then briefed us on the next day's programme. We all were required to fall-in at the parade ground where the roll call was to be

---

[50] Beds

taken and GTIs (Ground Training Instructors) would be present. The first day was spent finding our feet on the ground and getting to know the place around. The first and the most important place that we came to know of was the mess for trainees. We checked the meal timings so that we don't miss it. At this stage, my training during NCC camps while I was in school came handy. Inside the billet on one side of my bed was Kuldip (Instrument Repairer Trade) and on the other side was Gurcharan Singh who had Armourer Trade. In the same billet was Mr Vohra of Instrument Repairer Trade from Delhi, a very crafty person but jovial by nature.

We all went to the mess and had our evening tea. The meal timings were also quite early. After tea, we reached our billet and got introduced to all other co-trainees. Kuldip and I somehow started hanging out together. We arranged our bags and belongings in and over the suitcases we had. Before we arrived in the billet, one plate, one mug and one spoon were kept on our beds for our use for which we were to sign the next day. We went to the mess again during sunset and stood in a queue to get our meals, which were served by the mess members. These trainees, who had arrived a couple of days before us, were detailed to do the job. They were assigned the job of mess members. After a sumptuous and peaceful dinner, we returned to the billets. We were the 51st intake of trainees. We were told to fall-in at the parade ground for roll call and for some instructions from the GTIs. At night, in the process of getting to know each other, we all boasted of our school and college life for sometime and then went off to sleep. In spite of being tired, a new place and a different environment made it difficult to sleep. Anyway, night passed very quickly and approached the daybreak. With so many trainees present in the billet, there was no need for an alarm to get up in the morning. Some of us rushed to the toilets and group baths. After the morning routine, I dressed myself and got ready, as if I was to attend some wedding ceremony. We all rushed to the playground on foot and started to fall in. GTI Corporal Kang, at the top of his voice, was ordering all of us to stand in straight lines and make no noise. It took us about 15 minutes to be ready to receive the instructions from the GTI. Suddenly, one Corporal came on a cycle and said something to GTI Kang. Thereafter, accompanied by Mr Kang, he started to inspect our lines and then as he came to me and Kuldip and said, 'These are the trainees'. Mr Kang ordered the two of us to fall-out and come in front of all the boys. We didn't know what was going on. After introducing himself as corporal Sharma, he said to both of us, 'I will tell you who is *kala* and who is *gori*'. He said something to Mr Kang and ordered us to do front rolls in front of all trainees. It was then that we realized that our remarks at the railway station, in Madras Central, had caught up with us. Anyway, there was no time and no scope to apologize. We started front rolling. GTI shouted, 'Do not stop till I tell you'. Mr Kang announced our names and told all the trainees what we had done at the railway station. For that reason, we were being given front rolls as a physical punishment. With no other choice, we started to do front rolls. Though it was a punishment, both of us being physically fit, started the rolls thinking it was a warm-up exercise for us before a major game. After about 15 front rolls, we slowed down slightly and heard GTI shout, 'Don't stop till I tell you'. I think corporal Sharma left for his class as he was undergoing Conversion Course at Tambaram. GTI shouted again, 'Stop and fall-in'. By this time, our shirts and pants were completely stained but we took everything sportingly and also realized our mistake. Thereafter, we learnt a lesson—to never pass any remarks on anyone.

All trainees were given some PT exercises and were asked to march up and down. After about half an hour, we marched to the equipment section for issue of the kit. The kit included one towel, two bed sheets, one *dari*[51] and two pillowcases. After this kit-issue-parade, we were marched back to the billets. We were instructed by the GTI to fall-in again on the parade ground at 1600 hours. During this fall-in, the GTI asked everyone about the game of his preference and made groups for different games like hockey, football, volleyball, athletics, etc. Kuldip and I opted for all games, including athletics. We were made to play football and volleyball on that very day and then we dispersed to get ready for dinner. Before we were dispersed, the GTI also briefed us about the gymnasium and its timings. We were elated to hear about it as we had never heard of such a sport before. While coming back to the billet, we visited the gym and found it packed with senior trainees. We

---

[51] Light cotton mattress

watched them do some normal exercises and weight-lifting exercises. I really got highly excited to avail this facility and build my muscles and body as a whole, since I was on the leaner side.

The next day was scheduled for a routine fall-in, PT and parade. After that, we were marched to our classrooms which were segregated tradewise. All Inst/Rep trainees were taken to a room where our instructor Sgt Rakha Ram was waiting. As we sat down at our desks, Sgt Rakha Ram instructed us to introduce ourselves one by one. After the introductions were over, he made us interchange the seats and mark them to be permanent for the period of training. The scope of the course was covered and we were informed about the tentative date of the completion of the course for passing out. Soon everything fell into a disciplined routine and I started enjoying my games of hockey and football. Every day something funny used to happen and someone used to narrate his experience in the class or in the playground. For the first time in my life, I went to a gym and started enjoying the gym exercises. At the end of two weeks, there was a test in the class on the portion, which was already covered by our instructor. The results were declared the following week. Even though my position was 4th in the class, I couldn't help being disappointed because I thought that I had a good control over English language. In introspection, it hit me that I should have put in more hours of homework. The next day, I saw Kuldip going somewhere after dinner with a book in his hand. I followed him and saw that he sat in the gym veranda, where tube lights were on and was studying there. On asking him what was he doing there and why, he explained that this was a quiet place where lights were available for longer hours. So, he could study at night without any disturbances. It was then that I realized how he stood second in the class, whereas, my position was 4th. From that day onwards, even I started to burn my midnight oil. From the next test onwards, it was a competition between both of us. I stood first in some tests and Kuldip stood second. Again, there were some tests where Kuldip stood first and I got second position. After a three-month training, our officer in charge of 51st Intake, Flt Lt Kaushal, came to the class and asked some questions to all the trainees. He appreciated Kuldip and my answers and wished us good luck.

In the training routine, the time flew by very quickly and our competitions kept growing intense. The challenge of standing first every time had stuck in my mind and I was really becoming very serious about it. In PT and games, we took extra interest. Kuldip and I kept taking part in every sport and kept winning the appreciation of instructors. I did much better in parades than the rest as I had NCC training in my school. In fact, my commands on morning parades had become the talk of the town and on our final passing-out parade, I even commanded the parade. As far as my Trade results were concerned, I was granted Aircraftman-1 classification. This granted me six months seniority over other trainees. Kuldip and Bindra were also granted Aircraftman-1 classification. Within a couple of days, our postings were announced and I was posted to No.47 Squadron, a fighter Squadron equipped with *Toofani* Aircraft (French made) and was based at AF (Air Force) Station, Halwara.

10

THRILLS AND TRIALS

At Air Force Station, Halwara

Our arrival at AF Station, Halwara, was an event by itself. A batch of 10 airmen left Tambaram for Delhi and for a few more AF stations in Punjab. We all travelled this long distance for the first time after our training in respective trades. Kuldip and I were made in-charge of the rest of the airmen. We took utmost care to see that the journey was uneventful. We started departing gradually as our destinations arrived, some to the units in Delhi and around. I had to get down at railway station Ludhiana. That was the closest railway station to my destination. After collecting my stuff and bidding farewell to other friends, including Kuldip Singh, I left the train and alighted at the platform. Now as per briefing, I was to look for a posting truck parked in the parking of the railway station.

After taking a round of the parking lot, I located a three Tonner with Air Force logo but the MTD was not there. I guessed that he might have gone to see someone off. So, I waited for a while and a little later, one Corporal in uniform arrived at the vehicle. I asked, 'Is this vehicle from Air Force Station, Halwara?' 'Yes, it is. Have you arrived on posting?' he asked me back. He also saw my joining instructions to confirm. He waited for another hour till some more airmen in civil clothes joined us and we left for the Air Force Station. The journey took us approximately 45 minutes. One of the iron strips supporting the roof of tarpaulin of the vehicle on both sides was loose, making a cranking noise. Most of the airmen were cursing and complaining of poor maintenance of the vehicle, whereas, I was enjoying the ride because it was my first experience. Actually, I was too excited to join a

Fighter Squadron and meet new friends. After a couple of stops within the family quarters, the vehicle stopped near Airmen Mess. By the time we reached, the lunchtime was over and I was already starving. I headed to the mess and requested if I could get something to eat. One of the mess members asked,'Are you a new arrival?' I promptly replied,'Yes, I am', and then he managed some rice and *dal*, which was the leftover food from the quota of guards on duty. I took all the rice and dal and went back to the dining hall, sat on a bench, close to a table and enjoyed my first meal at AF Station, Halwara. After enjoying my simple yet filling meal, I left the dining hall, picked up my baggage but did not know where to go for accommodation. In the meantime, a Corporal came in uniform and pointed towards the tented accommodations. He mentioned the newly posted airmen would have to spend at least two to three months in the tents. Later on, squadron DWO (Discipline Warrant Officer) would decide when to shift the airmen to the squadron billets. I entered one of the tents with empty charpoy. I put my bedding on that and my suitcase below the bed. After seeing a new face, couple of airmen came to me, introduced themselves and started sharing a lot of 'gen' (information) about this new AF Station. I enjoyed the chit-chat with my new mates and didn't realize that it was already time for tea. We all rushed to the mess and formed a queue with mugs in our hands. This was our time of fun and jokes. Someone would say something and then others would cut in and add their version of the jokes. Even the mess members were not spared and a lot of remarks were passed on them too. I enjoyed all of this quite silently and patiently since I was new to the place. After tea, someone announced that we all had to fall-in for PT or run, and thereafter, head for the games of our choice. It was difficult to find my nicker (half Pants) in my luggage, but somehow, I managed to pull out one from my suitcase, which was fully creased and perhaps not even washed since its last use. Anyway, I enjoyed the PT and games and on the very first day, I impressed everyone with my hockey skills.

Now the routine started by reporting to my Squadron Orderly Room. I was seen by my DWO, and thereafter, he took me to the Adjutant. My Squadron Commander was Squadron Ldr DA Lafontaine, Flight Cdrs were Harry Chithwal and Mohan. Squadron Pilots were Subaramu,

Mascarenhas, Subaiya, Rajiv Verma and Gupta. These are some of the names that I can remember now. On the first day after my Adjutant's interview, I was taken to my section—Instrument Repairer's Den and it was in a tent. Sgt Balakrishnan was section in-charge and 2 i/c was Sgt Daulat Ram. Other airmen of my section were AC2 Ramaswami, Chetan and Verma. I immediately sensed that due to less manpower in the section, I needed to work for longer hours. I was mentally strong and focussed. I took the responsibility seriously and with the approach of a student, requested Bala and Sgt Daulat to start teaching me the DI (Daily Inspection) schedule for *Toofani Aircraft*. Anyway, the very first day went in meeting other sections of different trades. I met Cpl Ajit Singh Engine Fitter, Cpl Mangal Singh Armourer Fitter, Aircraftman (AC) Pruthi Airframe II. Soon we all became friends within a few days. The other airmen were AC Jay Raman, LAC R Singh, LAC Ram Lal and many others. All were very kind and nice to me and time seemed to pass quickly and joyfully.

One day, Sgt Bala told Cpl Daulat Ram and me that one of our aircrafts had a repeated snag of Turn and Slip Indicator (TSI) giving wrong indication. A repeated snag was viewed very seriously by all squadron pilots. The three of us discussed the rectifications that were done in the past. Sgt Bala said that the continuity test of the wire connecting the TSI is good. It has been repeatedly checked, TSI has been calibrated and declared serviceable (passed). After all the discussion, I volunteered to give it a try to identify the reason for the snag. We got the Canopy and Ejection Seat removed to have a free access to all the wires leading to the front instrument panel. The time was 2 in the afternoon, and the day was quite hot. I got into the cockpit with a continuity and resistance check meter. It took me at least 10 to 15 minutes to trace out all the connecting wires from the secondary source of supply to the front panel instruments. From those bunches of wires which were very nicely cleated to the floor of the cockpit, I was to trace out a single wire connecting to the TSI. After a struggle with the cleated wires, I assumed and guessed that the wire I had traced going to the TSI, was the one causing the trouble. After a little brain storming, I started the continuity test of that wire; the test was perfect. Now I did not know why the instrument was giving wrong readings in the air when it was perfect in performance on ground. I was going into a kind of frenzy and frustration for not being able to solve the problem. Anyway, as I was determined to solve the puzzle, I sat in the cockpit and started visualizing why something was going wrong with the TSI in the air. This was the time when I remembered a saying my father used to often tell me, '*Duniya vich koi cheez namumkin nahi hai*.'there is not a thing in this world, which is impossible to achieve. Now the idea struck me that I should speak to the pilot who had flown the aircraft the last time. That would give me some lead to work upon. I got up and left the aircraft and went inside my section and shared my idea with Sgt Bala, who, in turn, told me that both the pilots who had flown the aircraft have discussed the snag with him and Cpl Daulat Ram. They explained—while turning the aircraft, in the air, the instrument suddenly misbehaved. In straight and level flight the instrument was generally behaving 'normally'. After listening to Sgt Bala, I came back to the cockpit and started visualizing flight conditions. Then and there it stuck me that (G) gravitational force during turns is making the instrument misbehave. This thought gave me the feeling that one more test was required to be done. I connected the external battery to the aircraft and switched on the internal battery and waited for some time for the instrument to get processed and start giving stable readings on ground. When TSI was erect and stable in horizontal indication, I took my screw driver and carefully inserted it among the bunch of wires leading to the instrument panel. I shook one bunch of cables left and right, up and down. Nothing happened. Then I did the same thing to the next bunch of wires and to my surprise, the TSI bank indicator moved a bit to show the bank. To confirm, I did this action two to three times and noticed a similar reaction-taking place. I became so excited that I exclaimed on the top of my voice, 'I found it! I found it!' I was sitting in the cockpit without an Ejection Seat (Pilot's Seat) so I was hardly seen by anybody from outside. Coincidentally, at that time, my commanding officer Squadron Ldr DA Lafontaine had come back from his flight and was walking towards his office, past my aircraft. He suddenly heard my loud voice and got alarmed and looked towards me and asked, 'Singh, what has happened?' I got scared that he might get annoyed with me. He, anyway, laughed and asked again, 'What have you found?' I came out of the cockpit and got down from the aircraft. I saluted him first and then explained about the repeated snag on the aircraft instrument and about my discovery. He patted my back and said, 'Keep it up and get the aircraft on line as soon as possible'. I saluted him again and replied, 'Okay Sir, we will try our best'. Commanding officer left for his office and I left for my section to report the detection of snag and the conversation with my commanding officer. Sgt Bala pacified me and accompanied me to the cockpit to see my findings. He was pleasantly surprised with my discovery. We traced the single cable connecting the TSI and confirmed the snag by shaking it again and again. We changed the cable and cleated as original and tested in a similar manner. The TSI was behaving absolutely normally. This incident gave me more confidence and a good standing in the section. After this incident, my workload had also increased almost two fold. I started to work from morning to evening with only a break of one hour for lunch, on four days in a week. This routine continued as I also cleared my reclassification to Leading aircrafts man (LAC).

Selection for My Flying Training

Sometime later, there was an entry for an officer-commissioning interview in our URO (Unit Routine Orders). I applied on being recommended by my section and within one week's time, my interviews had started. To my surprise, Flying Officer Subaya, adjutant of our squadron, took my first interview. Since I was to be interviewed by my commanding officer, apart from a few questions, my adjutant became my guide and gave me some helpful tips for answering some questions. After an hour, I was taken to CO's office for the interview. I was made to sit and was asked if I was feeling comfortable to which I replied, 'Yes, Sir'. My CO asked me very simple questions besides asking one general-knowledge question. Since I used to go through the newspapers regularly and used to read *Current Affairs* magazine, I answered all his questions with precision, thus, impressing him. He then asked about the pilot aptitude test and the Control Surfaces of an aircraft, and then went on to ask, 'If you pull back on stick (Control Column), what will happen to the aircraft while in the air?' My answer was that the aircraft will start going upwards, that is, it will start climbing. Likewise, he asked me about all sorts of communications. My answers were more or less correct. He finally signed my application and recommended me for interview with Station Commander Wg Cdr Banerji. After four days, the Station Adjutant called me and my interview was planned at about 1300 hours. I was called in the Station Commander's office and made to sit across the table in front of Wing Commander Banerji. The first question that he asked me was, 'Why do you want to become a pilot in the IAF?' I replied, 'Sir, I am a son of a farmer, who can barely afford fees of my younger brother and sister. If I become an officer in the IAF, I shall earn a handsome salary and I will support my father's farming and fees of my younger brother and sister. They will be able to study well and join some profession. That way, we will be of some service to our nation collectively'. At that time, I did not know what his reaction was. However, after a little pause, he congratulated me and recommended my application for further and final interview at Air Force Selection Board in Dehradun. This recommendation earned me a great deal of confidence and respect among my unit personnel. My friends Cpl Mangal Singh, Cpl Avtar Singh, LAC Pruthi, LAC R Singh, AC Kharkal and Lac Jayaram were very happy and they arranged a small party to celebrate my achievement. We all enjoyed a cup of milk and biscuits. As a matter of fact, Cpl Mangal Singh and Cpl Avtar Singh started preparing me for my commissioning interview. I owe a great deal of gratitude to all my friends who always have guided me to advance in my career. I think I had managed to create an environment of good will and co-operation among my friends. I knew it very well that interdependence is better than independence and would pay far greater dividends. As I belonged to a joint family, I always remembered my father setting a good example by teaching interdependence within each other and how successful it would be in all fields. He also sometimes talked about those families who did joint farming ventures together. I had explicitly understood that interdependence certainly has higher values than independence. My friends always saw a ray of hope in me for higher values and higher ambition in my career. They were always appreciative of my cooperation and a forgiving nature. On Tarmac, where the most operational and technical activities were going on, I used to help my other tradesmen to complete their tasks, passing them tools when they required getting inside a restricted space where it was difficult to go in or come out every now and then. Also, the tools were not allowed to be taken to those compartments with a fear that someone might forget a small tool inside and that may lead to an accident on the start of the engine of the aircraft or it may happen in the air, which could result in a major accident.

It was mid of 1962 when the Air Force Selection Board at Dehradun called me for an interview and Pilot Aptitude Test. With a lot of prayers of my friends and blessings of my Squadron officers and other Ranks, I left for Dehradun. On the very first day, the pilot aptitude test consisting of a drum and controlling of a light had started. There were some written questions on instrumentation and technical-knowledge questions that were quite easy. With God's grace, I managed to pass all the tests and cleared for the rest of the interview procedures. The difficult part was obstacle clearance, which was a physical test, which, like the written work, was not as easy. The group discussions and talk on a subject given by the Ground Testing Officer (GTO) was really challenging. But thankfully, with Waheguru's help, the result was in my favour. After four to five days' stay in Dehradun, the indications were positive. However, official intimation was to be sent by the board to my Command HQs. I returned to the squadron and found my friends jumping with joy as the signal had arrived just the same day of my arrival at AF Station, Halwara. I was called by my adjutant to the flight commander's office. All my officers were there to greet and congratulate me. I was already flying sky-high with joy and excitement. My Squadron Cdr Squadron Ldr DA Lafontaine was overjoyed; he hugged me tight and congratulated me. On the same day, I was also called by the station adjutant and was taken to Station Cdr, Wg Cdr Banerji, who shook hands with me and congratulated me. For the next 15 to 20 minutes, he advised me on how to proceed further and what was expected from me during pilot's training. He also explained the further procedure, which I was to follow. The next step was my medical examination at CME, New Delhi.

One batch of six airmen was called by CME, AF (Central Medical Establishment, Air Force) for medical examination. When my turn came for my preliminary medical examination, I was called in a room where one lady medical officer was sitting. As I went inside and greeted her, she asked me to remove my clothes. As soon as I heard that, I quickly left her room and went back to the waiting room. I was stupefied—

how could I remove my clothes in front of a lady? Anyway, I was called again and told the same thing. This time, I went in another room where a male medical officer was present. 'Why are you here?' He asked and added, 'You should have been in the next room'. I immediately told him how the lady was asking me to remove my clothes and how impossible that seemed to me. He replied, 'Damn it! She is a doctor. She has to do the preliminary medical test on you. Go and apologize, otherwise your medical will be cancelled and you will be sent back to your squadron'. As soon I heard that, I quickly ran back to the lady medical officer and apologized and got my medical examination completed. The whole medical examination took three days and I cleared it with good remarks, being a hockey and a basketball player. After completing my medical examination, I had a drinking session with my cousins from Gondpur Village, *Sada Nanka Pind, that is,* from my maternal side, whom I had met there. They got me drunk and the next day, I kept throwing up the entire time. Anyway, to feel better and hydrated, they gave me many glasses of *nimbupani*[52] to drink. On the 5th day, I started by train for AF Station, Halwara, via Ludhiana. My squadron mates had received the message, which was passed by signal from CME, New Delhi. As soon as I reached my billet, many colleagues came over to congratulate me on clearing my medical test, which was the last hurdle before a call for training. Though all other friends were happy for me, the happiest man on the earth that day was Cpl Mangal Singh because he saw in me the potential of a pilot. The next day was a very memorable day for me. My Adjutant took me to my Commanding Officer who was overjoyed and had only kind words for me. He advised me to do well during pilot's training. My section mates and seniors were also excited that at least one of them was making to the pilot's stature. My morale was sky-high and I was determined to do well in pilot's training.

---

[52] Lemonade

11

SKY IS THE LIMIT

Stay at Pilot Training Establishment—Allahabad

The second signal followed from Air Head Quarters that I was to report to PTE (Pilot Training Establishment), Allahabad, for pilot's training. That was my initial training. Mid-term training was to be in PTS (Pilot Training School) Jodhpur and advanced pilot's training was supposed to be either in Secunderabad or Begumpet, depending upon the stream of selection (Fighter pilot's training at Secunderabad and Transport pilot's training at Begumpet). My farewell and departure from AF Station, Halwara, was a memorable event. All my friends came up to Ludhiana Railway station to see me off. So much so, Mangal, Ajit and Pruthi had tears in their eyes but deep within, they were extremely happy that one of their best friends was going for pilot's training. The train journey up to Allahabad was uneventful. At Allahabad Railway Station, I met a couple of more cadets and together, we reached Cadet's mess at PTE, Allahabad. I thought we were the first ones to arrive and no one else was there. However, a little later, one senior cadet appeared and introduced himself as Shergill. We were now a part of 85th pilot's course. One batch had already gone to Jodhpur directly. We, the 85th-course-boys, got together and I and Swaran Singh Banga became roommates. Due to some altercation, we chased Shergill out of our block and made fun of him. He left our block but reported the matter to our Physical Training Instructor (PTI). The next day, when we assembled for a health run in the morning, Banga and I were asked to fall-out in front of the whole course. The instructor then asked us to front roll in front of everyone. We did that and were told that Shergill was from a senior course and all were supposed to obey and respect him. And so, we did for the rest of the stay of Mr Shergill. Our ground subject classes started. Banga and I started working hard in practise and kept scoring very good marks (100%) in our tests most of the times. The instructor seemed quite pleased with our efforts. The following officers were in staff: Chief Instructor Group Captain Phillips, Chief Flying Instructor Squadron Ldr Birch and Squadron Ldr Malik. My flying instructor was Flt Lt Baldev Singh, a complete gentleman. His briefings for flying were very elaborate and thorough. Our flying was to start after a final test of ground subjects, including Emergencies on HT-2 Trainer Aircraft. We were given plenty of cockpit drills and practise of emergencies while sitting in the cockpit. This included blindfold check of various switches and levers in the cockpit.

Finally, the time had come for the experience of an air trip. Time was passing very fast every day; we used to hope for the flying to start soon. Before the air experience, we were given all ATC (Air Traffic Control) procedures and runway orientation while standing at the ATC Tower. Thereafter, I was taken for taxiing the HT-2 on the Taxi Track and Runway. Procedure for leaving dispersal, entering taxi track and tires-check at ORP (Operational Readiness Platform) before take-off were completed. Entering runway and line up for take-off was also very well-rehearsed. Even Taxi back to dispersal and switch off procedure was covered very well.

My first air experience was a unique one and I remember each and every step distinctly. My instructor, Baldev Singh, put me in the front cockpit of HT-2, strapped me up and gave me cockpit drill, including blindfold check of switches and levers. He felt happy and satisfied and got in the rear cockpit. He asked me to start up the engine as he had taken clearance from ATC. We both had intercom and were getting ATC signal at strength 5. We taxied out of dispersal and followed the taxi track. The nose of the aircraft was blocking the view of taxi track, as it was a tailwheel aircraft. To look for a clear way, we had to weave the nose of the aircraft on the taxi track. We got the tires checked, followed by our vital actions before line-up. My instructor took permission to line-up. My instructor demonstrated the line-up and I followed him on controls from the front cockpit. After the completion of line-up, I did my vital actions before taking off. The instructor obtained permission from ATC and started to open the throttle, I left the brakes and finally, we rolled forward for take-off. The instructor carried out take-off when I followed him on controls. He pattered the take-off procedure. We got airborne and soon we climbed to some altitude; I started to feel that our aircraft was standing still in the air and was not moving forward. I immediately conveyed my feelings to my instructor. He told me to look at the air speed indicator on the front instrument panel. When I looked at it again, it was reading 75 mph. Even after that, my sensation of being stationary in the air did not go away. Thereafter, he levelled the aircraft at about 3,000 feet and made me look at the tree line on my right. I did so and found the tree line going back slowly. Now my notion of being stationary in the air started to change. Then he descended down to 2,000 feet and made me see trees and other features moving back at a much faster speed. Then we climbed to 5,000 feet. I understood the difference and the feeling of being stationary in the air had gone away completely. Thereafter, daily flying went on as per the syllabus prepared for initial stage. One day, my instructor asked, 'Do you want to be a fighter pilot or a transport pilot?' I don't know why but I replied that I wanted to become a Transport Pilot. He really shouted at me and said, 'No, I want you to become a Fighter Pilot and I shall prepare your base for that. I want to see you as a Fighter Pilot'. From that day onwards, I changed my mind and started to prepare to become a Fighter Pilot. My instructor started spending more time on aerobatic manoeuvres. In HT-2 aircraft looping, manoeuvre was difficult for me. Nevertheless, with the help of my instructor, I mastered the art of looping whenever he was with me. Solo loops in HT-2 aircraft were prohibited. Finally, it was time for passing out from PTE, Allahabad. I had secured my position in the top 5 in my elementary stage.

Stay at Jodhpur for Intermediate Stage Flying Training

After all farewells, we were sent to Jodhpur for intermediate stage flying on T6-G aircraft. Since our 85th course was split into two halves, one half of us went for initial training at Allahabad and the other half was sent for initial training to Jodhpur. We reached Jodhpur AF Station and settled in. On the first day, the roll call surprised us when we heard a senior cadet shouting, 'All *Allahabadies*, fallout separately'. Sure enough, he indicated to us and told us that we lack proper discipline. They, being from Jodhpur Flying Training School, acted as if they were superior and called us *Allahabadies*—an undisciplined lot. These sorts of remarks continued for over two weeks, until we reported the matter to our chief instructor. Anyway, the stamp of Allahabad stayed with us for the next three and a half months of training. Our flying and ground instructors were quite efficient. Flt Lt Joe Bakshi, a very tough and hard taskmaster, was my instructor. We were three cadets with him—SS Bains, Dhillon and I.

In Jodhpur, one very interesting incident took place. On our first introduction in flights, Squadron Ldr Ammanula asked to give our names turn by turn. When my turn came, I shouted, 'Cadet Harbans Singh Sahota!' He corrected me, 'You mean to say "Harbans Singh Dakota"?' Everyone had a good laugh and I repeated, 'Sir, my surname is Sahota'. He said once again, 'Okay, it's Dakota. And I will call you Dakota'. Throughout my stay in Jodhpur, he continued calling me Dakota. Anyway, after a couple of days, I also started enjoying his shouts for which he was very famous.

Since our instructor, Bakshi was a hard task master in his style of teaching to fly, both Dhillon and Bains asked for a change of instructor. Bakshi later asked me if I too wanted to have a change of instructor. But I clearly said, 'No, I want to continue with you'. I think that made him happy and he took a lot of interest in my training. Once, during regular discussions, I mentioned to him that I wanted to be a Fighter Pilot. From then on, he concentrated more on my aerobatic skills. The difficult part was looping aerobatics. He made me perfect in that manoeuvre. In my solo flying, I used to enjoy my aerobatics and perfected my looping manoeuvres. My instructor was very happy with my progress. One time, during the night-flying phase, I created a serious emergency. It went like this—we were on a dual cross-country sortie. After completing the short cross-country, we joined circuit flying for Jodhpur runway. The Jodhpur runway was lit with gooseneck lights. As we came on downwind side of the circuit, my instructor asked me to change the fuel tank selection to full tank side. He asked me to do this because the engine had started making noise as if it would turn off out of fuel starvation. I put my hand on the fuel cap and turned it to one side, which happened to be the wrong side, as in that portion, there was no light. As we came to the final approach, our aircraft engine started coughing and the instructor shouted, '*Haraamzade! Fuel tank change nahi kiya!*' I quickly put my hand back on the fuel tank selection lever and turned it to the other side. Our engine nearly flamed out, but due to fuel injection just on time, it picked up again. Anyway, we landed that approach, and the instructor took over controls and brought the aircraft to dispersal, switched off and went out of the aircraft in a hurry. He straightaway went to his office. As soon as I reached the crew room, I got the message to meet my instructor. At first, he congratulated me for my reaction and said, 'We were very lucky to get the engine back on time or else we would have to force land the aircraft, and at night, God only knows what would have happened!'

Then began the other phase of debriefing, rolling with abuses—'*M****d, b**nc**d, kutta, harami*—you would have killed yourself and killed me too. It all happened because you did not listen and follow my instructions!' I immediately told him that I did change the fuel selection but to the wrong side. That is why it had happened. And as soon as he had shouted again, I had changed the selection once again. Luckily, this time it happened to be the correct selection. He said, 'Okay, do two things immediately, one, get into the cockpit of one parked aircraft with a torch and know the selections of fuel tanks. After that, pick up your parachute on your shoulders, and start running on the tarmac until I tell you to stop'. Believe me, that night was a real nightmare for me. I kept on running slowly on the tarmac and kept on going. I must have carried on for one hour. I was sweating and feeling thirsty, but could not stop. I was almost fainting when my instructor called me to his office. He told me that from then on, I would never make that type of mistake ever again; a mistake, which could have led to a disaster. He also told me that in flying, we must know exactly what to do, especially learning by instinct all the actions in the air and on the ground. From that night onwards, my training went absolutely trouble free. Rest of the stay at Jodhpur was quite ordinary as far as flying was concerned.

Since I was a hockey player, I was in the AF Station Jodhpur Hockey team. Gp Capt. Radhakrishnan (station commander) was also a very good hockey player. We played four matches with other teams, and during a match with the army team on our station ground, I was playing at centre-forward position and my station commander was playing as centre-half position. He passed the ball to me on the top of the Dee, which I could not stop, and missed a chance to score a goal. Thereafter, I received a big shouting for that mistake. Anyway, I scored the winning goal and finally earned his pat on my back.

Stay at Hakimpet for Final Stage Flying Training

After passing out from Jodhpur, we were split into two streams. One for fighter pilot training was sent to Hakimpet and the second stream was for transport pilot training, which was sent to Begumpet. Since I was in fighter stream, I was sent to Hakimpet, along with other cadets. There was nothing extraordinary in the arrival and settlement at Hakimpet cadet's mess. We were allotted rooms and two of us, Banga and I, became room mates like before. Training routine commenced and we all learnt and followed instructions well. Here we were allotted a bicycle each, for commuting to classrooms, flying squadron headquarters and flight offices. Our ground subjects training had also started and we were divided into two Flights, namely, A and B. My name was in A flight. Our Chief Instructor was Squadron Ldr Rajeshwar Singh. He was also well known for shouting at the cadets. My flying instructor was Flt Lt Daniel and we were only four cadets with him—Bains, Bhattacharji, Saini and I. Our ground subjects, along with emergencies, checklist and cockpit drills had also started. At first, my instructor demonstrated experience local flying area familiarization, circuits and landing. This was known as dual instructional flying. The first solo fly wasn't exceptional but thankfully, uneventful. At this stage, my confidence in jet flying had started to build up. We were to prepare ourselves for each mission (sortie). After the general handling phase came the formation-flying phase. I had no problems whatsoever in these phases. Ground subjects training was also going on simultaneously. Flt Lt Salins was teaching us Aerodynamics and Gyro Gun Sight. I understood GGS very well and was well ahead of other cadets because I had studied the Gyro theory very well in my training at Tambaram. After the ground subject test, our navigation phase started, taking the aircraft on a triangular trip at stated heights in a progressive manner. The day I was to go for a triangular cross-country at 20,000 feet, the weather was bad. A lot of low and medium level clouds were there in the sky. We were all waiting for the weather to improve, but it was taking its own time. At this juncture, my CI, Rajeshwar Singh came to our crew room and asked, 'Who all are going for navigation?' I raised my hand, and he asked, 'To what height do you have to go to?''Sir, at 20,000 feet', I replied. He immediately enquired, 'what are you waiting for? Why don't you go?''Sir, too many medium and high clouds are present and one cannot even see the sky from the ground', I replied.'Pick up your parachute and come out with me', he ordered. I followed him. He took me to the tarmac where the aircraft was parked. He said, 'Look up; do you see a hole in the clouds and the sky through that?''Yes sir', I answered. He quickly told me to go to my earmarked aircraft, start up and take off. His instructions were, 'You should climb overhead, and go through that hole and set a course for the first leg of navigation and climb to 20,000 feet. Complete your triangular navigation and return'. And I, like a good cadet, did just the same. As I took off, I entered clouds at about 1,500 feet and turned onto my first leg of navigation. I was on instruments and occasionally glancing out to look for the hole. It was not there but I kept climbing up and broke clouds at 15,000 feet and finally, I saw the clear sky above the clouds. Since these clouds were sheet-like, it made a very beautiful flat-looking surface and I enjoyed my flight. I steered the course and went by time only as map reading was not possible due to any contact with the ground. I turned on time for the second leg and steered the course with a fair amount of precision. Then I turned onto the third leg on time. There was no contact with the ground even then. On the third leg, towards the Hakimpet Airfield, I had marked my descent point on the map with time. Since there was no contact with the ground, I started the descent on time. I descended through the clouds, steering the marked course meticulously and expected that after breaking the clouds at some level, I would see the Hakimpet runway. For some reason, my NDB (non-directional beacon) was not locking properly. It was wandering to either side. Anyway, I was very confident that I had followed the courses and time meticulously. I was also confident that I would see Hakimpet runway in front of me. I broke the clouds at 1,700 feet. I only saw barren land in front. There was no sign of the runway in front of me. Now the real panic had started. I took a 360-degree turn to ascertain my position. In panic, I could not even recognize my own local flying area. Every feature looked different to me. Now I started to call my Homer at Hakimpet. Due to the low height and distance from the airfield, there was no response from Hakimpet Homer frequency. I changed over to Begumpet Homer frequency and called a couple of times. From there also I got no response. All the while, I was orbiting at the same place. Now I wanted to see my fuel for further endurance. My aircraft Vampire Mk-52 had five fuel gauges. In that panic, while flying at low level and totally uncertain of my position, I could not even add up my fuel. I only had an idea of fuel since it was calculated for the navigation purpose. I completed the 360-degree turns thrice and then it suddenly struck me that I should raise my height to get a better response from one Homer frequency. I started my climb and entered the clouds; this caused me further panic and I started palpitating. I remembered to go on my instruments and kept on orbiting at the same place. As I crossed 2,500 feet, I received Homing from Hakimpet airfield, I followed the instructions and set course to home towards Hakimpet. All this time, unsure of my fuel, I prayed to Waheguru to save me. I told Homer that I was in clouds and have no contact with the ground. I was told to descend to 1,500 feet. While descending, I broke clouds at 1,700 feet. I was steering the homing course and flew for 10 minutes at 140 kts, which means I was approximately 23 NM away from the point which I should have seen after the descent. I somehow finally landed safely and taxied back to my Tarmac. Before my landing, my CI and Flt Cdr were informed about my getting lost on the navigation trip. I was called by my CI Rajeshwar Singh. He asked me what had happened. 'Why did you ask for Homing while carrying out three leg navigation? That means, your planning was poor', he stated. I showed my map markings, times and fuel marked on the map as well as on the card, which was prepared for the navigation. He was satisfied with the preparation. Then he asked me, 'Do you know what went wrong?' I replied, 'Throughout, I had no contact with the ground due to the clouds. I turned on time for each leg.' He explained that since I did not have contact with the ground, visual corrections, depending upon the drift, due to actual winds at that level, I had drifted excessively and finally after my descent, I was far away from my expected place. He then advised me that, 'In future, if this happens, get Homing while you're at height and make corrections for a descent direction'. I realized my mistake and apologized for not following the correct procedure. He warned me to be careful in future navigation sorties.

Thereafter, all my training went very well. I stood third in my fighter pilot stream in both the results, including flying and ground subjects. In the whole course, that is, 85th cadets' course, I was at the fifth position. From transport pilot stream, Badhwar was first and Alvinder came second. From fighter aircraft stream, Tambe was first, Venugopal was second and I came third. For the 85th course, transport stream pilots were placed above the fighter stream pilots. So, the seniority was fixed by service numbers as follows:

1) Bhadwar
2) Alvinder Chand
3) Tambe
4) Venugopal
5) HS Sahota (me)

Now for passing out parade, there was a selection for the parade commander. The selection, based on who delivered effective commands for the parade, was among the three of us—Teju Asthana, Alvinder Chand and I. Finally, Asthana was selected as the Parade Commander, I was selected to be Flight Commander for Fighter Stream and Alvinder Chand was selected to be Flight Commander for Transport Stream.

After the passing out parade, we were given ranks of a pilot officer by our A.O.C. in C. (Air Officer Commanding in Chief) of Training Command. Finally, after becoming pilot officers, we congratulated each other and attended a high tea party, which was arranged by Air Force Station, Hakimpet. Our instructors congratulated us and we had a chance to meet our A.O.C.in C. in groups during the tea party. I, therefore, was commissioned as a pilot officer on 28 October 1963.

With Vampire Aircraft in Hakimpet

First to become Pilot Officer

Commanded Fighter Pilots Flight

12

BEING A PILOT OFFICER

Posting to No. 24 Squadron AF

My posting was already declared and I was posted to No.24 Squadron, AF, along with Pilot Officers Mann, Bains, Saini, Sidhu and Rehman. This Squadron was equipped with Vampire MK-55 and MK-52 and was placed in a Far East Air Force Station. Squadron Ldr M M Singh commanded the squadron. Squadron had six Staff Pilots. We were very thrilled to start our flying. After about two weeks, we were told that the squadron is placed in an OPS AREA where no training flying could be carried out. Therefore, for our training flying, the squadron was to be moved out to a peace station. This process took about three months and, in the meantime, we were utilized to carry out the Base Ops. Duties. The officer on duty would stay for 24 hours and would be replaced by the other pilot officer among our group. One day, we all were called by our Squadron Commander and were told that we did not know how to answer phone calls coming from Command Headquarters (HQs) properly. I could not understand why this happened as I had been answering all the calls from Command Headquarters correctly. Anyway, after a couple of days, we came to know that Pilot Officer Sidhu was on night duty a few days ago and a call had come from our SASO (Senior Air Staff Officer) at our Eastern Air Command HQ. Somehow, the line at that moment was not very clear and signal strength was low, and Sidhu said, 'Sir, you are very dim, I cannot hear you'. This reply was objected to, resulting in our *peshi* (report) to Squadron Commander. It became the talk of the Camp and every time we were in the bar, we rolled in laughter while raising this incident.

When I was in Ops. Area, my flying bounty hours became a problem since we could not fly fighter aircraft. Command Headquarters cleared my conversion on MI-4 Helicopters as I was the senior-most pilot officer among the trainee pilots. However, when I was to go on Solo Flying on MI-4 Helicopters, message came from the HQ that I, Pilot Officer HS Sahota, was a Fighter Pilot. I could not be made a Captain on MI-4 Helicopters. I could be given a Second Pilot Certificate and in future, fly as a co-pilot in MI-4 Helicopters. Thereafter, I flew to almost all the forward area Helipads in NEFA along with other senior pilots of 105 Helicopter Unit. I was also cleared to fly as co-pilot in Otter Aircraft. I flew 13 hours in that aircraft, which was good for two months' flying bounty, as I needed only six hours for a month. On one of the Station Flight Safety meetings, some hot discussions took place between both the Squadron Commanders (C.O. Otter Squadron. and our C.O.). I was told to remove the logged hours page from my logbook. However, thereafter, I was attached to one of the Dakota aircraft squadrons where I just managed to complete the flying bounty hours.

Our Squadron. moved to AF Station Kalaikunda in West Bengal. Our Air Movement was completed within one day but our Train Party took about five days. This train was loaded at Chabua Railway Station in Assam. We loaded all of the Ground Equipment belonging to our Squadron. We also loaded dry rations and livestock and chickens nicely packed in Bamboo baskets with good breathing facility. There were four officers, including me. I, being the senior-most Pilot Officer, was made in-charge of the train party. I also had 15 SNCOs, 50 Airmen, 12 NCEs and 10 civilians. The train left Chabua Railway Station with a lot of fanfare. Rest of the SNCOs and Airmen left for Kalaikunda Air Force station by different trains.

Our train reached Hasimara Railway Station where we had planned our lunch to be prepared and served to all travelling by this special train. Our train was parked on the spare track and we chose one open place to prepare our meals. Our cooks got ready to prepare the meals as one of them went to the basket in which chickens were carried. By mistake, he opened one basket wide open and, to his surprise, one chicken flew out of the basket. In his attempt to catch that chicken, other five too escaped from the basket. Within seconds, they went out of the train compartment as the door was open. Now that cook was shouting for help. Within a minute, most of the men started running behind the chickens to catch them. Chickens ran and got under the parked train. There was a lot of commotion and noises of different kinds to lure the chickens. It was quite a scene to be watched! Some of us were serious but many were laughing like mad men. I was busy in directing the 'Operation catch the chicken'. All the men somehow managed to catch five chickens but the sixth one flew and landed up on top of a train bogie. We had a very tough time to catch that one. One of the SNCOs borrowed a very long stick from the station master. He scared the chicken with the stick and managed to get it fly back to ground. And finally, we managed to make a barricade and caught that last chicken. In a revengeful attitude, that chicken was the first to receive the deathblow by the cook for the stew. Then the other five of them followed the same destiny.

We finally reached Kalaikunda Railway Station on the fifth day. All the other Airmen and NCEs who had arrived earlier were present at the Railway Station to greet us and off load the equipment and carry it to Airforce Station Kalaikunda. The story of catching the chickens at Hasimara Railway Station had become the talk of the Airforce Station. It amused even those who were not part of this episode to a great extent.

We all settled at Kalaikunda and were given tented accommodation. Our daily routine for Ground Subjects refresher studies had also started. Finally, within two weeks, our flying had commenced. Dual checks were given by our Squadron Cdr, Squadron Ldr MM Singh. He was surprised that those who had flown the helicopters were pushing the control column forward instead of the control column coming back for take-off and climb in the fighter aircraft (Vampire MK-55). However, in my case, it was a very gentle push on the control stick and I corrected immediately on his instructions. In subsequent take-offs, I did not display that tendency. Plt Offr Saini, my course-mate, had a lot of problems and finally Squadron Cdr recommended him for transport aircraft flying. He had to leave our fighter aircraft stream. We all were upset but this decision of Squadron Cdr was based on the reactions and response required for fighter flying, keeping the flights and his own safety in mind. This decision had scared me to some extent while at the same time it made me extremely cautious before making any silly mistakes. Pre-flight briefing needed full attention and finally proper execution of each mission (sortie) was essential. My complete training went very smoothly and I completed 200 hours of flying on Vampire Aircraft. My Armament Phase was very well appreciated by my Flying Instructors as well as by my Squadron Commander. There was a small break and we were to be posted to different fighter squadrons. During this time, I applied for one month's annual leave. To my absolute joy, it was approved and I left for home, thrilled to join my family members. On reaching my hometown, I was given a very good reception with local band and *dholak*. In fact, on the third day after my arrival, my parents had arranged *Akhand Path* at Baba Dharam Das ji's Gurudwara. There was *bhog* ceremony, followed by *shabad kirtan* by local *ragies* and *langar*[53] for everyone who attended the ceremony. We all did a lot of *seva* in that ceremony. While I was enjoying my leave, I had spent about 7 to 8 days in my village, and then a very strange incident took place. One Pandit, Narain Das ji, used to come from a nearby village for collecting *atta* from all houses of our *mohalla*. One morning, aftertaking a head bath, I was sitting on a *peerha*[54] with my hair open, enjoying the sunshine. That's when I heard the voice of Pandit Narain Das Ji. He was reciting some Sanskrit slokas while entering our house. He looked at me and called my mother and told her, 'This boy will go *saat samunder paar*'. On hearing this, I laughed and told my mother, 'Please give him *atta* in a big bowl because he is trying to win your favour for that since mothers are always keen to know about good things happening to their children'. My mother was very happy to hear that as pandit ji was repeating his *bhavishya vani*.[55] My mother excitedly asked him what it meant and he happily repeated himself, 'This boy will go to a foreign country soon'. Before this could blow out of proportion, I corrected panditji and my mother and told them how it was not possible as I was in Defence Forces and by the time I reach back to my unit, my new posting would be out. I would be joining my new Squadron, flying

---

[53] A communal free kitchen arranged by Sikhs to serve common people
[54] A small stool
[55] Future-telling

much faster in a better aircraft. Anyway, Panditji left our house and went ahead to other houses. On the next day, at about 2:30 in the afternoon, one postman came to our house with a telegram. Generally, in villages, telegram would indicate some bad news. So, with deep fear, I received a telegram from the postmaster after signing in his book. Before I could read it, my mother shouted, 'Did anyone die among our relatives?' I had to pacify her not to think negative and allow me to read the contents. To my great surprise, the telegram read, 'Leave curtailed. Report back to unit immediately'. I slapped my forehead and cursed the hell out of that Pandit who said I will go *saat samunder paar*. And here I lost my leave and also moments of further fun in the village with my brothers and sisters. On hearing this, my whole family had become depressed. But I had to obey the orders since this telegram was from my unit Adjutant. With a heavy heart, I started packing with the help of all my family members and left for Kalaikunda the next day.

'SAAT SAMUNDER PAAR'

Advanced Fighter Gunnery Course in USA

I reached my station on the third day at night. I tried to get some 'gen' as to what had happened and why was I recalled from leave. I got some information that I and pilot officer Maan were required to report to our unit Adjutant immediately after arriving. The next day, as soon as I reported to my unit Adjutant, I was congratulated by him and he said, 'You are selected for a course abroad'. Thereafter, he explained the type of course, which was an Advanced Fighter Flying course on F-86-F Saber Aircraft, under a scheme of Military Assistance by the American government. From 24 Squadron, only Maan and I were selected and from 45 Squadron, Asthana, Mitroo, Shishodia, Sandhu and Grewal were selected. A total of seven pilots were selected and fortunately, I was senior to them all. Thereafter, all of us were sent to New Delhi for medical and other formalities at Air HQ before proceeding for the said course.

I was over whelmed on hearing this news of my selection and wanted to share this good news with my family. The only means of contacting them at the earliest was by a telegram. I'm sure they were as excited about the whole thing as I was and their blessings were with me.

Medical examination was routine check-ups for all, which we all had cleared. After that, we were briefed by our Operations Director Group Captain, Ganja Bose. He prepared us for the final interview with the Chief of Air Staff-Air Vice Marshal (then), Arjan Singh DFC. During the final preparation, even our knowledge about America was checked and revised by Gp Capt. Bose. Among various questions of military and political concerns, he asked me a direct question—who killed President John F Kennedy? I was not sure but I said Mr Ruby and for this answer, I got a furious shouting for which he was well known in the Air Force. In the meantime, Shishodia had whispered the correct answer in my ear and I quickly corrected myself, 'Sorry, Sir. The name was Lee Oswald'. On hearing this, he spared me. On the same day, we were taken to Air Chief's office where Chief gave us a very good advice and mentioned, 'You all are the ambassadors of the Indian Air Force as well as of India. So, keep the flag flying high, work hard and learn as much as possible about the new aircraft as well as the functioning of the USAF'. Thereafter, CAS congratulated me and put the Flying Officer's Rank upon me, saying, 'You have a great responsibility on your shoulders. Keep up the discipline and keep your course together'. Thereafter, we all saluted our Chief of Air Staff and left his office along with G/C Bose. After we came to G/C Bose's office, he told me that this was an Acting Rank on me and as Flying Officer, I was the leader of the course. Then he advised, 'All of you must do well in flying and get some Laurels to the Country'.

Next day, we collected our official passports and took all the jabs (injections required to enter the United States) which gave us a fever. However, with a bit of relief, we finally left for USA by Air India flight on the next day in the evening. This was our first experience to fly in a Civil Aircraft and, more so, in our prestigious airline. Onboard, we were given special treatment which I cannot forget. Since liquor was for free, Sandhu Asthana, Maan and Grewal had a ball of a time. Only I, Sishodia and Mitroo sipped on soft drinks. However, all of us made plenty of noise onboard and disturbed some co-passengers too. I had to apologize to the co-passengers for the disturbing behaviour of my officers. Thereafter, our journey to our destination was uneventful.

Stay at United States, June 1964 to January 1965

On reaching the United States of America, we were received by a Captain of the USAF and were taken to the respective BOQs (Bachelor Officers Quarters). My quarter was a two-room set with a refrigerator in the drawing room, which was generally called sitting room. All quarters had the similar arrangement. We all admired and felt the difference

Receiving A to A firing trophy; Training Squadron Nellis USAB;
Clark Couty Sheriff's Posse Rodeo San Antonio

On the wing—Teju Asthana and Grewal
Standind left to right- Mann, Self, Sishodia, Sandhu and Mitroo

between tented accommodation and AC quarters with a refrigerator and a telephone for local use. In fact, trunk calls (long-distance calls) within the US were free. Next day, we were taken to a hall where the station Commander (called Base Commander), who was a Colonel dressed in a fine uniform with all medal ribbons, was waiting for us. His chest was full of ribbons. We all felt very much privileged to have such a Base Commander. He welcomed us and ran a tour of the station with very interesting slides. Thereafter, he came around and met all of us. While shaking hands and introducing ourselves, we were saying our Ranks as Flying Officer and Pilot Officers. Then, one of the Junior Officers with a Rank of Major told us to call our ranks as 1st lieutenant (Pilot Officer) and 2nd lieutenant (Flying Officer). So, throughout my stay, I was called 2nd lieutenant. This was US Air Force Base, Lackland, where we were to undergo American English Course. This was basically to understand instructions and normal conversations as there was a great difference in accent between our English and American English. We carried on for three weeks in the classroom, practicing the language and Air Radio instructions from different Flying Towers. This was all on audio CDs using headphones. After passing this test, we were taken to another place known as Randolph US Air Force Base. There, we started our flying on T-33A aircraft—all dual flying. We were given sufficient training in sector flying, re-joining circuits via various entry points. My instructor, Major Getchel, was a fighter pilot, and was very happy with my handling of the T-33A aircraft in the air. Everyday, our first mission take-off used to be at sunrise, which used to be approximately at 05:45 hrs, with a temperature of minus 10 degrees. All of us did fairly well and completed this course with great ease. These two Bases were in Texas around a city known as San Antonio.

On completion of this course, we were to move to Nellis US Air Force Base in Nevada State, which was quite a distance from San Antonio. We were given 10 days to join the next duty. All of us decided to drive to Nellis Air Force Base. We had two cars with us in the Lackland Air Force Base. One was Plymouth and the other was Ford. We set course for Nellis AFB—I, Mitroo and Maan in one car which was the Plymouth; and Asthana, Shishodia, Sandhu and Grewal were in the Ford. We were travelling together, keeping a safe distance between the cars. This journey was a historic one as we had to drive through places like the Sahara desert, which was the hottest and extremely hostile region. Luckily for us, the highway was under construction and police patrolling was very frequent. However, to keep our car engines a bit cool, we bought canvas water bottles, filled them with clean water and hung them in front of the car engines. This way we kept our car's engine temperature within the limits. We also got cool drinking water from those bottles. With prayers on our lips, we crossed the so-called Sahara region very comfortably. We finally reached our first destination—a place called Flagstaff city in Arizona State. From there the famous Grand Canyon was very close by. Utilizing the time that we had, all of us went to visit that place and really enjoyed our sightseeing and took a lot of pictures as this was a unique experience for each one of us. After spending one night in Flagstaff, we set course for Nellis, US Air Force Base.

In the cockpit of T-33 Star Fighter Aircraft

As we were entering the main gate of Nellis AFB, we were stopped, our identities were checked and we were briefed by one sergeant, who guided us to our BOQs. Each BOQ was a set of two rooms, one sitting room with a fridge, and the other had a bed with two easy chairs—a very comfortable accommodation. We had a day free to ourselves so we organised our rooms and made our study tables ready with a table lamp each. On the second day, I got everyone out of BOQ and reached our Flying Squadron where we were to start our ground subjects and briefings for flying. I was to fly F-86F Saber Aircraft in this base. This was a single seat aircraft, not a trainer aircraft, used for dual checks and instrument flying checks. Anyway, for this reason, we were given enough dual training in T-33A aircraft at Randolph AFB. Our flying training started on a very good note at Nellis AFB. My first take-off in F86F was a formation take-off. My instructor was in a lead aircraft and I took off formatting closely with him.

This was called formation take-off in which all commands were given by the instructor on the radio, calls like Line up, Open Throttle and Rolling were said. After getting airborne, instructions like Undercarriage UP, Flaps Up and reducing/adjusting the power for further climb were given. My duty was to format my instructor's aircraft with proper adjustment of power and control my own aircraft in the right position.

The Instructor took me to the flying area/sector where I was shown some major landmarks in the sector for flying. Since at one time there would be three to four formations flying at the same time, our flying area was divided in different segments and was marked by degrees. One had to fly and do all the air work in the allotted sector only. After a good amount of flying, our Gunnery Phase had started. We were to fire rockets, guns and drop practice-bombs, too. The range area was shown to us and a very nice plotting system of Air-to-Ground work was briefed to us. We also had two pilots from Coast Guards USA and two pilots from Vietnam for our course. The major competition was between the US Coast Guard pilots and us. Almost towards the end of Air-to-Ground Phase, began our Air-to-Air Phase. The following sketch depicts target, path of the tow aircraft and firing aircraft.

In India, we had done plenty of Air-to-Ground work but Air-to-Air work was something extensively new to us. At the end of these phases of flying, our results were very encouraging. Even though we won three trophies, the Air-to-Ground guns trophy went to the Coast Guard pilot from USA. Here are the trophies that we could bag:

- Myself: Air-to-Air Gunnery Trophy.
- Maan: Air-to-Ground Rocket Trophy.
- Shishodia: Air-to-Ground Bombing Trophy.

Now let me tell you about the fun and frolic during our stay at Nellis Air Force Base. Las Vegas city, which was well known for nightlife and gambling machines and night shows, was only 25 miles away from our base. We used to finish our flying by 1700 hrs in the evening. The sunset used to be approximately at 1915 to 1930 hours. We quickly used to come back to our BOQs and after bathing, get ready and set course for Las Vegas. We did a lot of hilarious antics for fun. I was once asked by some local men, 'Are you a Maharaja?' to which I replied, 'Yes, Maharaja of Hoshiarpur'. I think those people had heard, read about or seen pictures of Maharaja of Patiala. That is why they asked this question. Many girls and women were keen to know about my turban, which they'd call a cap. I used to correct them by saying that it is called a turban and it is a five-meter long cloth which had to be tied on the head. They would not believe it and wanted to see. For that I used to fix a day and time and take one turban and tie it in front of them. They were very surprised to see the technique of tying the turban as it was something they had never seen before.

We finally completed our course and passed out of Nellis Air Force Base, USA, and left for India by air. We reached New Delhi. After settling down in our mess, all of us had to report to Air HQ. We presented the three trophies that we had won to our Director OPS. He was very happy and proud of our achievements. He congratulated the three of us one by one. Thereafter, I was required to submit a report on our training. We got together and prepared a meticulous report which was well appreciated by our Director OPS. Since our postings were out, we were then dispersed to different Air Force Squadrons.

14

ESCAPING DEATH

Posting to No. 32 Squadron AF

Standing- VP Singh, Chinoy, Teja Gill,
Raj Kumar Jayant Singh (C O), Madan, Shyam
Sitting- Self, chander shekhar, Ratnaparkhi, Iyer

With Station Commander Adampur Gp Capt Lloyad

I was posted to No.32 Squadron AF, based at AF Station, Adampur. While I was in New Delhi, I had managed to witness the Independence Day Parade on 26th January, 1965. It was quite animpressive parade. On 27th January, 1965, I left for Adampur. My Squadron was equipped with Mystere Mk-IV aircraft which was a very good aircraft for Air-to-Ground weapons firing. It also had a built-in gun which could be used for Air-to-Ground as well as Air-to-Air firing. My training at Adampur started with a dual check on Vampire aircraft as Mystere aircraft was only single seat aircraft. For all dual checks and Instrument Flying, only Vampire aircraft was utilized. During my training, a lot of interesting things had happened. The worst of them was, one day during training, I was to fly a sortie with partial fuel in drop tanks. The aircraft Form 700 was signed up by all technicians and the Supervisor. I also signed and accepted the aircraft. This was a requirement before the sortie/mission of the aircraft. That day, my chase pilot was Flt Lt Ratnaparkhi—an excellent flyer who carried out my briefing very thoroughly for the exercise which we were to carry out in the flying sector. After start-up and radio contacts, I started to taxi the aircraft followed by Suresh. We did our vital actions before lining up for take-off and got our tires checked. I obtained the permission for line-up and we both lined up for the take-off. Suresh was to take off 10 seconds later. I obtained the permission for take-off and on clearance from ATC, I opened the throttle and commenced take off after giving radio/ R/T call for the same. As I was rolling, my aircraft was pitching up excessively. I tried but could not control the aircraft. My aircraft pitched up and got airborne prematurely. In the meantime, Suresh overshot me on my right. But since my aircraft had pitched up so much, it stalled and did a leafing action. While it was coming down like a leaf, I pushed the stick forward and wanted to recover but there was hardly any height. It hit the ground on three points—tail, right wing tip and then on nose wheel. My throttle was fully open, the aircraft started rolling in Katcha Ground/Runway shoulder. I brought the aircraft on the runway and by this time, I had covered ¾th of runway. I closed the throttle and wanted to stop the aircraft, but due to excessive speed, my brakes were not responding as per my convenience. I was approaching the arrester barrier, which was in down position. I saw the cable of the barrier and after kicking the rudder; I headed for the cable as the barrier was down.

Fortunately, my right drop tank got entangled with the Arrester Barrier Cable and I also had entered the soft ground at the end of the runway. My aircraft stopped while turning 60 degrees from the runway direction. As it stopped, I opened the canopy and switched off the battery and other necessary switches. When I looked inside the cockpit, my aircraft nose wheel strut had pierced the cockpit and was

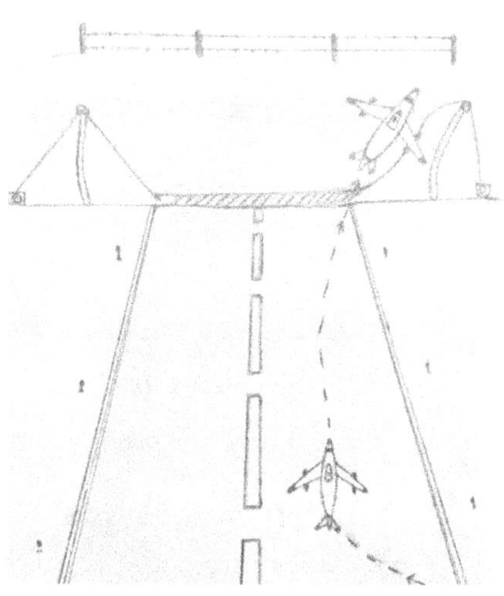

appearing between my ejection seat and the control column. Had it hit the ejection seat, it would have fired and maybe I would've even died that day. But Waheguru was kind to me and I got saved by a thread's margin. I immediately jumped over the left wing and then on to ground. I saw that the arrester barrier cable had cut through the drop tank and there was a fuel leak, which caught fire. I quickly put a lot of loose mud over the fire and managed to put it off. In the meantime, fire tenders, ambulance and one more vehicle arrived with six–seven airmen. They all took over the scene and I was put into the ambulance and was taken to the MI room (medical inspection room) for my medical check-up. With god's grace, everything was all right and no alcohol was found in my blood.

A court of inquiry was ordered and tried to find fault with me as I had recently come from USA after my training. Many thought that I was doing some stunts during take-off. I sincerely did nothing of that sort. The court of inquiry had found out the real reason for the pitch up of the aircraft. For partial fuel in drop tanks there had to be blast weight put into the top front compartment of the aircraft, which was meant for that. This weight would take care of excessive pitch up tendency because of the fuel shift to the rear of the drop tanks due to sudden acceleration during the take-off. The blast weights were not put in the nose compartment of that aircraft. Let us not get into further details as I would like to leave it at this stage since it's a service matter.

15

INDO-PAK WAR, 1965

My training continued and we were progressing in our tactical formation flying phase and had gone through the minor tactics in the air. This is when the Indo–Pak War of 1965 had started. I, Mitroo, Boparai and Iyer were all U/TOps and were not allowed to take part in the OPS in the beginning stage. There were four senior ex-Mystere pilots on instructional duties in the Training Command Stations who were attached to our squadron; namely, Rodrigues, Bains, Mangat and J Singh. Wing Commander Rajkumar Jayant Singh was our Commanding Officer, Squadron leader Teja Gill was our flight commander and other staff pilots were FltLt Ratnaparkhi, FltLt Dara Chinoi and FltLt Muzi Hussain.

During that period, innumerable things had happened which unfortunately cannot be discussed because of the security reasons. Initially, we were not allowed to take part in the OPS as we were U/T OPS on type (Mystere Aircraft). We kept requesting our CO to allow us also to take part in the OPS. I was finally allowed to carry out patrolling duties, which were known as CAP overhead, and around Adampur Air Force Station. The senior pilots initially led us. As we gained experience of two missions each, thereafter, any two of us used to pair up and carry out the CAP duties. This patrol flying was in an elliptical pattern around the airfield. During this pattern, we were to look out for enemy. If they attempted to attack our airfield, we were to pounce on them and shoot their aircraft. We were also covering each other's tail at the same time. Enemy did not attack our airfield during the day. They, however, did attempt to attack during the night. Their bombing was very accurate in destroying our crops around the AF Station but they could not hit any of the installations

110

at the Airfield. Our airfield remained fully functional throughout the operations.

When the operations were going on, one hilarious incident took place near our officer's mess. It was slightly dark in the evening and one of the personal bearers was bringing tea in a big kettle. On the same day, due to the fear of enemy paratroopers invading our airfield, we had deployed Airmen with rifles in and outside the fence of the airfield. As this bearer came out of the officer's mess gate and came on the road, there was a siren for lights out and getting into the trenches. This bearer, on the other hand, was merrily walking on the road towards the officer's quarters to serve tea to his officers. At that time, one of the airmen patrolling parties arrived from the opposite direction. It was pitch dark but one of the airmen sensed a movement on the road and got into panic, because as per his thinking, all the personnel were supposed to be in the trenches since warning by siren was already given. The airman challenged the moving figure, 'who is there? Halt and put both hands on your head!' The bearer took his own sweet time to stop, which probably annoyed the airman a bit. He again challenged and shouted very loudly. The bearer now stopped and put one of his hands up while the other kept holding the tea kettle. On seeing this, the airman got further agitated and shouted, 'Put both your hands up!' On hearing this, the bearer shifted the teakettle in the other hand and raised his empty hand again. Now the airman got scared by his actions and thought that maybe one of the infiltrators had a gun in one hand. The airman shot a bullet of a 303 rifle. It was a sheer luck that the bullet had hit the tea kettle and not the bearer. The poor bearer got so scared that he threw the kettle on the road and ran back to the officer's mess. This incident was later investigated upon. It all happened in a panic and fortunately, no one was hurt.

During Indo–Pak war of 1965, a very strange incident took place. A formation of four aircraft had been sent for attacking some place in Pakistan. On their return, the formation was bounced by enemy Sabre aircraft. All four aircraft got separated and started escaping using their tactics. In the formation Flt Lt Hussain was number 4. He was chased by one Sabre aircraft. He took a bit longer to shake-off that enemy aircraft, and as a result, his engine flamed out due to shortage of fuel.

He was only 30 NM away from Adampur Airfield. He had no choice but to eject. In those days, all the villagers were very alert because they were made aware about the Pakistani paratroopers who might be air-dropped around that area. They saw someone come down with a Parachute. They all nabbed him on ground, thinking him to be enemy paratrooper, . His flying suit had his nametag, Hussain. The Moment the villagers read his name, they thought that he was a Pakistani paratrooper and instead of helping him, they started dragging him and one guys had even hit him on his head. He kept telling them that he is an Indian pilot from Adampur Air Force station. But the rowdy crowd did not believe him and almost tried to kill him in a rage. After a little while, Air Force Rescue Party reached the spot to save him and rescued Flt Lt Hussain, who was bleeding profusely. He was immediately given first aid and was taken to the Military Hospital. It took about three months for him to recover from the injuries. He was a brave soldier and also a very daring fighter pilot who did his job excellently. I'm sure he was well awarded by the Air Force authorities later on.

16

BEGINNING OF A NEW CHAPTER

Indo–Pak War of 1965 finally came to an end within a few days and all became normal and we resumed our routine of flying training. While I was at AF Station Adampur, my marriage engagement ceremony was fixed for April 1966. Since my village was in the local flying area of our Squadron, on the day of the ceremony, a fly past of four aircraft in close formation was carried out. Over my village by my Flt Cdr Teja Gill who led the formation. They made a couple of runs over my village, in fact, over my house exactly at the time when my engagement ceremony was going on. The whole village was overjoyed seeing the wonderful display. I got married the same year on 27 November 1966. All my Squadron mates attended my wedding as my wife's village was also close to AF Station Adampur. My wife Mrs Gian Kaur Sahota was a BA and B.Ed. During those days in Punjab, it was considered to be a brilliant qualification for girls. She did her BA from Lady Shri Ram College, Delhi and B.Ed from Ludhiana. Thus, we began our married life together. Air Force Station, Adampur, provided us a fine accommodation. After some time, our squadron moved to Air Force Station, Ambala and all the families also moved to Ambala Cantonment. There I was given a temporary accommodation. Since all the squadron families were in the same area, we had a wonderful circle of friends and enjoyed our stay. We were blessed with our first child, a baby girl, and named her Tejinder Kaur. She was born in Military Hospital in Ambala Cantonment on 5th January, 1968. In the same month, I had to start my conversion on MIG-21 aircraft. During my stay at Ambala, I was selected for MIG-21 aircraft flying and was sent for advanced medical check at Aero Medical Institute located at Bangalore. The

113

medical check was very tough and strict. I, being a player and in regular practice of hockey and basketball games, managed to clear my medical. As I came back to the Squadron, a signal from Air HQ was received for my MIG-21 conversion. I reported to MIG-21 conversion Squadron No. 45 based at AF Station, Chandigarh. I cleared my ground subjects and emergency training. Flying started with a big bang. Since I had gone from Mystere a/c which used to take 3/4th of the runway to get airborne, the MIG-21 Trainer a/c on my first dual-check was a classic take-off. Assisted by the instructor from the rear cockpit, and take-off run with the afterburner, my aircraft got airborne much before reaching half of the runway. Everything was happening really fast and the radius of my turns and loop was so big that I wondered how to manage my flight. Sure enough, after landing, which was demonstrated by the instructor, I received a good rap and he commented, 'Mr Sahota, you have not flown the aircraft, the aircraft has taken you for a ride'. It meant that I couldn't manage my flight to his satisfaction. These remarks did put me in a spin for the time being, but I started with a stronger will to improve in the next training missions. My instructor was Squadron Ldr AK Mukherji who later on became the Director of Air Staff Inspections. After my successful conversion training, I reported back to my Squadron.

Posting to No. 4 Squadron AF

I then got posted to No. 4 Squadron stationed in the Eastern Region. During my stay there, I completed my OPS training. Wg Cdr Ak Mukherjee was posted as chief operations officer at A F Station, Tezpur, before moving to Air HQ. One day, he decided to fly a 1 Vs 1 mission with me. It so happened that I did not let him count 10 in the air and took a camera shot after coming behind him. After landing during debriefing he remarked, 'Sahota, you flew your aircraft very intelligently'. That's when I recalled his debrief during my conversion training on MIG-21 aircraft. His remarks were put in my Blue Book. This time again, I presented my Blue Book for his debrief to be written in that. He put the above-mentioned remarks in my Blue Book and signed it. I think it was god's blessings that helped me keep my promise.

I had lot of achievements and successes at the station. But, at the same time, I also had to undergo a lot of harsh words and criticism of my Flight Commander, Squadron Ldr Keith Lewis ji. His criticism certainly made me even stronger. I took everything on a very positive note, however, there were situations when I also felt that his pressure and harsh words were to discourage me even when I used to be correct in my work and flying. I was adjutant of the unit with multifarious duties. I used to fly more than any other pilot in the unit. This was generally seen in monthly summaries of flying to be signed by the Flight Commander. His sore point was, 'I had given to you so many ground duties and you still managed to fly more than others'. In fact, every afternoon, I used to work very hard even when others use to relax in their rooms. I also used to do Airmen's Mess management in the evening regularly. My working hours were from 0600 hours to evening 1900 hours with one-and-a-half-hour-break for lunch.

My attitude was, 'If you have the spirit of understanding and taking everything in a positive way, you will enjoy each and every moment of life, whether it's pressure or pleasure'.

'*In my knowledge, nobody has ever died from over work, only from over worry*'

–DrWayne Dyer.

During this period, one officer looking after the MlG Simulator went on two months' leave. To load me with some more work, my Flt Cdr detailed me as officer in-charge of that simulator. I took the advantage of this post and in addition to supervising flying practices of other pilots, I used to fly for every day one Instrument sortie under the hood. As a result, my instrument flying ability improved two fold. After two and a half months, the Aircrew Examination Board's team had arrived at our station. Flt Lt Deshpande flew with me in trainer aircraft to check me for my instrument flying ability. With Waheguru's grace, that sortie was an exceptional one. He was very happy with my Instrument Flying ability. After a few days' stay at Tezpur and flying with many other pilots, the AEB Team returned to Hindon AF Station. To the surprise of me, my CO and Flt Cdr, I was selected for an Instrument Rating Instructor course (IRI). At that time, I had only Green instrument Rating and I was a Flt Lt. This course was held at Hindon AF Station along with three more pilots. During this course, Squadron Ldr Tarlochan Singh, known as Tango(he later on retired as Air Marshal), took me up in an MIG Trainer aircraft and made me fly inside the clouds for 20 minutes. This was a real test of my ability. In this course, I stood first among four pilots. And then I returned to my Squadron with flying colours.

When I was posted to AF Station, Tezpur, our accommodation was very interesting. I went alone to Tezpur, since my daughter was only five months old. I had to leave my wife with her parents in New Delhi. No family accommodation was readily available at that time in Tezpur. I got one *Basha*[56], made with the help of local people and called my wife to join me. I told her that I got one *Basha* constructed for her and Tenju, my daughter. She had no idea what it was but became very happy to hear the word *Basha* thinking it to be a palatial house. I also kept it a secret till she saw it herself. She travelled by air from Delhi to Tezpur. She was welcomed by not only me but all the squadron officers and families. We were invited to the ladies room in the officer's mess for lunch. She kept asking me about our *Basha*. When I took her to the *Basha* and told her that, that was

---

[56] A hut made of Bamboo Chatais

our home, the picture which she had in her mind was shattered. Anyway, she reconciled very quickly and started enjoying Air Force life again. Thereafter, we kept moving almost every two years to different units. Before shifting from Tezpur, we were blessed with our second child—a baby boy—on 27th November 1970. He was born in Military Hospital at Tezpur and was named by the AF Station Ladies as Tejpal Singh.

We made many friends while we were at Tezpur and some of them are still in touch with us and are like family to us. We were very fortunate to have met them. One such family was Mr Kuljit Dhanoa and Hardarshan Kaur Dhanoa. We got introduced to them through a cousin of mine, Kirpal Singh, who was working in a shipping company at Tezpur. Thereafter, we used to visit each other often. They were a big help to us when I was admitted in the Military Hospital for my appendicitis operation. In fact, they used to bring nutritious homemade soups and food for me as the hospital was in the town, closer to their house. I recovered at a speed with all their affection and care. Then again when Gian was in the hospital for the delivery of our second child, she was looked after by them in spite of Hardarshan having to look after her own new-born child. We used to visit them often and enjoy authentic Punjabi food at their place. Even after they shifted to Chandigarh, we were in touch and still are after almost 50 years! Unfortunately, we lost Mr Kuljit Dhanoa some time back. We pray to god to bless his soul for he was a man with a large heart.

We, in the military service, learn very early in life to adjust ourselves in any situation. After all it is the people, the colleagues who mattered and not the material things. Our motto was 'work hard and party hard'. All of us were like family there and would be going together for picnics and outings. This brought a lot of comradery among us.

Source: Bharat Rakshak.com

Air Chief Marshal Arjan Singh DFC visited AF Station Tezpur in 1968 where No.4 and No.28 MIG 21 Squadrons were based. I was in 4 Squadron at that time. The Station Commander Gp Capt Bharat Singh along with the two COs Bertie Weir (4 Sqn) and S K Mehra(28 Sqn) can be seen in the photo. Rear Row Standing L to R : U V Lagad, Herbie Sahota (myself), Keith Lewis, C D Chandrasekhar, A B Dhavle, "Maxie" Mullick . Front Row Standing L to R: S K Gulati, Sardesai, (Doc) Virendra Singh, Lawrie Menezes, G L Daniel, Gp Capt Bharat Singh (OC Tezpur), Wg Cdr R A "Bertie" Weir (CO 4 Squadron), Air Chief Marshal Arjan Singh, S V "Bo" Pathak, Wg Cdr S K Mehra (CO 28 Squadron), S "Kitcha" Krishnaswamy, A J S "Black Leader" Sandhu, D R "Natty" Nadkarni, Sanjeev "Popo" Sahay, V K "Chic" Bapat and J Sukrut Raj (From Wg Cdr G Balasubramaniam's collection)

17

RISKS AND REWARDS OF AN IAF OFFICER

Posting to No. 8 Squadron AF-1971 And Indo-Pak War 1971

From No.4 Squadron, I was posted to No.8 Squadron based at AF Station, Pune. Wing Cdr AK Sen was commanding the squadron. Now, with my experience of being a fully Ops Pilot, I was given more responsibility to manage flight commander's office under Squadron leader Vijian and Squadron leader HandaVrC of 1965 Indo–Pak War. After a couple of months of flying, the Indo–Pak War of 1971 had started. Being an Air Defence squadron, we got split and were sent to two places for air defence duties. One half went to OPS location in western sector and the other half was deputed to carry out Air Defence of Bombay Domestic and International Airport, Bombay City, dockyard, Trombay and Tarapore Power plants. Half the Squadron was operating from Bombay Airport itself. Wing Cdr Sen with Flight Commanders Handa and Manbir Singh commanded detachment at Western Base. Squadron Leader Vijian commanded detachment at Bombay and I was his assistant as senior-most pilot. We had four more pilots with us and we managed the Air Defence during the OPS. During the period of operations, one very miraculous incident took place. That night I was on ORP (Operational Ready Platform) duties. At night we used to go in a single aircraft and fly in contact and under cover of radar, deployed somewhere near Bombay. I was ready in the cockpit since a long time and no order had come to get airborne. Squadron Ldr Vijian was to relieve me. He came to me and asked me to go and take rest as he took over the duty of cockpit readiness. Sure enough, after about 12 to 13 minutes, the order came for Vijian to get airborne as one aircraft was detected by radar and was declared hostile because it was heading towards Air Force Station, Poona (Pune). Squadron Ldr Vijian

119

was guided by the controller from the Radar Control Room. It was a very good interception and the controller ordered Vijian to fire, thus instructing to fire the missile at the perfect locking range of the missile. Squadron Ldr Vijian was a very matured flyer (pilot). As soon as the order came to fire, he saw a blinking light on that target aircraft. He quickly sensed why the enemy aircraft should have blinking light. He did not fire his missile and called to the controller. Then he decided to go close to that aircraft and find out more details. As he went a bit closer, he saw—it appeared a big aircraft and all wingtip lights were turned on. He informed the controller. Thereafter, he called on International Bombay Tower Frequency and contacted the pilot of target aircraft. It was a French Airline Aircraft, which was drifting away from Delhi–Bombay route because all navigational facilities were switched off at Bombay airport. When this was happening, it appeared on the radar tube that this aircraft was proceeding towards Poona, hence, mistaken for enemy aircraft. I must tell you that because of Squadron Ldr Vijian's maturity and intelligence, a very big disaster got averted. I will also tell you very frankly that if this interception had come up when I was in the cockpit, the fate of the Airliner and passengers would have been different. I would not have thought anything else when controller had given the order to fire. In the thrill and excitement of War, I would have obeyed the order and would have killed all innocent passengers. I think that God saved the Airliner and passengers by putting Squadron Ldr Vijian in my place in the cockpit of aircraft on ORP. I also thanked my Waheguru for saving me from being called a 'murderer'.

During the War, I flew many operational missions, including the one where I chased enemy aircraft escaping into the sea after dropping their bombs in the sea near dockyard of Bombay. Before I could close-in to missile locking range, I was ordered to break the chase as I was going quite deep into the sea. The main reason was, if one ejects that deep into the sea for any reason, the quick rescue would not have been possible as infrastructure for the rescue would take more time at night. Any delay in rescue operation might result in pilot's death because of shark-infested sea. As the war ended within a few days, both the detachments returned to AF Station, Poona. India won the war and our squadron suffered no loss during the entire operations. After all the elements had returned to Base Station, we had a wonderful get-together at the station to celebrate as a matter of pride. Our wing officers took lot of interest to make the party a grand success as well.

After a couple of months of training and OPS flying, the Directorate of Air Staff Inspections (DASI) inspected my squadron. The highest authority for air staff inspections at Air HQ Gp Capt. Dhotiwala was the director at that time. All our groundwork and air work were inspected. Inspectors flew with us in different phases of flying to assess our abilities in the air. Air-to-Ground Firing Phase was also assessed. Our squadron was 'average' in all activities. As an individual, my performance was assessed as 'average'. Debriefing for my flying missions was good and Air-to-Ground firing work was much better, even then my assessment was 'average'. I, however, promised myself that I need to improve more and need to work harder to earn better assessments in future. My don't-cry-over-spilled-milk approach was very helpful for me to quickly recover from setbacks. I recognised this aspect of my nature and helped my friends and colleagues understand that it is productive flexibility rather than an I-don't-care attitude.

> *'Life knows no failures, failure exists only for those*
> *Who are always comparing themselves with others'.*
>
> –Sadhguru

During my stay in 8 Squadron, I encountered a very serious emergency while carrying out Dark Night Flying Practice in MIG-21 aircraft. I was flying at an altitude of 7 km. I was practicing level, climbing and descending turns. This mission was of 40 minutes. As 20 minutes passed and I was in a level left turn, I noticed a decrease in the Main Hydraulic Pressure. I was still figuring out the reason and thinking what problems I was going to experience. I abandoned my mission and started the return journey to my base AF Station, Pune. Before I could inform the ATC at Pune, I noticed, my Emergency Hydraulic Pressure had also started to drop. I realised that it was going to be a failure of Total Hydraulic Pressure. I immediately called the ATC Pune and declared the emergency. I was told to re-join circuit and land as soon as possible. I was almost 50 km away from the base and had 1800 litres of fuel. Watching both the Hydraulic Pressures dropping fairly fast and realising that if both the pressures come down to zero, I will not be able to lower my undercarriage, I quickly reduced my speed and lowered my undercarriage. All three wheels came down and got locked. I got green indication in the cockpit. Now both the pressures dropped, main pressure came to zero but emergency was at about 40 psi. I tried lowering the flaps to take off position, the flaps came down. But the control column movement started becoming heavier. In that condition, with minimum stick movement, I came on long finals. I decided to make approach and landing with partial flaps. I realised that if I operate any other services operated by Hydraulic Pressure, my control column will become solid or freeze and landing might not be possible. At that stage, I had 1600 litres of fuel. Normal landing fuel should not have been more than 1100 to 1200 litres of fuel. Due to the fear of my control column becoming solid or rigid, I could not consume the excess fuel. In that condition, the landing may not have been possible and ejection from the aircraft would be the next option, resulting in loss of an aircraft and pilot injuries while landing with a parachute in the dark night. However, I continued the approach, kept both hands on the control column, occasionally manipulating throttle to control speed. I made an overweight and partial flaps landing. Fortunately, it was a reasonably smooth landing. My control column became solid during the landing run. Had it happened in the air, the outcome of the mission would have been very dangerous. On completion of the landing run, I cleared the aircraft on the ORP and switched off the engine and battery. The rescue party at ORP quickly opened lower panels of the aircraft and found out that the leak was in the lower portion of the engine. Again, if the leak was on the upper portion of the engine, the hydraulic fluid falling on the outer casing of engine might have caught fire due to contact with very hot portion of the engine. Secondly, if there was any delay in landing by me, it could also have been a huge catastrophe.

In the year 1972, we all had our first exposure to cinema shooting. A famous movie named *Hindustan Ki Kasam* was being made on some incidents of 1971 war. This was, in fact, the first war movie made on Air Force, which showed many flying scenes for which the entire crew of the movie had come to Air Force Station, Pune. The hero of the movie, Raj Kumar, was acting as an Air Force pilot and Sqn Ldr Manbir Singh and I had the privilege to do most of the flying for the aerial shots. We also had a chance to interact with the producer and the director. My wife and I also acted in a party dance scene and were thrilled to see us in the movie. This episode had become the talk of every conversation for the coming years. Another exposure to movies happened during our tenure at Pune. Some shots of the famous movie *Silsila* were to be shot at the Air Force Base as the actor Shashi Kapoor was acting as a pilot. I again had the privilege to do the flying scenes for the movie, and of course, it was a pleasure to meet the great stars of the cinema world.

18

THE JOURNEY FROM ONE BASE TO ANOTHER

Posting to No. 28 Squadron AF 1973

Bhalla, Myself, Gp Capt Karan Yadav Station Cdr AF Stn Tezpur, Wg Cdr Ramachanderan—Second Picture—Left to Right—Mrs Sahota, Mrs Yadav, Gp Capt K Yadav, Myself and Wg Cdr Janak Kumar

Figure of 28 with Wg Cdr Ramachandran in the center

I got posted to no. 28 Squadron from no. 8 Squadron. My new unit was located in the Eastern region at Tezpur. Wg Cdr PM RamachandranSC was commanding the Squadron while Gp Capt. Karan Yadav was commanding AF Station, Tezpur. My Air-to-Ground gunnery, rocketry and bombing work was appreciated by all, including my Station Cdr in this squadron. After a few months of normal flying, the DASI team came for inspection. This time the director was Gp Capt. MellyWollen. After the inspection of all the units at the station, my Squadron was assessed as average plus. This time my individual assessment was 'aboveaverage'. This was an honour and a great improvement from my last assessment by DASI. During my stay in this squadron, I had earned my first citation for Vayusena Medal. The citation was written by Gp Capt. Karan Yadav himself on 22 March, 1976. The same is reproduced below:

1. Squadron Leader Harbans Singh Sahota (7663 L) F (P) has been on the posted strength of No. 28 squadron. Air Force w.e.f. 01 Aug 74 as a Flight Commander.

2. During his stay in this squadron, Squadron Ldr HS Sahota has been working extremely hard with sincerity and great dedication to his profession. Even personal hardships have not deterred him, as was evident when during the illness of his father, he made do with casual leave and continued working hard. He has put in sustained, strenuous effort often well beyond working hours and has contributed largely towards the squadron meeting and all its tasks successfully. As a Command Examiner, he took keen interest in the Instrument Flying Training in the squadron and it was in small measure due to his efforts that the unit Instrument Rating State was considerably improved and the squadron won the Instrument Rating Trophy for 1974–75.

3. After he qualified as a Fighter Combat Leader in February 75, he was put in charge of the operational Training of the staff Pilots in the squadron and this task, too, was carried out by him very creditably. His own results in armament work are very good and provide a good example to the other pilots in the Squadron. He scored an average of 8.5 yards in R/P firing during SCEMEAC 1975, and the combat mission led by him was also assessed as 'Above Average' by the DASl team during their visit in 1975.

4. Squadron Ldr HS Sahota has shown dedication to his profession and applied himself to his tasks with keenness from the very beginning of his career. When he had 200 hours of experience on Vampires, he was selected to undergo the Advanced Fighter Gunnery Course in USA which he completed successfully. He took part in the Indo–Pak operations in 1971, flying Air Defence missions in the Western sector on Type 77 aircraft.

5. His professional skill, presence of mind and cool handling of potentially dangerous situations have averted many an accidents—a few examples being, failure of after-burner on take-off in a Type 77 aircraft, inadvertent deployment of the tail chute during take-off in a Type 66 aircraft, and complete failure of main hydraulic system in a Type 77 aircraft during dark nights.

6. For his professional skills, high devotion to duty, hard and diligent work, I recommend Squadron Ldr HS Sahota for the award of Vayu Sena Medal.

However, I was not awarded the medal that year.

During my stay with No. 28 Squadron, a very interesting incident took place. Our range firing phase for our U/T OPS pilots was coming close. They all were given dual checks for range firing and now they were ready for solo missions at the range. Their Range Firing practices were required to be supervised by the Flight Commander. At that particular time, only two of us, senior Flight Commander Squadron Ldr Thunder Gandhi and I, the no. 2 Flight Commander, were present. My Squadron Commander detailed me to supervise Firing Practices of U/T OPS pilots at the Lakhimpur Range while performing the duties of RSO (Range Safety Officer). Range party consisting of about 10 airmen, four civilians, two NCEs and one three-tonner vehicle had left for range six days in advance. They were required to mark the bombing and rocket-firing target with lime and arrange gunnery targets (15 feet x 15 feet framed canvas) and put them in position. Our communication to and from the range was by signal only. We sent a signal to the range party—'Squadron Ldr Sahota reaching Lakhimpur Railway Station by Tezpur–Tinsukia passenger train for RSO duties. He will reach on Monday morning at 0500 hours. Arrange pick up from Lakhimpur Railway Station. Firing over the range commencing at 0730 hours on the same day'. I boarded the train at Tezpur railway station at 2100 hours on Sunday. It was a metre gauge train and had stopped at many stations before Lakhimpur. The duration of the journey was about 8 hours. I had carried along bedding with me and the journey was very comfortable. I slept on the lower berth in the train. There was no rush in the train as only two to three passengers were in the same bogie. As I reached Lakhimpur railway station, I got down with my baggage at the platform and expected that the range party would send the transport along with two or three airmen to take me to the range. The distance to the range from railway station was about 5 km but the road to the range was through a thick jungle.

I waited at the railway station till 0530 hours but no transport had come to pick me up. At that time, I thought that our signal might not have been received or the transport might have broken down. I handed over my bedding and a bag full of my personal clothes to the stationmaster and requested him to hand over the same to the Air Force driver (MTD) as and when he would come. I left for the base since time was running short and the first formation of 02 aircrafts was planned to be over the target (TOT) at 0730 hours. The route from the range to the railway station was circuitous, so, I set course on foot through the paddy fields and took a shortcut to the road. When I hit the road, it was the opening to the jungle. It was early in the morning and I kept chanting the prayers of Waheguru and kept walking fearlessly through the jungle. As soon as I reached near the range, the airmen on duty on range tower spotted me and quickly sent a vehicle to pick me up. When I reached the Main Quadrant, I heard the noise of 02 aircraft formation and at the same time leader of the formation called on range frequency. I cleared them to join range circuit and carry on the range work. If I were not in the range tower, no one would have cleared them to fire. They were to return to the base. It would have been colossal loss. As these two aircrafts finished their range work, they returned to base and immediately 02 more came over the range. This range work for other pilots carried on till 1400 hours. Thereafter, we went for lunch and some of the airmen told me some hair-raising incidents. The jungle on both sides of the road between Lakhimpur and the range was infested with wild elephants, wild boars and lions. They, in fact, had heard the roar of a lion only two days ago. After hearing this, I also felt that I should not have taken the risk of crossing the forest on foot but at the same time all those airmen present on the range, started treating me like a hero and praised my daring act by saying, 'service before self'. I returned from range after one week while some of the range party members were replaced two to three days earlier. They had reached AF Station, Tezpur, and spread the word around that Squadron Ldr Sahota did a very daring act and set an example of 'service before self'.

When I came back to the station, many officers and men congratulated me for my daring act. This news had reached my Station Cdr Karan Yadav. He called me to his office and gave me a rap for being stupid. He scowled, 'Damn it! You would have been eaten by a lion in seconds or may be the wild elephants would have killed you'. I apologized and told my story of not letting the range mission be aborted for which I took the risk of walking and ignoring the danger less known to me. I think the saying that 'ignorance is bliss' is very appropriate here. After that he congratulated me and said, 'You are lucky to have escaped possible death'.

Even in this Squadron, I flew more than other pilots. You will be surprised to know how I managed it. All the aircraft after periodic servicing were to be 'air tested'. Our R&SS used to service the aircraft and put them up for 'test flight'. I volunteered to carry out the air tests as it had to be done in a full Pressure Suit. In Pressure Suite, pilot would perspire too much while manoeuvring the aircraft on ground before the take-off and after the landing. This was a sore point for some pilots. I started doing Air Test Flights on Sundays as well. I got my wife trained by a technician to down the Pressure Suit on me, so, almost every Sunday, I used to carry out one Air Test Flight with my wife, downing my Pressure suite on me effortlessly. There were some Sundays when I carried out two Air Tests as well. It was quite a tiring venture but I did it with full dedication.

After some more time with the squadron, I was selected for the FCL (FighterCombat Leader) course. The course was in TACDE, AF. During the course at TACDE, all my assessment phases of flying went very well. I had some difficulty in 4 Vs 2 phase. Wg Cdr SK Mehra warned me verbally for poor performance in one mission. Anyway, I picked up all the debrief points and showed a good improvement in the rest of the missions. Also, my Air-to-Ground Firing Phase was so impeccable that Wg Cdr SK Mehra showered me with praises. I finally passed with good grades. In fact, I came 2nd in Ground Subjects, 3rd in Flying Phase and 1st in Air-to-Ground Weaponry Phase among eight pilots. After passing out, I was back in 28 squadron.

Caricature made during FCL course

When I was in No. 28 Squadron at Tezpur, four young pilots were posted to us for conversion on MiG-21 (FL) aircraft. During the course of training, a picnic was arranged in one of the weekends by the younger lot and we all proceeded in our private cars and motorcycles. Since all the families were invited for the picnic, we also took a big vehicle to carry our food, drinks, some chairs and matresses. Two cooks and four other helpers also accompanied us in that vehicle. We reached the picnic spot—about 45 km north of Tezpur, in the hills, just off the main road from Tezpur to Bomdila. This was a very picturesque location. We all enjoyed a sumptuous meal along with drinks while engaging in several games. Some of us, the ones more adventurous, did some short trekking too. Finally, we decided to return around 4 in the evening. We all packed all our belongings and left the area together in our repective vehicles. Two younger pilots, Sandhu and another pilot behind him on the rear seat, left a few minutes before us. As we all hit the road, we saw a herd of elephants blocking our way. We had to wait for the herd to clear the road. Somehow, Sandhu along with his pillion youngster had cleared the area where we all were held. After the elephants cleared the road, we all moved and started our journey towards AF station, Tezpur. On one side of the road were high hills and the other side was steep low-lying area full of creepers and shrubs dotted with tall trees. While driving ahead on the road, at a bend, we suddenly saw two men, entangled in creepers and covered in mud, pushing a motorcycle up the low-lying area. It was quite a very funny sight to behold, but we immediately stopped to help them. As we all got down from our vehicles, someone shouted, 'Oh! They are Sandhu and Arora!' It was then that we recognised them as our guys! Anyway, we finally helped them out of the mess and pulled the motorcycle out of the bog. They quickly got onto the bike and finally left for AF station. When we reached home, we came to know from the squadron doctor that both of them were badly bruised and Sandhu also had a deep cut on his right leg. I immediately met them and wanted to know the reason for their fall. Sandhu replied, 'Sir, we were going straight, the road suddenly turned right but we didn't and so went straight into the *khad*[57]. This thereon became the joke of the duo as we kept teasing

---

[57] Ditch

them with this dialogue throughout their stay in the Squadron. They became a good laughing stock of all the Squadron parties.

Posting to No. 4 Squadron AF—Second Time

After a few months' stay, I was posted to no. 4 squadron at Tezpur itself. In fact, it was an exchange posting between Surjit Singh and me. At that time 4 squadron was under move to AF Station, Bareilly. After winding up all the work, I lead the last 4 aircraft formation to Bareilly. We flew there for about four months and had settled down well. Then the DASI team arrived for their inspection of the wing and our squadron. This inspection went very well. Our squadron was assessed 'Above Average'. Wing Cdr OP Sharma, my Commanding Officer and I were assessed as 'Above Average' as well. In this visit Squadron Ldr Tipnis, as a member of the DASI Team, flew a slow speed handling sortie with me in the MIG-21 Trainer aircraft. During debrief of the sortie, he remarked that for the first time as an inspector, he had enjoyed the slow speed handling of an MIG-21 aircraft. Squadron Ldr Tipnis retired as Chief of Air Staff in later years.

Posting to No. 21 Squadron AF, 1977

After another four months of stay in 4 squadron, I was posted to no. 21 squadron, based at Poona. This squadron was converting onto MIG 21(Bis) aircraft from Gnat aircraft. Squadron was handed over by Wg Cdr Honky Mukuty to Wg Cdr DN Rathore. There were two more Squadron Ldrs above me in seniority, namely, Frisky Verma and Ratnaparkhi. We all started flying as some of the pilots were already converted on to MIG-21 (Bis) aircraft in Russia. I completed my conversion in no. 21 squadron. Within three to four months' time, Squadron Ldr Verma was posted out, followed by Squadron Ldr Ratnaparkhi. With this change, I had become no.1 Flight Commander of the squadron. There was a great responsibility on my shoulders since our squadron was given the task of converting some more squadrons onto MIG-21 (Bis). We converted many pilots of other Squadrons which were being equipped with MIG-21 (Bis) aircraft. Ours being the first MIG (Bis), squadron was visited by many civil dignitaries and also by the Chief of Air Staff. In fact, our AOC in C had visited us twice and our SASO had visited four times. I used to play a pivotal role in NDA Flypasts and demo Aerobatics in the Squadron for the visiting teams of Staff College and NDC officers. It was here where I earned my next citation, which was written by Wg Cdr DN Rathore on 4 April, 1978.

1. Squadron Leader Harbans Singh Sahota (7663 L) Flying (Pilot) has been on the posted strength of No. 21 Squadron A F w.e.f. 01 Feb 77. Since 20 June 77 has been functioning as Flight Commander. As the first squadron to be equipped with Type-75 aircraft, this unit has been engaged in converting new pilots to Type-75 aircraft, who in turn would be posted to new Type 75 Squadrons. Throughout the year 1977 and at present, the unit continues to be engaged in this task. A total of 61 pilots' conversion has been carried out by the unit as on 01 Apr 78. All this, apart from the continuous Operational training of its own pilots, has been achieved without a single accident or a near accident situation. This achievement was made possible by sheer dedication and hard work of the Flying Supervisors in the unit who took the utmost care to formulate and follow where necessary review of the Flying Training Methods was being followed to ensure maximum training benefit with maximum safety of aircraft and aircrew operations.

2. For his very significant contribution in the administration of flying in the unit during this crucial period of intensive Type 75 conversion training, I recommend Squadron leader Harbans Singh Sahota (7663 L) F (P) for the award of Vayu Sena Medal.

In the year 1979, on one NDC Team's visit, I was to lead Four Aircraft Formation for Bombing at Lohegaon Range. Our AOC Air Commodore Jain and Gp Capt. SK Kaul as Chief Operations Officer had made very elaborate arrangements at the range. Seating arrangement was made at an elevated platform. PA System and a commentator was also arranged to announce to the NDC Team members regarding our Range Work and particularly our Bombing Mission of Four Aircraft. Unfortunately, that day happened to be a cloudy day but clouds were expected higher than our bombing circuit over the range. Anyway, after much briefing and coverage of emergencies, in case we encounter low clouds over the range, all four aircraft got airborne one by one. Each aircraft had 10 seconds gap for take-off. I did one loose circuit to facilitate the other three aircrafts to join me in loose formation as briefed.

We proceeded to a preselected point for RV. We just made one orbit over the RV point and were told on R/T that the Range was ready and we were cleared for safety run. Safety run means, fly over the target at your pull-out height. As soon as I went past the target, I pulled up for climbing to my range circuit height. I entered clouds at 1,000 m and found that the layer of clouds was very thick. I was to climb to 2.3 km of height. At 2.3 km, I was still in clouds. I quickly called my formation members to abandon the circuit, turn outwards and proceed to the R/V point. No.2 at 1.5 km, No.3 at 1km and No.4 at 500 m and at R/V point; if the weather is clear, join-in tactical formation if possible, otherwise, they would have to orbit at respective heights and wait for me. I was orbiting over the range and was in clouds. When all the three aircrafts positively cleared the range area, I did one more orbit of the range and descended very slowly below clouds. All the while, I was talking

Target and Safety Run

to the RSO (Range Safety Officer) on R/T. Since it was a show for the NDC team, I informed the RSO that I was going to try an unconventional circuit at low level and will try to bomb the target. Sqn Ldr. Adi Gandhi was the RSO; he took permission from the COO, Gp Capt. SK Kaul, MVC (who later retired as Chief of Air Staff) and RSO informed that I was cleared to do that. I carried out range circuit just below the clouds, almost touching the lowest layer of clouds, which was approximately at 1,000 m height. Now the other problem was—due to the low height, the entry speed and bomb release parameters would change drastically. Within a few seconds, I worked out my parameters and made circuit at 1,000 m and came in for bomb release. With god's grace, all worked very well and the bombs had hit the Target Pin (Direct Hit). I was later told that RSO, COO and NDC team members were jumping at the range in joy. Later in the afternoon, all of them—my CO, COO, AOC and NDC team leader—came together to my Squadron and congratulated me for the marvellous range work. The leader of the NDC team, having visited some ranges in other sectors, informed that they had not witnessed such a splendid display before. I once again thanked Waheguru for blessing me with high-class appreciation of all senior officers. This news reached my Command HQ. My SASO, Dushyant Singh, rang up to congratulate my CO and me. Sure enough, my SASO visited our Squadron after two weeks and handed over one commendation letter by the AOC in C, Central Air Command, AF to my CO. He personally congratulated me and conveyed the appreciation of the AOC in C. This commendation was presented to me by the AOC on a Station Parade. In the commendation, there was a mention of some more my exceptional abilities as a flight commander.

In the same year, I had earned one more citation by Wg Cdr DN Rathore, which was written on 05 Apr 79.

1. Squadron leader Harbans Singh Sahota (7663 L) Flying (Pilot) has been on the posted strength of 21 Squadron AF since 01 Feb 77. After completion of his own training, Squadron Leader Harbans Singh Sahota (7663 L) Flying (Pilot) has been functioning as Flight Commander. As Flight Commander, one of his tasks has been to supervise operational as well as conversion flying training in the squadron. As the first squadron to be equipped with Type

75 aircraft, this unit has been engaged in converting pilots from other fighter aircraft onto type 75 aircraft. Throughout 1977 and 78 and also at present, this unit continues to be engaged in this task. A total of 91 pilots have been converted till date onto Type 75 aircraft by this unit. This achievement has been made possible by sheer dedication and hard work by the Flight Commanders and other Flying supervisiors of this unit, who took great care in formulating ground training and flying training programmes for conversion pilots and ensured effective and successful execution of the programmes, with maximum safety to aircrew and aircraft. Even though Squadron Leader Harbans Singh Sahota (7663 L) Flying (Pilot) is not a qualified flying instructor, his professional knowledge, hard work and devotion to duty has greatly contributed in achieving this task. He has been carrying out instructional flying efficiently and competently and has flown 530 Sorties in 400:25 hrs during his present tenure in the unit.

2. For his significant contribution as a Flight commander and as an instructor and for his supervision of flying training in the unit during this crucial period of intensive Type 75 conversion, I recommend Squadron leader Harbans Singh Sahota (7663L) Flying (Pilot) for the award of Vayu Sena Medal.

In the same year, I received one more commendation by the Chief of Air Staff (CAS) from Air HQ. It also had described my abilities and achievements as Flight Commander. I think I was the only officer to receive two commendations in a year. CAS's commendation was also presented to me on the Station Parade. It was a proud moment for me, as two commendations in a year had become the talk of Air Force Station, Pune.

After two months, I requested for leave as my wife and children were very eager to visit my hometown. My leave for 30 days was sanctioned. It so happened that the day I was to leave, my Squadron had arranged *Bara Khana*[58] for all the Squadron members with their wives and children. On the same day, we also had one function in our AF Gurudwara for which my AOC Air Cmde NC Suri had given me the responsibility

---

[58] A feast

as President of Gurdwara Management Committee. It happened to be a Sunday. One special team of renowned *ragies* were performing in Gurudwara. The whole programme in Gurudwara was to be followed by a *langar*. All arrangements were to be supervised by me. I became too busy while looking after the arrangements in both the places. Our Station gurudwara was about 2 km away. My wife and I were running between both the places to organise everything well. Since it was a Sunday, village Lohegaon had its routine vegetable and fruits open market too and all the buses running between Lohegaon and Pune were overcrowded. I had to take a bus to reach the railway station. My train, Poona–Delhi Express, was scheduled to leave at 1305 hours. I finished all the commitments, picked my wife and children along with our baggage and reached the bus stop at 1205 hours as the bus generally used to take about 20 to 25 minutes to reach Pune Railway Station.

We were standing at the bus stop just behind my CO Wg Cdr DN Rathore's house, missing most of the buses as they were overcrowded due to the reasons mentioned above. The time was running out and I began to have a sinking feeling in my mind that my tickets would go waste if we did not make it to the Railway Station and board the train on time. Then, as a last resort, came another bus, which was supposed to leave our stop at 1225 hours. If we missed that one, our booking and tickets would, sure enough, have gone waste. The bus came from Lohegaon packed with passengers and it did not even halt at our stop. Now we began to panic and prayed to Waheguru to send someone for our help. In a few minutes, I saw Wg Cdr Rathore approaching us on his scooter. It was anunusual sight. He had just sent his car to the MT Section and came to the rear of his house and saw us stranded there. He was aware of my train timings. Since his car would take a long time to come from MT Section, he started his scooter and came to the bus stop. In the meantime, one more person on scooter had offered to help us. So, one can only imagine how we had left for the railway station—my wife and son along with some baggage with Wg Cdr Rathore on his scooter and my daughter, along with my bed holder, and me were loaded on the other person's scooter. We all left for the Railway Station only in a hope that we will be able to catch the train. When we finally reached Poona Railway Station at 1320 hours, we had left all hopes of catching the train. As we reached the station, a coolie asked us which train we had to board. As I mentioned Poona–Delhi Express, he quickly said, 'The train is at platform no. 3 and has not left yet'. What a sight it must have been when we all, with the help of Wg Cdr Rathore, picked up our baggage and ran through the rail tracks between platforms no. 1 and 2! We managed to climb to platform no. 2 and again picked the baggage and ran to platform no. 3. When we saw one door of the passenger bogie open, we quickly threw the baggage in and all four of us jumped into the bogie. As we entered the bogie, the train whistled and started moving. Wg Cdr Rathore waved and heaved a sigh of relief; so did we. It seemed that as if some godly power had held the train for us, and it was God who had sent Rathore and one more *farishta*, whose name I still do not know. I never met him or had seen him thereafter throughout my stay at AF Station, Pune. I believe in Waheguru and my prayers. He only had made it possible for us to reach the railway station and had held the train until we had boarded. He knows everything; and I have complete faith in Him. The train left at 1330 hours. This delay of 25 minutes of a train—known to leave on time every day—only Waheguru could explain!

In fact, when I came back from leave, one day, Wg Cdr Rathore told me that, 'I very rarely go towards the back of my house. On the day of your departure for leave, some godly power had forced me to go behind my house and then I saw you at the bus stop and noticed you all were still there, whereas, at that time you should have been at Pune Railway Station. Then some godly power made me rush and check on you'. He also expressed his surprise about the late departure of the most punctual train. According to him, it was all God's doing.

We were very pleased to finally reach my village Garhdiwala. We had to change the train first at Delhi then at Jallandhar and then we had to go by bus from Dasuya to Garhdiwala. Bibiji and Bapuji were overwhelmed to see all of us and we even caught up with many relatives and friends during our stay there. By now my elder sisters were married off and had left for their husband's home. My younger brother Harbhajan Singh and my younger sister Amarjit Kaur were also at home. My sister was teaching in Khalsa High School and my brother was working as a basketball coach in the same school. My children were very excited to see farm life and they would always be upto some mischief like riding buffaloes, chasing goats and hens. We also had some hens in a coop at home and the kids found it very amusing to collect eggs and feed the hens. They seemed to treat them as pets but we didn't have the heart to tell them that the chicken curry, which they relished so much, was from the same source. In the *haveli* we also had some buffaloes and they used to wait for their milking time.

The very next year was a traumatic year for us because we got the news of the sudden death of my father-in-law, who had suffered a heart attack, in March. We had just recovered from this mishap when we received the sad news in the same year in August that my father too had left us for his heavenly abode. In spite of my best efforts, I could not reach on his funeral due to my service duty and distance of travel. This loss could never be recovered. The next year was even more tragic because in April, my younger brother, Harbhajan suddenly died in an accident and left a very big void in my life which took a long time to heal. Well this is what life is...all we can do is accept what is served to us by the Almighty and eventually move on.

19

FINDING THE LEADER WITHIN

Deputation to Nigerian Air Force as an Instructor Pilot

After returning from leave, I got involved in normal flying activities of the squadron. During that time, our board for Wing Commander rank was going on at Air HQ. My name, meanwhile, was declared for deputation to Nigeria for flying training and OPS training of the Nigerian Pilots. Wg Cdr DN Rathore was selected to be the Team Leader. Squadron Ldr Surjit Singh and Squadron Ldr DS Sant were also selected to be a part of the training team; seniority wise list was as follows:

- Wg Cdr DN Rathore
- Wg Cdr H S Sahota (myself)
- Squadron Ldr Surjit Singh
- Squadron Ldr DS Sant

Air HQ informed me that I was cleared for the rank of Wg Cdr Rank but the deputation requirement was one Wg Cdr and three Squadron leaders. If I was prepared to go on deputation in the rank of Squadron leader, my Wg Cdr rank and seniority will be maintained until I returned. I accepted to go on deputation. All four of us left for Nigeria along with our families and children since the deputation was for two years. During this deputation, I did a lot of work in improving the flying procedures, making the SOPS and Pilot Orders, briefing techniques and night-flying procedures. I was told by a senior Nigerian MIG pilot that the MIG aircraft was not capable of night flying and they are not prepared to take chances in venturing into night flying. I convinced them that MIG-21 aircraft was an all-weather flying aircraft. Night flying capability of a pilot is an essential part of training and OPS requirement. They were very deficient in Instrument Flying skills as well. I, along with my colleagues, made night-flying procedures, SOPS and Instrument-Flying procedures. In day flying, Nigerian pilots were quite proficient but they needed more practice and experience in night and instrument flying. The base, where we were stationed, had a full-fledged standard runway, standard lighting and Arrester Barrier on both ends. The surprising part was, there was only one taxi track from the tarmac with a hanger. The taxi track was approximately 100 yards long to join the runway but had no lights for taxiing the aircraft in the night. To make the taxi track fit for night taxiing of aircraft; I bought wires, holders and ordinary 15-watt bulbs from the market. I pegged the wires with holders and bulbs on both sides of the taxi track and made a connection in the hanger with a switch for putting these bulbs 'on' and 'off'. Just to flay their fear of night flying, Wg Cdr Rathore and I got airborne at night. It was a moonlit night. Rathore performed some aerobatics overhead at night and I orbited away from the airport for sometime. When Rathore landed, I came overhead and carried out aerobatics, including loops and barrel rolls as well as a couple of low-level runs over the runway, followed by landing. It was only then that the Nigerian pilots got convinced that the MIG aircraft was capable of night flying also.

During this deputation, I used to carry out all liaison visits to the Nigerian Air Force HQ at Lagos. Somehow, all the Nigerian pilots liked my training ability, both on ground and in the air. They kept giving feedback to their Station Cdr and he, in turn, was sending feedback to the Nigerian AF HQ. In appreciation of my sincere and good work, the Chief of Air Staff of NAF wanted to extend my stay for one more year for which he asked my willingness through his OPS Director. This happened when I was on a liaison visit to the NAF HQ. I immediately requested for an interview with the CAS and informed him that before coming to Nigeria on deputation, I was cleared for my Wg Cdr rank. My Air Hq would be waiting for me to reach India as soon as the deputation period is over. If I do not reach on time, I may lose a chance to Command an MIG Squadron. It appeared to me that he was convinced with my logic. In spite of that, his staff at AF Station, Makurdi, delayed my departure for two months. All of them kept telling me that their Chief would speak to the IAF chief for the extension of tenure. However, I kept on insisting to leave as soon as possible. Finally, they cleared me to leave for India.

When I went on a deputation to Nigerian Air Force, the whole family moved together and had a ball of a time in Nigeria. From there we visited UK, France, Italy, Switzerland, Netherland, USA, Canada and Singapore. It was an excellent opportunity for Tenju and Tipi to see the world. My children studied in Nigeria for two years and my wife got the opportunity to work as a Mathematics teacher in a teacher's training school. We went on many family road trips together and explored Nigeria too from northern side, Kano, to southern PortHarcourt. We went on wildlife safaris and visited many tourist places on the way. This was an excellent exposure for all of us, as we had never visited any African country in the past.

I feel that in my opinion these travels to unique places and interacting with the local people makes us more acceptable and liberal towards different cultures and traditions. It makes us open minded. We learn a lot from each other and start looking at the world as an integrated whole. At a deeper level, we realize that after all we all are humans first with the same basic feelings and emotions. This creates a feeling of universal brotherhood and so I recommend that everyone must travel to different parts of the world and India. This can put an end to racism as well.

Command of No. 21 Squadron AF

After coming back from Nigeria, I reported to the Air Hq and there, I met Gp Capt. SK Mehra Director OPS (who later on retired as Chief of Air Staff). He informed me that I was to go to Pune and take over the command of no. 21 Squadron AF. The signal of my promotion to the rank of Wg Cdr and posting to 21 Squadron was already out. After getting this message, I flew in civil aircraft to Pune. On the next day, I reported to the AOC, AF Station, Pune, Air Cmde NC Suri (who later on retired as Chief of Air Staff). I felt privileged when he put the Rank tapes of Wg Cdr Rank on my shoulders. He also gave me an informative talk for about half an hour on weaknesses and strengths of my Squadron and my role in the Station as Squadron Cdr.

Thereafter, I came to my Squadron and found that the Squadron was deployed on OP Location for practice OPS. The Squadron was split in two detachments and both the detachments were deployed on two different Op locations. All the pilots and serviceable aircrafts were out. Only one technical officer, Flt Lt Mishra, who was looking after the base, received me. He took me in the Squadron Hanger attached with all the technical offices and tool crib. There were also some Airmen who were manning the sections. They—including orderly room staff and DWO's (Discipline Warrant Officer) staff—were introduced to me. Thereafter, we all had a cup of tea and some snacks. I spoke to all of them for about 15 minutes and left with Flt Lt Mishra who took me to my office. After spending a few minutes in my office, he took me to the R&SS Hanger. There I met Gp Capt. Gursharan Singh, Chief Engineering Officer, who later on retired as SMSO (Senior Maintenance Staff Officer) at Air HQ. He briefed me on the R&SS working arrangements, including the planned servicing schedules of my Squadron aircraft. My Squadron was supposed to return after a week or so. I utilized this time to go through the Pilot Orders and Instructions, Squadron Diary and various Administrative Orders. Wg Cdr SAB Naidu, who was CO of 21 Squadron before me had left for Air HQ for onward journey to Nigeria on deputation. Senior Flight Cdr, Squadron Ldr Denny Nayyar was officiating as CO. On arrival of the detachments and settling down at AF Station Pune (Home Base), Squadron Ldr Denny Nayyar formally handed over the command of 21 Squadron to me on 08 February, 1982.

My duty now was to address my officers and all technical personnel, including civilians, so that I make them aware of my plans, policies, requirements and expectations from them. My talk was long but full of target setting, encouraging them to work fearlessly and display discipline in all walks of duty and off duty. Though I started with my introduction, some of the officers and airmen already knew me as I had served in the same Squadron as Flt Cdr before proceeding on deputation to the Nigerian Air Force. I would like to mention an encouraging and befitting gist of my speech which I had delivered without referring to my script—

"I want all of you to be proactive, which means creating or controlling a situation rather than just respond to it after it has happened. For any work situation or armament phase, etc., always start with the end result in mind. While planning, put first things first and always think positively of a win-win situation. Mostly, people jump to conclusions without understanding a situation and argue with less knowledge. So, you must always seek first to understand and then be understood. You must empower and synergize the people placed below you. Give a kind of vitality and enthusiasm with positive ideas and attitude to all placed below you. Also, keep your saws sharpened and react to situations before they become a problem. No one is as strong as you, only you can tackle your fears and work fearlessly to gain ascendency over every situation. Fear is the only factor, which can force you to hold back. With courage, you can win any situation and tackle any problem. I also quoted my father's saying, 'whatever seeds you put in the land, and the same crop will come up for you to reap.' What he meant was, 'what you sow, so shall you reap.' I, thereafter, insisted that there is no shortcut to success. Mainly, our problem is lack of perceiving, understanding and interpreting any situation. We devote more time to fixing our shortcomings than to developing our strengths."

Actually, I spoke for about half an hour, covering all aspects of Squadron life. My talk was so motivating that all of them started cheering loudly and promised that they will do their best during their stay with the Squadron.

'Should you encounter a problem along your way, change your direction but not your destination'.

A few more aspects like the management of airmen's messes, welfare and flight safety were also discussed. Thereafter, we all had tea and dispersed for respective duties. The next day, I started my flying after a dual check by Squadron Ldr Denny Nayyar. After a couple of days of flying, I observed that after morning Met and ATC briefing, we used to rush to the Squadron, conduct quick briefings for respective exercises or missions and get airborne. I realized that this type of rush for trainee pilots might become a Flight Safety Hazard. I devised a system where we would have combined briefing in the Squadron before the mission briefings. We started this system and continued for a few days. I added one more thing that at the end of Squadron briefing, everyone was to remain seated in his respective chair, relax with closed eyes and concentrate on aircraft emergencies or may be on god. The duration of this exercise was for five minutes. We continued this system, which resulted in a delay of 20 to 30 minutes of our pack-up time. The dividends of this exercise were to be seen later on but the immediate effect of delayed pack-up started to pinch my Flt Cdrs. However, I managed to convince them and named the system 'Let us sit for five minutes and finish them quickly'.

This meditation mantra did not come to me overnight. It was my daily routine. I used to spend 10 to 15 minutes meditating before going to bed. I followed this practice right from my school days. While in the service of air force, I started practising in the morning as well as before going to my work. It helped me get rid of the clutter in my mind and improved my concentration and self-control. Meditation is a process of calming the mind and an affirmation of the individual relationship to the universe. Meditation is an art of self-realization, power of silence, love and curiosity, making us aware and awareness leads to achievements, sometime beyond your own imagination. Meditation needs consistency. Remember, meditation is not a quick fix for your problems. You have to practice it all your life. I meditate every day and I can tap into my meditative state of mind to resolve any of the problems. This practice improves concentration, kindness, love, empathy, and health, improves attention, boosts energy, and finally, makes you successful in any of your endeavours. With just a little effort, we can all achieve healthier minds. Investing just 10 to 15 minutes of attention to mind-fitness can pay enormous dividends.

People say cats have nine lives but all of us know, a man has only one life. So, all your goals and targets must be achieved within this life. You have to be positive and spread positivity to others. Meditation makes you a positive individual. Your positive attitude in you will give you inner strength to cope with any situation. Once you are thinking positively, the same attitude is expressed towards others in all situations. Your work situations, day-to-day pressures of work or external factors can be depressing but your inner strength, which you gained by your daily dose of meditation, will take care of everything; and put you in control of even very difficult situations. To win the confidence of others, you have to be sincere and be honest and love all who come in contact with you. This means, respect everyone in whatever capacity they are involved with you or are around you. Meditation also inspires you to learn the art of happy living and cultivate, in your mind, qualities such as compassion, contentment and humility. My daily dose of meditation is paying me rich dividends in my day-to-day life.

Meditation is a tool we use to regulate our thoughts. Meditation to be used as a means and not as an end itself. It is the right step towards shaping our life in the right direction. Meditation is to focus your thoughts on one object. The right object is the heart chakra, which is the area in the centre of the chest. We should rest our thoughts on the divinity inside us and stay on that thought. This way our thinking becomes gradually slower. We bring our mind to a very relaxed and calm state. Here we feel our consciousness as a mirror of who we are. We accept our strengths and weaknesses. We use our will power to focus on the positives and resolve to change our thoughts to be in tune with spiritual values of patience, acceptance, tolerance, compassion, kindness, universal brotherhood and unconditional love. This way we transform ourselves to what we want to achieve and what we want to become. That is why it is said that our thoughts shape our destiny. Here, I would also like to mention that our meditation helps us control our thoughts. Sometimes, before we realise, bad and negative thoughts enter our mind and get seated and slowly start changing our life, as we rarely understand the cycle of thoughts, which leads to our destiny.

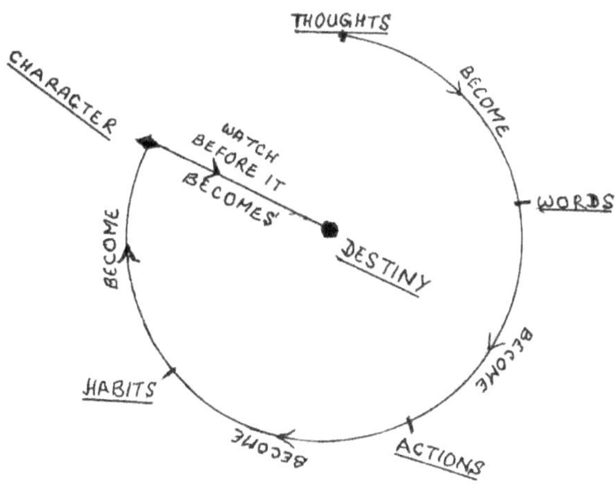

Cycle Of Thoughts

Our thoughts become words that direct our actions, which in turn become habits that lead to our behaviour, which leads to character and eventually become our destiny. We need to train our mind to think positive and that training is done by meditation. Therefore, meditation is a process, which will check our bad, negative or unwanted low categorised thoughts before they follow the cycle to become our destiny.

After my stay of two months, Air HQ assigned my Squadron with a Conversion Role, but at the same time, my Squadron's operational role was not changed. So, it became a dual role Squadron. Within another week, Air HQ posted eight pilots from Hunter Aircraft Conversion Unit to my Squadron to be converted onto MIG-21 (Bis) supersonic aircraft. We needed a huge infrastructure to start the Conversion Training. My tech officers took upon themselves the responsibility to create the required infrastructure out of the Squadron resources. I did not ask for any additional funds from HQ Central Air Command or Air HQ, New Delhi. My Flt Cdrs and Tech Officers covered ground subjects for trainee pilots. Even Conversion Flying Training had started in full swing. All the OPS pilots were to be kept in good preparation for our OPS Role at the same time. I led all the Fly Pasts for NDA, passing out parades and executed low-level aerobatics displays as well for various defence teams and civilian dignitaries visiting Air Force Station, Pune. Our armament phase was to start in June 82. For that purpose, all the aircraft, which were to be utilized for Air-to-Ground armament work, were to be harmonized. I personally checked all the harmonizations. This process paid us rich dividends. Later in the year, Inter-Squadron Gunnery Meet of HQ CAC, IAF, had started and we won the overall championship with Individual Guns Trophy—won by my staff pilot Squadron Ldr Sahni. Maintenance Trophy and Trophy for Best Squdron of Hq CAC, IAF.

Hq CAC, IAF Inter-Squadron Gunnery meet 1982-83
Sobti, Deepak, Sasoon, Self, Iyer and my Tech Offr Mishra

Training flying for eight ex-Hunter aircraft pilots was also progressing slowly. Our armament range firing was also going on almost every three to four months. In the year 1983, my Squadron maintained 100% serviceability for two days and flew all aircraft on the Squadron strength, on both the days. This was a very rare achievement. The AEB visited my Squadron, all my pilots passed the written examination and most of us got our Instrument Ratings renewed. The DASI Team from Air HQ inspected my Squadron and gave 'Above Average' assessment. In the same visit, my performance was also assessed as 'Above Average' with all my staff pilots scoring an 'Average Plus'. I kept my pilots, tech officers, airmen, NCEs and civilians very well motivated and insisted them to work with full dedication and enthusiasm.

Briefing Air Cmde Upkar Singh DASI-1 on
Slow Speed Handling of Mig-21 (check mission)

We were continuing with normal conversion and OPS flying for some time. Then came the Second Gunnery Meet of HQ CAC, IAF. In this Gunnery Meet, my Squadron had won the Overall Championship once again and I had bagged the Individual Rocket firing Trophy. The other trophies that we won were as follows:

- Best Fighter Squadron of CAC, IAF.
- Command Flight Safety Trophy.
- Best Maintenance Trophy.

Standing—First Row—Sinha, Neeraj, Nambiar, Chhabra
Second Row—Sachdeva, VP Singh, Sasoon, Self, Bhatt, Jain, BP Singh
Sitting---Alfa Yadav, Bhatt, Srikant and Panikar

In the year 1983, one OPS ASI signed by Gp Capt. SK Mehra was issued to all flying squadrons and their base stations. All individual pilots were to be assessed for their excellence in Air-to-Ground armament work. They were to be awarded with STARS as follows:

- Air-to-Ground Bombing with 'Above Average' result—One Star.
- Air-to-Ground Rocket Firing with 'Above Average' result—One Star.
- Air-to-Ground Guns Firing with 'Above Average' result—One Star.

The most difficult part was that all the sorties/missions were to be assessed from the start in the squadron where they were posted. If even one sortie/mission result were not 'Above Average', the pilot for that phase would be disqualified. As per this OPS ASI, I was the only pilot in the IAF who had won three stars. Initially, it was difficult to accept but a team lead by Wg Cdr MV Singh from HQ CAC, IAF, cleared me after inspection of all the Range firing records kept with the AF Station, Pune. This team sealed all records sheets. It appeared that it was not enough, so one more team lead by Wg Cdr SAB Naidu from Air HQ was detailed to verify the relevant records. This team also returned fully satisfied, and finally, I was awarded with a certificate and a badge with 'THREE STARS' and with an inscription 'MARKSMAN' of the IAF. I am very proud of this achievement because till date, no one has achieved three stars! Becoming a Marksman of the Indian Air Force was only possible due to the mindful and deliberated Armament Firing practices with utmost dedication, discipline, clarity and a spirit to win. During that time, Wg Cdr Charlie Brown (who retired as CAS later on) was awarded two stars only and many other pilots were awarded only one Star each. I can safely say that I am the proud MARKSMAN of the Indian Air Force. I kept the IAF Flag Flying High, *'Touch the Sky with Glory'*.

In the same year, trials for a new concept of aircraft readiness had started in my Squadron. This concept was known as 'Crew Chief Concept'. Gp Capt. Gursharan Singh was the President, I was a Flying Member and two more Tech Officers were also members of this team to complete the trials. This was a herculean task, which took three months for completion. At the end of the trials, we were required to submit a report and give a presentation in Air HQ on its viability and final acceptance of this model for the rest of the flying units. Anyway, for various reasons, this concept was not accepted.

Briefing AOC in C –CAC, IAF—Air Marshal DA La Fontaine on crew chief concept AOC AF Stn Pune Air Commodore EG Salins looks on. Crew Chiefs in the back.

In the same year, during the Golden Jubilee Celebrations, an Air Show including Ground Display of weapons and different aircraft was organised at Air Force Station, Pune. The Air Force Formation Aerobatics Team known as Thunderbolts was to perform. Before the Thunderbolts arrived, I performed solo aerobatics over the static display, which was witnessed by approximately one lakh (1,00,000) people present on the ground for the static and air display. As I was touching down for landing on the runway, Thunderbolts lead by Gp Capt. Ben Brar (who later on retired as Air Marshall) arrived over the airfield and performed wonderful formation aerobatics, which further more thrilled the people present on the ground. Thunderbolts operated from

Nasik Airport. After the display, they landed back at Nasik Airport. The public wanted to see the pilot who performed solo aerobatics in MIG-21 (Bis) aircraft. Since I was present in the AF station, I was taken in an open Jeep to the site of static display. On seeing me, they shouted, 'Our dare-devil fighter pilot!' Some of the Senior Officials from Pune shook hands with me and remarked, 'Your aircraft was dancing in the sky like the famous actress Hemamalini's dance in some movies'. This grand air show was conducted under the direct supervision of Air Commodore Salins, AOC of Air Force Station, Pune. He was also mighty pleased with my display of low-level aerobatics.

I earned my first citation as Squadron Commander, which was written by Air Commodore EG Salins on 23 Apr 83.

1. Wing Commander Harbans Singh Sahota (7663 L) F (P) has had an illustrious career over the last 20 years of his service wherein he was entrusted with prestigious appointments and qualifications like Flight Commander of a MIG-21 Squadron, Command Examiner, Fighter Combat Leader and on deputation to Nigerian Air Force. His performance in the execution of all his duties has been consistently commendable throughout his career, which brought credit to the units, which he served within the IAF and won the appreciation of a foreign air force by his noteworthy contribution in discernibly enhancing the flying training effort of that country. He has displayed exemplary and most creditable performance in his personal flying as a fighter pilot where he has had an accident-free record during the last 18 years of his service flying a total 2,673 hours out of which more than 2,250 hours on MIG-21 variants.

2. Wg Cdr H S Sahota took over the Command of No.21 Squadron, AF on 08 Feb 1982. Right from the onset, he infused a high sense of professionalism among his squadron personnel to achieve the highest standards in operational training as well as conversion commitment entrusted to his unit.

3. No 21 Squadron (his unit) was entrusted with the task of conversion on Type 75 aircraft of the pilots of the IAF in addition to the operational task in Air Defence as well as a Ground Attack

role. Wg Cdr Sahota, by his dynamic leadership, inspired his team to enhance the flying effort of the unit. He organised the conversion training in a methodical manner to accelerate the training of the inexperienced, Type 77 and ex-Hunter OCU pilots. In the interest of the service, he took no service leave during 1982, in order to meet the conversion commitments with proper supervision.

4. Wg Cdr H S Sahota set a personal example of the high order which was worthy to be emulated by his Squadron pilots and maintenance personnel. He achieved above average results in weapons delivery both in air-to-ground and air-to-air phases. His solo low-level aerobatic displays to NDA cadets, DSSC visiting teams and during Golden Jubilee celebrations at No. 2 Wing AF were not only morale boosting and inspiring the young cadets but also brought credit to his squadron and the station and won laurels for the Air Force amongst the vast civilian population.

5. His meticulous planning, personal example of highest professional skills, devotion to duty and diligent execution enabled his Squadron to achieve praiseworthy results in all spheres of activity which enhanced the operational preparedness as well as provide positive promotion to flight safety. His squadron was thus able to achieve an accident-free record for the year 1982–83. In the field of maintenance, his unit had the honour of achieving 100 % serviceability twice during the year.

6. I strongly recommend the award of Vayu Sena Medal to Wing Commander Harbans Singh Sahota for his diligence and sincerity of effort, dedication and devotion to duty, consistent display of commendable personal performance and professional skill and accident-free record during the last 18 years of service and for the dynamic leadership as a Squadron Commander to inspire his unit personnel for enhancement of flying effort and accident-free record of the squadron in the best traditions of the Indian Air Force.

President of India Shri Giani Jail Singh Ji congratulating both of us on the award of Vayu Sena Medal. CAS, IAF-Air Chief Marshal Katre introducing the recepients and their families

After the static display, our normal routine of training and OPS flying continued. I had a big challenge in front of me—of progressing the conversion training of eight inexperienced pilots. However, my staff pilots were well motivated and we met the challenge squarely and managed to bring seven of them to U/T OPS stage, however, only one of them could not make the grade. He was posted out for Helicopter Conversion. Other seven pilots got posted out one by one to various other MIG-21 squadrons. In the year 1983, we had far too many visits of civilian dignitaries and I did most of the briefings and low-level aerobatics displays for them. Year 1984 started with my low-level aerobatics display for the NDA cadets. On 26th January 1984, two of my staff pilots and one technical officer were commended by our AOC in C. I WAS AWARDED WITH 'VAYUSENA MEDAL' BY THE PRESIDENT OF INDIA. CAS commended one more Tech Offr Sqn Ldr Ahluwalia of my Sqn.

In May 1984, there was an NDA passing out parade and as usual, I was to lead three aircraft flypast for that parade. For the same parade, our CAS, Air Chief Marshal Dilbagh Singh was the Reviewing Officer. The entire parade was to pass in front of the Saluting Dais twice, and both the times, as the last column goes past the Dais, the aircraft formation comes in front of the Reviewing Officer to receive the salute. For the first run, my formation came over the parade ground and in front of the Dais on time. There was a loud applause from the public witnessing the parade. For the second run, which was from a different direction, there were thick low clouds in our path for the run. Location of NDA being in the hilly terrain, descent below clouds could not be made. We had to take a detour to get below the clouds. As a result, the flypast was delayed by 8 seconds. For that period, our CAS was waiting on the Dais for the formation to arrive. As the formation arrived overhead, he saluted and left the Dais and there was a loud applause again from the public. The liaison officer told this to me later in the evening. After landing back, I found that the CAS was coming to the AOC's office before departing to New Delhi. I reported to my AOC and informed him about the error I had made. We waited for the CAS to arrive as I was preparing myself for the rap from him. As soon as the CAS saw me standing near the office of my AOC, and before I could even salute him, he said,

'Sahota, congratulations! It was a nice show. In the second run, the low clouds' must have put you off. After hearing this, I did not give any excuse; I said, 'Sir, it was my fault, I miscalculated the time, since I had to take a detour because of the low clouds on our way for the run. I am very sorry for the delay in the second TOT'. Thereafter, the CAS shook hands with me and entered my AOC's office. Interacting with the CAS was a privilege, which only a few could have in those days. I was lucky to have met him. After some time, the CAS left for New Delhi in his special aircraft.

Deepak, myself and Malesh

Air Chief Marshal Dilbag Singh
Visiting Air Force Station Pune

During March or April of 1984, a wonderful incident had taken place. The DASI team was visiting my Squadron, and at that time, everyone knew that all the missions on the range by Wg Cdr Sahota were 'Above Average'. However, one member of DASI, Wg Cdr Sukrutha Raj, was not convinced of my abilities and still had a doubt. Just to prove his point, he asked me to lead Four Aircraft formation for Bombing Mission on the Range which was already active as some other Squadrons were utilizing the range. After planning the mission and fixing up all arrangements, I got four aircrafts loaded with two practice bombs on each aircraft. I chose my team with three more of my staff pilots. Raj gave us the Time Over Target (TOT). I was to work backwards for my start of aircraft, taxi, take-off and navigation at low level and attack/ release of bombs from a pull up attack. During this mission, Raj was to orbit over the range to check our TOT and bombing results visually apart from the Range Officer's plotting of bomb hits. I made the TOT exact on time as per my watch and released the bombs after pull up attack. The Range Safety Officer reported,'Direct hit'. My second aircraft bombed at 20 yards, third bombed at 15 yards and fourth bombed at 25 yards, following which we all regrouped and then came back to the base. Raj followed us and as soon as he reached the crew room, I requested him to attend our debriefing of the mission. He only had one complaint that the TOT was minus 02 seconds as per his watch. We did synchronize our watches before starting the mission. When I asked about the bombing results, he said 'Hats off' to the results. Finally, he was convinced of my abilities!

During my Command of 21 Squadron from 08 Feb 82 to 08 Jul 84, my Squadron achieved accident-and-incident free record. My Squadron won Gunnery Meet Championship for two consecutive years, and was adjudged as the best Squadron for the same period. In the second Gunnery Meet, I also won Individual Rocket Firing Trophy. I would like to give all the credit to my Staff Pilots, Technical Officers and all Technical personnel, including NCEs and civilians for these achievements in the best traditions of the IAF.

During this tenure as commanding officer of No. 21 Squadron AF station, Pune, my wife Gian Kaur Sahota, intimately known as Gian Ji, took over the responsibility of Welfare of squadron families and later on station families too. She has been a good dancer and lecturer and a housewife. She used to enjoy arranging cultural programmes for ladies and children. Ladies club was always very actively involved in organising functions and she would willingly participate and organise.

Both the children also enjoyed participating in various programmes on stage. Children also learnt a lot about welfare activities by volunteering for AFWWA (Air Force Wives Welfare Association) activities. I must add here a little bit about AFWWA, which plays a very important role in our Air-Force life. Other than many activities handled by AFWWA, it manages a shop, which runs on very nominal profit for the convenience of all the families on the station. Those days, ladies on volunteer basis did the sales. The association also takes care of the families of Air Warriors in times of distress like after the death of an Air Warrior, a lot of financial assistance and moral support is extended to them. There are scholarships for meritorious students too. They are managing many vocational ventures at the same time. A lot of classes are organised on the stations for the ladies and children. When we stay at remote stations away from city, then all the AFWWA activities provide a great way of keeping everyone involved and bonded together. We celebrate all the festivals of all religions together, be it Eid, Ganesh chaturthi, Guruprab, Christmas, Dussera, Diwali, Holi, Durga puja, Onam or Pongal. So, this way we have the real feeling of 'Unity in diversity'.

I was glad that my entire family used to actively take part in all such events. Both my children, Tenju and Tipi (nickname of my son) did well in studies. Besides academics, they both were very good badminton players. In fact, Tenju had even won the Badminton Championship of Western Region School held in the year 1983–84 while Tipi used to play badminton, basketball, football and squash, and had also won the Badminton Championship of Eastern region Air Force Schools in 1988–89.

During our stay in Pune, we had made good friends in civil with which we are still in touch. We used to go to MG road, Pune, for our monthly shopping together. This was a monthly trip as the Air Force Station was about 15 km away from the city. We used to spend half a day shopping and then have a sumptuous lunch of dosa and idly at Mangal Vihar restaurant. There were some fixed shops like the Budhani mixture wala, Laxminarayan chewda wala, Monginis bakery, grocery store, etc. where we would visit frequently. There was an ayurvedic store that we liked to visit for some medicines. Rasik Bhai owned this. His wife, son and daughter-in-law were also all very affectionate and friendly so we would often spend time with them during our visits. Rasik Bhai would show us his small-scale production unit of ayurvedic medicines, which he used to supervise himself. They also used to visit us at the Air Force Station. It is because of such people and their kind affection, which made our stay so memorable!

Posting to Air Force Station Jamnagar

In July 1984, I was posted out to attend Higher Air Command Course in Secunderabad. On completion of this course, I was posted to AF Station, Jamnagar and worked for two months in the office of the Chief Operations Officer. I did review many of the Station Flying Orders and Instructions under the guidance of Gp Capt. Lagad. Since we had served together in one of the MIG-21 Squadrons, I had a very nice and fruitful short-stay at Jamnagar AF Station.

My family did not accompany me as my daughter, Tenju, was in class 11 and Tipi was in class 8 at that time and I didn't want to disturb their studies. They stayed back in Pune and retained the accommodation there. They were well taken care of at the station and were very comfortable as it was a known place.

Attachment to HQ South Western Air Command IAF at Jodhpur

Thereafter, I was attached to HQ South West Air Command at Jodhpur to perform the duties of OPS-1. When I reported to my Air-1 Air Cmde, Brahmawar, I was told that there had been no OPS-1 in the command for quite some time. When I reached my section, I found that piles of files were kept on the table for action. OPS-1 was also required to conduct morning briefing for the AOC-IN-C, SASO and all other officers posted in the command. On the third day, I was taken by my Air-1 to our SASO Air Marshal, Man Singh, for introduction and briefing. Air Marshal Raghavendran was the AOC-IN-C of SWAC, IAF.

There was a lot of pending work in the office of OPS-1. To get the train on the track, I started working morning and evening with just one-hour-break for lunch. Within the first one week, I managed to clear all the pending work. In the next week, I started conducting the morning briefing. It went on for about two weeks and I was also required to cover the range firing results of the Squadrons under SWAC, every day. On many occasions after the briefing, my AOC-IN-C used to call SASO in his office and used to give a rap to the Squadron Cdr whose one odd pilot had a bad result in Gun firing or Rocket firing or bombing. I saw this happening for almost every day. I waited for two more weeks. One day, I took permission from my Air-1 to meet my SASO. Air Marshal Man Singh called me. He asked me if everything was all right with me and if I had finished my pending work. I replied, 'Yes Sir'. He then told me that he had seen me working on all afternoons and said that he liked the hard-working officers. He then asked me to keep up my hard work. I took that opportunity and requested if I could be permitted to cover the armament results of the Squadrons under SWAC in the morning briefing on weekly and monthly basis instead of daily basis. He thought for a while and told me to go and meet the AOC-IN-C and request him for the same. Thereafter, I requested AOC- IN-C's PA, if I could get an appointment with my AOC-IN-C. He said that he would let me know after taking time from him. On the same day after about an hour, I was called by the PA and told that the AOC-IN-C had agreed to see me. I quickly reported to my AOC-IN-C. He gestured me to sit on a chair in front of him. He asked me, 'What is your problem?' 'Sir, no problem as such. I want to discuss something about the coverage of armament results of the Squadrons in the morning briefing on everyday-basis', I replied. 'What is wrong with that?' he asked. I answered, 'Sir, I personally feel that the armament results should be compiled and covered in the briefing on weekly and monthly basis. This system will give us a better picture and then the Squadron with 'below-average' results can be informed or warned instead of doing it daily. He said, 'Okay, but can you produce the slides within 15 days, separately for Guns, Rockets and Bombs results on weekly, monthly and six-monthly basis for all Squadrons under us?' he inquired. 'Yes sir', I answered. He said, 'Alright, go ahead and let me see how it appears'. After that, I came to my SASO and informed him about AOC-IN-C's decision. He said, 'Damn it! How can you do this work single-handedly in such a short time? I will attach one more officer to your section'. 'No sir, let me try, I will produce the slides on the 15th day', I replied. He thought for a while and then said, 'Go ahead and good luck to you'. In my section, I had one Sgt and two Corporals. I briefed them about the workload and urgency. Thereafter, we started working day and night to complete the next-to-impossible herculean task. To my AOC-

IN-C's surprise, I projected the slides on the 13th day. After looking at the results both, my SASO and AOC-IN-C, were surprised and said that we were unnecessarily pulling up the Squadron Cdrs on a daily basis. On the same day, my AOC-in-C called me to his office and congratulated me for my innovative work.

Posting to HQ Eastern Air Command IAF at Shillong as CFS & IO

From Jodhpur, I got posted out on promotion to the rank of Gp Capt. to HQ Eastern Air Command, IAF, to take over the duties of Command Flight Safety and Inspection Officer. I took over my new assignment on 14 October1985. I had two more officers under me—Wg Cdr Dhami, a pilot from transport aircraft stream and Squadron Ldr Aggarwal from technical stream. For the first time in the IAF, CFS&IO was placed to work directly under the AOC-IN-C. My AOC-in-C, Air Marshal KD Chadda, called me on the third day of my joining the duty. He welcomed me and at the same time told me that EAC, IAF had far too many accidents and our rate of accidents were very high in the IAF with 8 accidents in the past and as well as in the current year. He told me to devise strict safety measures and pass to the Units under this Command. If needed, he asked me to visit all the stations and personally give the current statistics on accidents to them. He further ordered to pass all the safety measures to avoid accidents in future. For that purpose, the AOC-IN-C placed one OTTER Aircraft with one pilot Squadron Ldr Sahu under my control. The aircraft and pilot were attached to the Command HQ. With the help of my staff, I took about 10 days to prepare all the statistics and my presentation with slides, etc. I visited all the stations and gave a presentation on aircraft accidents and safety measures. Besides that, I also gave them my 'mantra of meditation', which I had followed while Commanding No. 21 MIG (Bis) Squadron at AF Station, Pune, where we had nil accident and nil incident during my tenure.

Almost all the Squadron Cdrs agreed with me and started following the system for their pilots of sitting in meditation for five minutes before flying in the morning. The result of this exercise was seen in the next year. In the year 1986–87, the aircraft accidents dropped to half the number, that is, only 4 accidents. Whereas, in the previous year, we had 8 accidents. My AOC-IN-C appreciated my efforts and work.

My family joined me at this place after a gap of one years. I was looking forward to having them over as it was a beautiful place and we all were together again. My son joined the school there and my daughter joined college in the city. It used to get very windy and cold in winter but used to be pleasant all throughout the year. Of course, one had to get used to the humidity and the perpetual rain there, the best part was the fireplace in our house, which was always a welcoming place to sit by. We all used to go for long walks and treks around the hills there. The picnics that we all went for, as a family and also as command families together were also very memorable. I, in fact, picked up the hobby of playing golf here as there was a beautiful golf course close by maintained by the Air Force Station.

During my stay at Upper Shillong, I started practicing Homeopathy system of treatment only by consulting books as I had a very keen interest in it. I had no formal qualification or certification. I found that since Upper Shillong was a cold place, children of NCEs and civilians working in command, suffered from perpetual cold and always had some problem or the other. I treated at least 30 children and 9 women with 100% success. By seeing this, some of the officers' wives also took my treatment and got cured of their illness. Two ladies were even cured of their heart trouble. After some time, it had become the talk of the Station that I was a good Homeopath. One day, something interesting had happened. On a Sunday, Mrs Chadda, wife of our AOC-IN-C, came to my house without any advance information. The time was 11 in the morning and her car MTD knocked at my door and told me that madam wanted to see me. Both, my wife and I, got really worried thinking what had happened because it's not normal for such a senior lady to walk in like that. However, we greeted her and started making a polite conversation. During this talk, Madam asked me about my Homoeopathic remedies. I got further scared, thinking that someone might have complained and that is why she had come to check. Anyway, in the next few minutes, to my relief, she mentioned that Mrs Ahmad, wife of Gp Capt. Ahmad, Command Logistics Officer, had mentioned to her about the cure of her heart trouble with my treatment. She further mentioned that she also thought that she had some heart trouble because earlier she used to go for long walks but lately, she couldn't even walk 25 yards as she would feel breathless. The heart specialist in Command Hospital had advised immediate surgery to her as two of her heart arteries were blocked. I frankly told her that I wasn't a qualified or certified Homeopath and I do the treatments only as a hobby and do it by consulting homeopathy books only. I politely told her that I was not in a position to start her treatment. She said that she was aware of all that and she still wanted me to treat her as she had faith in my medicine. I told her that I would like to inform AOC-IN-C before starting her treatment. She told me that I need not worry as she had already discussed it with her husband. Thereafter, I felt quite confident. I asked her a few more questions and finally started her treatment. I gave her one week's medicines and told her to walk every day as many yards as possible without going out of breath. After one week's treatment, she started to walk about 200 yards without going out of breath. And soon, with three months' treatment, she started to feel normal and averted the surgery. This was an achievement for me as I was able to treat such a major illness.

This is how my very fruitful tenure ended at Shillong and I again had to be relocated to another place.

Posting to Air Force Station Tezpur As Chief Operations Officer

After some time, I got posted to AF Station, Tezpur, as Chief Operations Officer. In fact, it was an exchange posting between Gp Capt. Surjit Singh COO, Tezpur, and me. This was the second time that there was an exchange of postings between both of us.

I moved to Tezpur along with my wife and two children, Tejinder and Tejpal. On arrival, both the kids joined their new school and college respectively. I took over the duties of COO with much fanfare. I also had a GL Section under me. The GLO was Lt Col Manmohan Singh. My AOC was Air Commodore AP Shinde. He was a very nice person and a good administrator. We had one MIG OPS Flying Training Unit (MOFTU), one Operational Squadron and one Helicopter Unit at the Station. MOFTU had strength of aircraft and personnel equal to two fighter Squadrons. This unit was converting Subsonic stream pilots to Supersonic stream. There was a great pressure of training the younger pilots. All the Unit Cdrs were very experienced and were dedicated to their training assignments and commitments. The staff of these units consisted of some QFIs and very experienced pilots. My job was to provide flying environment and keep the Station in operational readiness. I looked after all the operational resources and support services, including communications and Air Traffic Control and Meteorological section for efficient conduct of flying. I maintained a high operational status of the Wing. The DASI Team on their visit appreciated my good work and control, as on some days, we used to handle 90 to 95 take-offs and landings including night flying.

During my stay at Tezpur, we also conducted Para Training of Army Personnel. I provided all the facilities to the launch of three transport aircraft and loading of personnel with parachutes. This training continued for four weeks in addition to our fighter training flying. Thereafter, HQ EAC gave me the task to prepare the base for paradropping of supplies in the forward area of Tawang Sector. I geared all the machinery for the task with the help of a unit of No.4 Corps, which was located at Tezpur. During my stay, I served under three AOCs, namely, Air Cmde AP Shinde, Air Cmde Sharman Tally and Air Cmde MS Vasudeva. There was a delay of three and a half months for Air Cmde Vasudeva's arrival due to IPKF duties. Air Cmde Tally had to leave for NDC course so the command of the station/wing was handed over to me for that period. During my command, I completed all the pending works in the Station. We had one sports stadium but it was abandoned due to the overgrowth of elephant grass. Being a huge area, manual labour was not enough to clear the tall grass. I had a very good liaison and rapport with Corps Commander of No.4 Corps. I requested Lt General Narhari for help. He, in turn, detailed one Mechanised Unit with heavy and light dozers to clear all the fields in the sports stadium. It is pertinent to mention that I provided airlifts out of wing resources to Two Corps Commanders for the forward area visits every now and then. Their names are:

- Lt General Dias.
- Lt General Narhari.

Both of them were very cordial with me and showed a lot of affection whenever we met at parties or official visits. After the sports stadium was ready, our SOA AVM Chaudhary from HQ EAC came for the inspection. He was very pleased to see the sports stadium with two football fields, one hockey field, one basketball ground and one volleyball field. He took the decision to hold Command's Annual Sports Meet at that stadium. I was detailed to conduct the Meet consisting of all sports at my station, which was to take place within one month of SOA's visit. This meet was a great success and my station won three trophies for the following games:

a) Hockey (I played as centre forward)
b) Basketball
c) Volleyball

Our love for travel took my family and me to many new places and so in the Eastern India, we visited Tawang, Sela, Tenga and Bomdila. This trip was very adventurous as the road at most of the places was very narrow and we had to face several landslides as well. I'm grateful to our army and Assam rifle friends who had organised our stay and sightseeing in all these places. We had a wonderful time travelling together. From Tezpur, we also visited Sikkim and Bhutan. We drove in our car from Tezpur to Chabua Far East. These places are so lush green that one has to see to believe it. The beauty of nature is one of the best in the country.

Base Commander Vavuniya During Operation Pawan under IPKF in Sri Lanka

During my tenure at Tezpur, I was also detailed as Base Commander Vavuniya in Sri Lanka for 'OP Pawan' duties from 13 May 1989 to 18 August 1989. This period was very crucial as IPKF was preparing to leave Sri Lanka. My base being the centre of operations would have been an easy target, but I played a crucial role in protecting my three helicopters, co-located Army Units and all assets, including men and materials. My helicopter pilots with full dedication carried on delivering the supplies to forward posts and casualty evacuation. I earned the appreciation of no. 4 Div Commander Maj. General Malik, AOC-in-C Southern Air Command Air Marshal Sen and VCAS Air Marshal NC Suri (who later on retired as CAS). During my stay at Vavuniya, I handled many tricky situations with courage and innovativeness.

When I reached Vavuniya, I was received by Brigadier H P S Mann Deputy GOC No.4, Inf. Div, which was located at Vavuniya Airfield. All the officers of my staff accompanied Brig. Mann. We were invited for tea at Officer's Mess No. 4 Div. and thereafter, we moved to the briefing room where I was briefed about the situation there. This is a normal procedure to be followed by any new incoming officer. An over view of the situation prevailing at that time along with the historical background was covered briefly. I was shown a picture like this, of the map of Sri Lanka. Where Tamil population dominated the shaded portion and Sinhala population dominated other portion. Tamil people were wealthy and intelligent and well educated. They held many key posts in the civil society. Many of them were also professors and teachers.

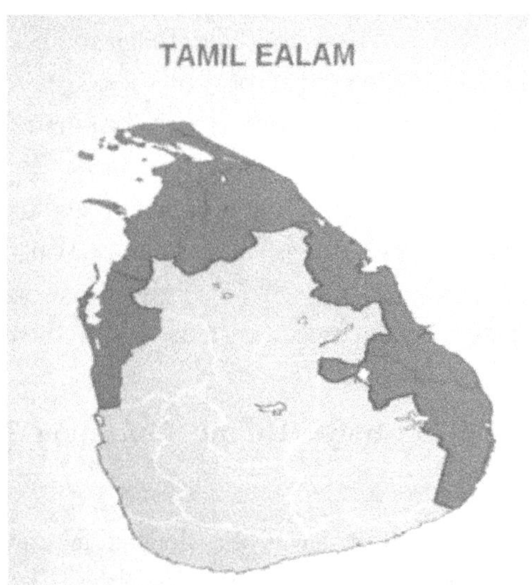

Shadded area is showing Tamil dominated area[59]

---

[59] *Independence was finally granted in* 1948 but the country remained a Dominion of the British Empire until 1972. *In* 1972 Sri Lanka assumed the status of a Republic. A constitution was introduced in 1978, which made the Executive President the head of state. Source-Wikipedia

According to the demographics given by wikipedia, The Sinhalese people make up 74.9% of the population (according to 2012 census) and are concentrated in the densely populated southwest and central parts of the island. The *Sri Lankan Tamil people, who live predominantly in the eastern and northern province* of the island, form the largest minority group at 11.1% (according to the 2012 census) of the population.

Whereas in 1987-1990 when the LTTE (Liberation Tigers of Tamil Elam) problem was at its peak the percentage of Sri Lankan Tamils was higher.

When Sri Lanka got independence, the first elected government was of Sinhalese. Within a short time, this government started putting restrictions on Tamilians. Tamil people were also denied jobs and posts. There were many other factors, which gave rise to resentment by Tamil people. They also demanded autonomy for their area. However, all this was not acceded by Sinhala govt. Whenever, they protested, the Sinhala govt. would treat the Tamil people badly and carry out atrocities against them. This gave rise to extremist groups and the main group was LTTE, which was later lead by young Commander Prabhakaran. However, when the situation went out of control of Sri Lankan govt., an accord was signed between Sri Lanka and India and the Indian Peace Keeping Force (IPKF, refer to footnote*) was sent to Sri Lanka to neutralize the situation by dialogue with LTTE, and to create a neutral platform for dialogue between Sri Lankan government and LTTE. This was the main reason why IPKF was initially sent there but over time due to political decisions on all sides LTTE became hostile against IPKF[60].

---

[60] Indian Peace Keeping Force (IPKF) *was the Indian military* contingent performing a *Peacekeeping* operation in *Sri Lanka* between 1987 and 1990. It was formed under the mandate of the 1987 *Indo-Sri Lankan Accord* that aimed to end the *Sri Lankan Civil War* between *Sri Lankan Tamil nationalists* such as the *Liberation Tigers of Tamil Eelam* (LTTE) and the *Sri Lankan military.*

The main task of the IPKF was to disarm the different terrorist groups, not just the LTTE. It was to be quickly followed by the formation of Interim Administrative Council. These were the tasks as per the terms of the Indo-Sri Lankan Accord, signed at the behest of Indian Prime Minister Rajiv Gandhi. Given the escalation of the conflict in Sri Lanka, and with the pouring of refugees into India, Gandhi took the decisive step to push this accord through. The IPKF was inducted into Sri Lanka on the request of Sri Lankan President J. R. Jayewardene under the terms of the Indo-Sri Lanka Accord.

The force was initially not expected to be involved in any significant combat by the Indian High Command. However, within a few months, the IPKF became embroiled in battle with the LTTE to enforce peace. The differences started with LTTE trying to dominate the Interim Administrative Council, and also refusing to disarm, which was a pre-condition to enforce peace in the island. Soon, these differences led to the LTTE attacking the IPKF, at which point the IPKF decided to disarm the LTTE militants, by force if required. In the two years it was in northern Sri Lanka, the IPKF launched a number of combat operations aimed at destroying the LTTE-led insurgency. It soon escalated into repeated skirmishes between the IPKF and LTTE.

The IPKF began withdrawing from Sri Lanka in 1989, on the orders of the newly elected Sri Lankan President Ranasinghe Premadasa and following the election of the *V. P. Singh* government in India. The last IPKF contingents left Sri Lanka in March 1990.

India's battle in Sri Lanka is often compared and called as 'India's Vietnam' by International Media.

Source: Wikipedia.

By the time I reached Vavuniya in 1989 (refer map of Sri Lanka), LTTE had turned hostile against the IPKF and a thick conflict was going on between IPKF and LTTE. I arrived in the midst of action and it was a war like situation then. In such situations the degree of difficulty is intensified when you can't differentiate between the enemy and the local population. On the base I had three MI-17 Helicopters for sending supplies and bringing in personnel for replacement. Also casualty evacuation was a routine feature as there were injured army personnel who had to be airlifted. In June 1989 IPKF was asked to leave Sri Lanka by the Sri Lankan govt. This was a sudden decision due to some differences between both governments. At this time the Sri Lankan defense forces also turned hostile towards us. What a dilemma it was being inside a foreign country, and suddenly on a base with no support from them. We were sitting targets for the LTTE now.

This situation became very tense and Vavuniya was to be fortified because all the supplies were coming from main land to Vavuniya by air. Both approaches to runway were required to be protected against any militant attack on approaching or taking off aircraft. For which, I worked out a plan and with permission of Air Headquarters, I was given a free hand to plan and execute the safety of the aircrafts. This task was carried out so well that no aircraft either approaching to land or taking off was attacked by any militant group.

During this time GOC of 4 Div. received a message to plan along with the Air Force element to evacuate around 600 Indians including diplomats and civilians from Hotel Samudra at Colombo to INS VIKRANT, Indian Navy ship that was to be anchored 25-30 kms away in sea. They were to be airlifted by helicopters, MI17s. This was a secret mission, and we were not to disclose our plan to any other authority. This planning was to be completed within three to four days. We were required to put up a plan to the Commander of IPKF Lt General Kalkat. The team was formed as follows: -

1.   Brigadier H P S Mann Team Leader.
2.   Brigadier Balsara Member (Commanding Officer Para Brigade).
3.   Gp Capt HS Sahota (Myself) Member (Commanding Officer Vavuniya Base) .

For the success of this Airlift mission a reconnaissance mission was considered a prerequisite since we were not sure of the LTTE's positions in the airlift planned areas, so we had to be very careful of secrecy and had to carry out our plans discretely. We were at Vavuniya, which is about 230 kms by road away from Colombo. We were to go by helicopter from Vavuniya to Hotel Samudra and area around it. Our plan was to fly at 600 meters AGL (above ground level) to avoid any ground to air fire. The next priority was to avoid Radar detection during our mission. We had to avoid Anuradhapura airport Radar by staying low level and out skirting the airport and staying out of Radar surveillance range. Next was Bandaranaike International Airport Colombo. Their Radar was also to be avoided. We were now to descend to 300 meters ignoring any danger of ground to air fire. We out skirted this airport also and managed to reach hotel Samudra, which was located almost between Bandaranaike International Airport and Ratmanala Airport. We found one Sri Lankan Army Unit very close to Hotel Samudra. We saw their Parade ground and landed there. We were seven of us in the helicopter, two pilots, three of us (members) and three Army soldiers with two rifles and one LMG (light machine gun). All of us were fully armed with revolvers hidden under the flying overalls. We also had ammunition boxes inside the helicopter. We had removed rear doors of helicopter before setting course for the mission for ease of firing from the helicopter if required.

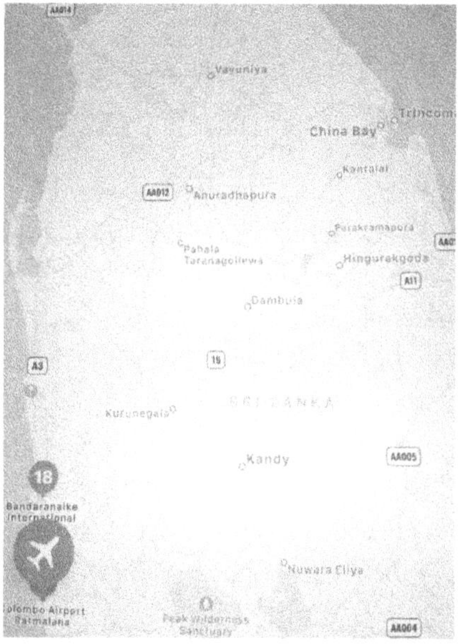

(Ratmanala Airport, was the only International Airport in Sri Lanka until the inauguration of Bandaranaike International Airport, Katunayake in 1967. Thereafter, it was being used as domestic civil airport. We suspected that this airport might be used by Sri Lankan Air Force to hinder our airlift operation, since the situation at that time was so fluid).

As we landed in the Parade Ground, one Sri Lankan Army colonel approached us. He shook hands with three of us as we came out. The other personnel remained inside the helicopter. He asked us suspiciously, "Why have you landed here?"

I promptly answered, "We have come to pick up one Indian Navy Captain from Hotel Samudra, but we found their parking lot in front of the hotel was not free, so we decided to land here and take your help to reach hotel Samudra". I spoke quite loudly so that this was also heard by captain of the helicopter.

He spoke from the cockpit and said, "Sir, I have received a wireless (R/T) message from a ground controller at Hotel Samudra. They are vacating one portion of parking lot. We can go and land there".

On hearing this we thanked that Army colonel and got back inside the helicopter. Our helicopter was fitted with fully loaded rocket pods, which could be used in case of any eventuality, which we didn't want to disclose to anyone, as it would have created a problem for us.

On our way back to Vavuniya Base, we took off from the parade ground, saw hotel Samudra from the air and planned our ground defenses as where to place LMGs during airlift operation. From there we set course for Ratmanala Airport just South- Southeast of Colombo. Again we landed on the R/W and carried out roller landing to see the complete defense of the area around and to survey if any Fighter aircraft of Sri Lankan Air Force were parked there. We found that there was no fighter aircraft, only 4 to 5 transport aircraft were parked there. Those aircraft looked like belonged to some local airline operating within Sri Lanka. We contacted the ATC (air traffic control) on International open frequency. The controller had too many questions to ask us. I told him on R/T that I will come to ATC for our further clearance. We parked our helicopter in front of the ATC. I decided to go alone and I told other people to stay inside the helicopter.

I also told them in case of any problem, "I will fire my revolver to indicate if I'm in danger so that you all can launch a rescue operation".

I climbed through the stairs to the ATC and met two controllers. They asked me many questions, as this was not a planned mission.

I answered, " We are lost and are short of fuel. We can only go up to Bandaranaike International Airport". I asked them for fuel on payment to which they refused and told me to go to the International Airport and get fuel from there.

Thereafter, I engrossed them in some polite conversation and in the meantime, I took the opportunity to take a good look of the Airport from the ATC, to help us plan our mission. Then I left the place after thanking both the controllers in a calm and composed manner. We took off from there, contacting the ATC on Open International frequency. From there, we went at a very low level and out skirted Bandaranaike International Airport. On our return journey, we planned to land at Anuradhapura Airfield. We kept calling Anuradhapura ATC on open International Frequency but there was no reply from ATC. However, we decided to land on the R/W and then reached ATC following a circuitous taxiing route. We noticed that everything appeared to be locked. We saw two fighter aircraft parked in front of a hanger. After taxiing the helicopter to couple of places around the ATC, we came back on the runway and took off for Vavuniya. After landing back at Vavuniya, we realized the danger involved in this type of Reconnaissance Mission. However, the success of Airlift Mission from Hotel Samudra in Colombo was assured to the fullest extent. We had worked out a plan to safely airlift personnel by going through the whole route ourselves. Somehow, this dangerous airlift mission was called off because of government decision and all the personnel were now allowed to travel safely by International Flights and also by Air Force transport aircraft. Well these are the situations one goes through in such circumstances where you always put yourself out to face the danger first to assess and plan missions. This is what makes defense personnel different from civilians where you are trained to put yourself in danger for the safety of others. It becomes your "Dharma" or duty to risk it all without thinking of the dangers involved.

Sometime in mid June, 1989, Indian army commandos were engaged in a thick battle in a jungle east of Vavuniya. Since the LTTE was entrenched in that jungle, there was a fierce battle going on. LTTE had suffered heavy casualties, but our three commandos were also badly injured. This commando Battalion was commanded by Col. Lidder which was co-located at Vavuniya. When Col. Lidder got the news of the injured, he came to my office and put in a request for casualties to be picked up. He showed me the location on the map, it was a kind of dry pond in the middle of the jungle. I quickly called the standby helicopter pilot and instructed him to study the map and pick up the casualties immediately. Both Captain and Co-pilot of the MI-17 helicopter pointed out that the area was very restricted and the pond though dry but was surrounded by tall trees and there was a danger of ground to air firing by LTTE hidden in the jungle. Anyway, Col Lidder assured me that the jungle around the pond had been sanitized by his troops and some of them were guarding the pond too. Now the next problem was to land the helicopter on the area surrounded by tall trees. Both the pilots appeared a bit nervous. However, to boost their morale, I volunteered to go on board with them. When Col. Lidder heard this daring decision on my part, he also decided to go on board with us. Our helicopter was loaded with rockets in pods on both sides for any eventuality. We took off for the mission of casualty evacuation as planned. As we reached close to the jungle. We realized that we could not descend below 600 meters above ground level due to the fear of ground to air fire by one odd LTTE person hiding somewhere in the jungle, for which they were expert. Anyway, we found the pond and the pilot did a daring vertical hovering landing. Casualties were loaded within no time and we performed a vertical climb to 200 meters AGL and set course back to base. This mission was a classic example of valor on the part of all participants. This story reached GOC No. 4 Div, Major General Malik for which he specially called me to his office and appreciated my daring action to save the lives of the injured troops. My job was only to provide a helicopter for casualty evacuation and brief the pilots to carry out the mission, but I took it to be my duty to boost the morale of the troops by going along.

There was another very interesting incident during my tenure as Base Commander at Vavuniya. Sometime in June 1989, Shri Premadasa

President of Sri Lanka unilaterally called for withdrawal of the IPKF by 29 Jul 1989. This new dimension in the politico military operation like 'Pawan' necessitated a qualitative change in military thinking, compelling the IPKF to be ready for any eventuality by strengthening our own defences against both ground and air threats from Sri Lankan Forces in addition to the threat of clandestine attack at our location by the LTTE. Situation became so tense, that we saw the Sri Lankan Forces taking position in the trenches on the other side of the R/W (runway). Commanders of Sri Lankan Forces could see us deploying our troops all along the R/W on our side. Brigadier Ratanasinghe, I knew the commander of Sri Lankan Army Brigade and Flt Lt Fernando, commander of commando unit and we were on friendly terms as we had interacted earlier officially and socially too. We had some common topics, as Brigadier Ratanasinghe was a graduate of Defence Services Staff College in India. As we were collocated we used to dine together at times.

One night I got a phone call from them and they appeared very scared and feared that IPKF was going to attack them at night. This might have been due to some wrong intelligence report on their side as there was no such intention from our side. I assured them that there was not going to be any attack from our side but if any one fires even a single bullet from their side, there would be 1000 bullets coming from our side as it was our duty to protect ourselves in self defence. Their location was on the Southern side of the Runway and our location was on the Northern side of the R/W. The following sketch depicts both sides on either side of R/W.

As the nighttime was coming closer, both these Commanders again rang me up and asked if there was any planned attack on them. This time I spoke to our Army commanders Col Lidder and Col Balbir Singh as their commandos were deployed on the Northern side of R/W. They told me that their troops would fire only if Sri Lankan Forces fire at them first. I also mentioned to them about the fear of Sri Lankan commanders. I once again spoke to both the Sri Lankan commanders and assured them that there would be no fire first from our side. But if any one of their troops fires even a single bullet, even if they accidentally fire; then our troops would not hesitate to fire back. Anyway, Brigadier Ratanasinge seemed to be satisfied with my reply. More so because his Brigade Hq. was a bit far from us and had many buildings for their shelter, in case of attack from our troops. Whereas, Flt Lt Fernando's unit was very close to the R/W and would have been an easy target for us. Therefore, he was not ready to believe me and then he finally thought of some plan to get assurance.

So after some time he called up again and said, "sir, if you are right, why don't you spend the night in our mess?" This way he wanted to make sure that there wasn't going to be any attack on them. Their mess was right opposite to our forces. I sensed that It was an open challenge to my courage.

I called two of my officers, Sqn Ldr Malik, Admin Officer and Sqn Ldr Menon Tech officer. I spoke to them and narrated the incidents and asked them to accompany me to their mess as I thought that instead of going alone it would seem like a casual interaction if three of us went there. There was no time to take any permission from senior authority, as there was no such ill feeling from our side. Anyway, both my officers initially were not willing to accompany me to spend night in Officer's Mess of Flt Lt Fernando as they thought that it was some sort of a trap.

I sensed that to motivate them, my reasoning was not enough. So I tried to reason emotionally, as I thought at that time to be the only way to pacify the Sri Lankan friends to stay calm. Manipulation of human emotions is the art of military leadership, which I adopted and they finally agreed to accompany me. After informing them of our decision the three of us reached Flt ft Fernando's mess at 2300 hours. Flt It

Fernando and his three officers were waiting for us. There was a sigh of relief as they saw us and were now assured of a safe night. As they all eased a bit some of the officers started playing cards. However, I had taken my pocket Gurbani book along so I sat in a comfortable place and started my prayers and went on till 0500 hours with small breaks in between. In the morning a smiling and grateful Flt Lt Fernando served us tea and snacks. The only solace was that there was no incident of firing from LTTE too, which would have created confusion. What a long night it was!!

Just to allay the fear of a friend, I took this decision knowing completely well the disastrous outcome of this daring act. I also knew that if some action had taken place that night, all three of us would have been in great trouble. This life-threatening situation did not deter me and prevent me from taking this mindfully daring decision.

I end this phase of my story with a quote from Guru Gobind Singh Ji, "Deh Siva bar mohe eh-hey subh karman te kabhu na taro. Na daro arr seo jab jaye laro nischey kar apni jit karo. Arr Sikh ho apne he mann ko, eh laalach hou gun tau ucharo. Jab aav ki audh nidan bane att he rann me tabh joojh maro.

Meaning:

O Timeless God give me this boon that I never refrain from doing the righteous act. Therefore, I shall have no fear of the enemy when I go into battle and with determination I will be victorious. That, I may teach my mind to only sing your praises. And when the time comes, I should die fighting heroically on the field of battle.

For a recognizable involvement in OP Pawan, dedicated hard work and positive support of all kinds to the IPKF, I was recommended for 'Yudh Seva Medal'. Air Commodore AP Shinde—Air Advisor to the IPKF, wrote my citation on 01 September 89.

1. Gp Capt. Harbans Singh Sahota was in command of Air Force Element Vavuniya from13 May 1989 to 18 Aug 1989. It was during this period that the political situation suddenly turned adverse, in that the President of Sri Lanka unilaterally called for a withdrawal of the IPKF by 29 Jul 1989. This new dimension in the politico

military operation like 'Pawan' necessitated a qualitative change in military thinking, compelling the IPKF to be ready for any eventuality by strengthening our own defences against both ground and air threats from Sri Lankan forces. In this critical situation, Gp Capt. Sahota, with his excellent professional background and combat experience, took all the steps to gear up his station for coping with the expected threat. With professional involvement, dedication and excellent ability to foresee the requirements of his station for future likely operations, he sufficiently motivated all the officers and men under him to face any adverse situation. He planned and reorganised his defences to counter the expected threat including the air attacks of clandestine nature.

2. During the very critical period from 25 Jul 1989, at Vavuniya four Mi-I7s were operating for daily Air Maintenance missions for the army. To save these Mi-17s from possible ground fire either by militant's clandestine attack or attack by the Sri Lankan forces, Mi-17s were dispersed every night by the Base Commander at well-planned locations with fuel and other Logistics arrangements in OP locations of Army. On the night of 27 Jul 1989, firing by militants took place around Vavuniya airfield. On 28 Jul 1989, during runway inspection in the morning, six bullet heads were picked up from the places where helicopters used to be parked for Air Maint Missions. Thus, due to Gp Capt. Sahota's foresight, meticulous care and planning, he saved four helicopters from possible damage. On the same night when firing broke out presumably between militants and one Sri Lankan post, one Bell helicopter of Sri Lankan Air Force mounted with guns got airborne and started firing very close to IPKF troops. Sensing the danger of accidental firing from helicopter in a dark night over our troops and mounted tensions between the IPKF and Sri Lankan forces Gp Capt. HS Sahota immediately drove his Gypsy in a cross-fire situation to ATC which was across the R/W about 1 km from the domestic camp. He ordered the helicopter to stop firing and land back. In that momentous situation, even one bullet accidentally fired in the wrong direction would have triggered off a skirmish between the two countries. GP Capt. Sahota took the risk of his life to avert the possibility of a conflict between the two countries.

3. Also to his credit, Mi-17s did air to ground rocketry for the first time under his direct supervision over Militant's hideouts in Nitikaikulam forest when he was on board, directing the fire. Army units close to the forest that militants fired back at their helicopter reported it but due to his meticulous adhering to the Standard-Operating Procedures, the helicopter was saved from ground fire. Yet another display of his valour, the officer directed seven Mi-25 gunship missions while being on board with full intelligence briefing against militant's hideouts in various places in Vavuniya sector. The gunships used to come from Trincomalee and without switching off; they used to get airborne to save time. Out of the seven missions he directed, five were very successful as per the radio intercepts by our communication intelligence at Vavuniya. During his tenure of three months at Vavuniya, a total of 656 tons of load and 13610 personnel were carried out on helicopters, which was an all-time high record for the base. This task was achieved without even a single accident or incident.

4. Also, this officer was specially chosen by the Air HQs (VB) to lead the Air Force component of one of the most daring and risky missions planned to evacuate about 600 Indian personnel including the key personnel of the Indian High Commission, in case of contingency which at that time seemed most imminent. Gp Capt. Sahota meticulously planned for the air aspect of this Commando Operation. He was sent on an initial recce of the expected scenario to the extent possible. The success of the mission, if ever it were to be undertaken, would have been assured mainly due to the officer's involvement and leadership.

5. GP Capt. Harbans Singh Sahota with his enthusiasm, dedication and sincere attitude to work and matching strength of character, remained as a shining example to his fellow officers and men, particularly during trying conditions. For his meticulous effort to save war machines, daring display of valour and for his positive attitude, ability to motivate his subordinates and display of leadership qualities and professionalism par excellence in the best traditions of the Air Force, Gp Capt. Harbans Singh Sahota is very strongly recommended for the award of Yudh Seva Medal.

7 Sqn boys visit प्रयाग
W/C Cdr Bakshi is in the Centre

After I returned from Sri Lanka, HQ EAC, IAF had its Annual Gunnery Meet for the fighter squadrons. HQ EAC also organised a competition of Air-to-Ground Firing for the Staff Pilots, Air-1, CFS & IO, OPS-1, all AOCs, all COOs and any other fighter pilots posted to the Wings. Being COO of AF Station Tezpur, I took part in the Front Gun firing and won the Command Gunnery Trophy. During my command of no. 11 Wing, my AOC-IN C Air Marshal Sinha visited my station once and SOA visited the station twice. Both were quite pleased, having seen the progress in flying, maintenance and general administration of my station. During my tenure as Chief Operations Officer, I earned one more citation, which was written by Air Vice Marshal D Chaudhury, Senior Officer In-Charge Administration, HQ Eastern Air Command, IAF on 30 Mar 1990.

1. Group Capt. Harbans Singh Sahota (7663) F (P) has been on the posted strength of 11 Wing, Air Force since 01 Sep 87. He has had an illustrious career over the last 26 years of his service holding prestigious appointments like, Flight commander of Three MIG-21 Squadrons, IRI/Command Examiner, Fighter Combat Leader, Deputation to Nigerian Air Force, Command Flight Safety and Inspection Officer, Chief Operations Officer and Station Commander, etc. His performance in the different assignments had been consistently very good. He has logged a total of 3,365 hours on various/fighter aircraft. His personal accident-free flying performance serves as an example for all the junior pilots on the station.

2. He has been working as Chief Operations Officer at No. 11 Wing Air Force since 01 Sep 87. Under his overall supervision and guidance complete operational flying training commitments have been fulfilled to the full satisfaction of all superiors. He involves himself in active flying and has been a constant source of inspiration to the young pilots

3. No. 11 Wing Air Force has been engaged in the crucial operational flying for MIG pilots, the task carried out by the station take on enormous amount of responsibilities. Coordination of the various disciplines of flying, various facilities like air traffic control, meteorological, communications and NAV Aids, etc., call for a capable man to carry them out. Gp Capt. HS Sahota has utilized

his drive and pushes to get the maximum out of these supporting agencies. He has been making himself available throughout the day and at odd hours and has guided the multifarious operations with his superior managements kills. He takes utmost care and ensures completion of the tasks laid down.

4. Functioning of Dullang Mukh Range under this base also places additional load on the Chief OPS Officer. His management of the Range and personal efforts has set an example for others to follow. His winning of Front Gun Firing Trophy for staff pilots during the Exercise—Eklavya1988–89 Gunnery Meet—has had an uplifting influence on the junior pilots.

5. This base, being strategically located, has a good number of air movements of defence and civilian VVIPs/VIPs that terminate or pass through this place. This calls for state-of-the-art preparedness and upkeep of the flying facilities. Gp Capt. Sahota along with his team has been very effective in meeting this important task. He has been often called upon to officiate as Station Commander, for periods at times, ranging up to two and a half months. He has been very successful in getting the Air Force land evicted from the possession of unauthorized people, who were entrenched there for so many years. The incident-free eviction reflects the acumen and management skills of the officer, as also his excellent tacit with the local civil government. The outcome of this has resulted in a clean look to the main entrance of this station. From the security point too, it has been a task of much importance. Under his command, the flying effort increased to 3,423 sorties from 3,270 sorties and serviceability of fighter fleet increased to 71.36 % from 60.75 % as compared to the previous quarter.

6. Successful completion of Para Refresher Training for the *Jawans* of 2 Btn Para Regt (Marathas) during Jan 89 and the support provided by Gp Capt. Sahota in the training has been appreciated by HQ 4 Corps. His coordination with IV Corps and 5 Din in the Tawang sector has won Army's confidence and GOC himself has appreciated it. This has brought a good name to the IAF and in particular to No. 11 Wing, Air Force.

7. A detachment of AN-32s from No. 33 Squadron based at this station for Air Maintenance to inaccessible areas of Arunachal Pradesh has been functioning and engaged in its task under the direct supervision of Gp Capt. Sahota. This cost-effective management of resources has proved to be a two fold boon, one, wherein the defence funds were conserved and the other, speedy and safe supply of rations and other equipment for the Army. Gp Capt. Sahota has thus promoted functional efficiency through his supervisory role in the air maintenance of such large proportions. He has been observed to be very methodical in his approach.

8. Gp Capt. HS Sahota has acquired the art of influencing and directing the men at his section to accomplish the mission set for them. He took special interest in the conduct of leadership courses for the officers and supervisory staff (JWO to MWO) at this station. His own lectures on leadership had deep, lasting effect on all supervisors. As Station Commander for two and a half months, he gave due emphasis to the welfare of the personnel and also their families. A mini medical camp was set up during Feb 89 for conducting medical check-up for the ladies and educating them for family planning. Immunisation Programme for the children was also taken up. Station Ladies' picnic and AFWWA Ladies' athletic meet were some of the steps introduced, which were widely acclaimed by the personnel of No. 11 Wing AF.

9. This station, being a premier flying base, required very strenuous work from the technical personnel and aircrew to keep the aircraft airworthy, as a result, a major part of their time is consumed in this task. For maintenance of health of these personnel, Gp Capt. Sahota introduced physical training for them thrice a week. His presence on such occasions and leading the contingent for long runs brought a positive effect on the personnel and resulted in overall improvement in their performances. Social and cultural aspects at the station were given necessary fill-up.

10. Gp Capt. HS Sahota has been unsparing in his efforts and devoted 12 to 15 hours a day to implement his ideas towards the betterment of this station. Whether he is busy in leading the flying effort, or

engaged in sports, cultural and social activities, he has been doing all this in a comprehensive manner. His efforts have transformed this station into a living entity buzzing with life.

11. For his diligence and sincerity of effort, dedication and devotion to duty, consistent display of commendable personal performance and professional skill and accident-free record during the last 26 years of service, and for dynamic leadership both as Chief Operations Office and officiating Station Commander to inspire his personnel for enhancement of flying effort in the best traditions of the Indian Air Force, I strongly recommend Gp Capt. Harbans Singh Sahota (7663) F (P) for the award of Ati Vishisht Seva Medal.

Memories of Tezpur

Tenju feeding cake on our wedding Anniversary

Receiving President of India Shri Shankar Dyal Sharma at Tezpur

Received Shri Darbara Singh At Tezpur

Receiving Prime Minister Shri Rajeev Gandhi at Tezpur

Handing over command of AF Stn Tezpur to Air Cmde MS Vasudeva

Being introduced to Air Marshal SK Sinha
AOC in C- EAC, IAF by Air Cmde Tally

Posting to Southern Air Command IAF at Trivandrum as Air-1

I reached Trivandrum on 7 January 1991. On arrival on the very first day, I reported to my SASO Air Vice Marshal Puri. He briefed me about my duties in general and after a cup of tea, he took me to the AOC-IN-C. My AOC-IN-C Air Marshal Chand was very pleased to see me that atlast, an Air Commodore was posted to fill the vacancy of Air-1 in his command. He discussed 'OP Pawan' for a while and briefed me about my role as Air-1. The scope of my duties was very wide as we were providing Air Support to Southern Army Command Units all over the Southern Peninsula. We were also providing Air Support to Southern Naval Command as well as Eastern Naval Command, including units in Port Blair. We were also supporting and providing Air Defence of CarNicobar Islands. Thereafter, I went around to meet the other staff officers of our Command HQ. I met Air Cmde Chhabra, CMSO and GP Capt. Panikar, Air-II who was also officiating as Air-I before my arrival. He briefed me on Male OPS and our future involvement for Air Support and Air Defence Responsibilities.

During my stay in SAC, I conducted two major exercises, one with Southern Naval Command and the second with Eastern Naval Command. I used to carry out all briefings and debriefings of the exercises. After an exercise around Port Blair and CarNicobar Islands, the debriefing was to take place in Port Blair. I was given three days to prepare the debrief and slides. I had two more officers to assist me. It so happened that I had very severe reaction of my hair dye on the very first day and had to be hospitalised to naval hospital in Port Blair. The doctor treating me was Commander Menon. I was given sedatives apart from other medicines to subside the reaction. The next morning when I got up, to my surprise I saw a lady doctor treating me. I was informed that she was wife of Cdr Menon. Her husband about my severe condition informed her. Mrs Menon remembered me from Pune, where she was my Squadron Doctor before her marriage, while I was Commanding No. 21 Squadron AF at Air Force Station Pune. It was a very pleasant coincidence. The couple took utmost care of me and they also used to bring me homemade food. Because of such good treatment, I was discharged from the hospital on the second day in the evening itself. Now I had only one day to prepare my debrief of the entire exercise. My assistants prepared the slides. I carried out the debrief with full confidence. Chief of Naval Staff was also in attendance for the Exercise Debrief. He, while summing up the debrief, appreciated my role in the exercise planning and execution of Air Support.

Air-1 SAC, IAF

During the same year, my daughter's marriage was fixed. We had the wedding ceremony at Air Force Station, Adampur, as most of our relatives were around that area. The AOC, Air Cmde. Boparai was my course-mate who extended all the required support for the functions. Since we were all so service oriented, my daughter got married to Flt Lt HS Basra, son of then Air Cmde. D S Basra (who later retired as Air Marshal). My son, at that time, was studying in second year of B.Tech. After meeting all the relatives and completing the family obligations, we were back in Trivandrum.

My stay as Air-1 in Trivandrum was very pleasant. I served under four AOC-IN-Cs. I genuinely enjoyed the appreciation of all of them—Air Marshal Chand, Air Marshal Bharadwaj, Air Marshal Mohan and Air Marshal Tally. While Air Marshal Sharman Tally was in command, he called me to his office and informed me that my extension of service had not been approved by the Government. I felt a bit upset but quickly planned my second career in Civil Aviation. I started all the preparations for my civil aviation licence (ALTP). Air Force did give me conversion on the Avro Aircraft. I will remain ever grateful to the Air Force for this help.

We continued our ritual of road trips here as well. We travelled to Kanyakumari, Vivekanada Rock and Rameshwaram. Kerala also is very beautiful and serene, that is why it is called 'God's own country'. We also travelled to Tirupati, Thanjavur and also to the most holy place of Keralite Hindus—the Sabari Malai temple. It was the three of us—my son Tippy, Gian and I. The trek to the temple was tough but we had thoroughly enjoyed it. As my wife was above 50 years old, she was allowed to go as they don't allow women below the age of 50 to visit the temple. It is good to know that now a lot of changes are taking place to allow women inside the temple. Anyhow, we had a memorable trip to sabari Malai Temple.

20

HOW YOGASANAS CHANGED MY LIFE

My Motivation for Yogasanas in 1985 When I Was Attached to HQ SWAC, IAF, Jodhpur

During my stay there, one day, my friend and I were going to Jodhpur town from our mess on a scooter. It was 1630 hours and so we stopped for a cup of tea at a cleaner-looking dhaba on our way. While I was sipping my tea, I saw an old man reading a newspaper without spectacles. Amazed by that, I could not resist myself from asking him the secret to his good eyesight at that age.

So, I went on to ask him, '*Shriman ji*[61], you are reading the newspaper without glasses, have you got your eyes operated for the replacement of lenses?'.

He replied, 'No, Sardarji'. I then asked him his age, and he answered, 'I am 85 years old and my name is Bhagwan Rathore'.

'What is the secret of your good eyesight and your fit physique?"

'Are you from the air force?', he asked. I then introduced my friend and myself. He told me that he was a retired teacher and now he was into teaching Yogasanas. For that he practised the yogic asanas daily.

I asked, 'Can I learn yoga too?' and quickly added, 'But I have time only in the evening as I have to carry out my duty upto 1430 hours every day'.

He then said, 'you don't have to practise difficult yogic asanas. You can stick to the easy asanas only which will give you maximum benefit to remain in shape and will also help you to maintain good eyesight'.

---

[61] Addressing one with respect

I noted the timings for my yoga class, thanked him and left for the city. I had a feeling—rather had faith—that the yogasanas would definitely benefit me.

On the given date and time, I reached his house and found that he had dedicated one room for teaching yoga. He made me sit in the posture of one asana and asked me to do breathing exercise for three minutes. Thereafter, he made me do on the spot running for three minutes. He told me that it is very important to warm up before starting any yogic asana or exercise. He made me do one asana in which I had to bend forward and touch my toes. He called it *Paada hasth asana*. The next one was *Dhanurasana* where I was to lie on my stomach and catch both my ankles and stretch like a bow.

After three cycles each of these exercises, he made me lie flat on my back and asked me to spread my legs and arms and relax. This he called *Shava asana*. I was amazed to have learnt this asana from him about which I had not paid much attention in any of the books on Yoga. He explained the importance of it and how to get maximum benefit from it. I learnt that while lying down in *Shava asana*, I must relax my body completely and imagine that my soul is about one foot above my body. It is an imaginative posture and pratise of *shava asana* after every set of yogic asanas must be done. The other three asanas were *Paschimotta asana* (preliminary leg pull), *Hala asana* (plough) and *Sarvaanga asana* (shoulder stand).

After learning and practicing these asanas, I was able to maintain my weight between 71 and 72 kg for 10 years from 1985 to 1995. Thereafter, till today, I am maintaining my weight between 72 and 73 kg. With the practise of Shava asana, I can relax myself anytime and have a good sleep too. I must thank Mr Bhawan Rathore ji for giving me this gift of a lifetime!

Yoga, a Necessity for All

What I realised is that warm up is necessary before these yogic exercises. It prevents muscle pulls and prevents toxic build-ups, which result in stomach acidity, heartburn, flatulence and joint pain.

One must practise these exercises daily in the morning on empty stomach. These simple four to five exercises will certainly transform one's life. Since the mind has a remarkable effect on the body, these exercises help one control and calm their mind too. While doing these exercises one can find their body, breath and mind working as one. All the systems get toned for better functioning. In fact, one's stress can also be relieved in a systematic manner. The other benefits of these exercises are—they help to have perfect equilibrium (balance) of mind, body and brain. It improves one's concentration tremendously. These yogic exercises are recommended to be a part of daily routine for students and adults in any profession. I, as a pilot, would recommend it for pilots of both sexes whether they're in fighter flying in defence services or in civil flying.

21

RETIREMENT AND LIFE THEREON

I finally retired from the Air Force on 31 January 1995. There was a very surprising Office Order, which was issued by Air HQ, New Delhi. In this Office Order, I was already cleared to the Rank of Air Vice Marshal. I, however, did not raise any query on the subject and happily retired as Air Commodore. I find myself to be extremely fortunate to have risen nonstop in my career graph and to have achieved the Rank of Air Commodore and retired with flying colours. My career in the Air Force was a very memorable one and may serve as motivation to the college-going students who may aspire to join the IAF.

I enjoyed a wonderful rapport with my peers and earned the respect of juniors and all the men I had commanded in the Air Force. I maintained the motivation of the men at the highest level at all times in whichever unit I had served. All of my achievements were only possible with willing cooperation and dedicated hard work of all officers and air warriors.

I believe that whatever work is assigned to anyone must be done with all sincerity and dedication. Each and every duty must be done with the best intentions for the service. The key to a contented life is that we must do selfless service without any expectation. Ultimately, what goes around comes around. Having faith in god and yourself always pays rich dividends.

Obtaining my ALTP Licence and Joining Jindal Iron and Steel Company as Chief Executive Pilot

After my retirement at Trivandrum, I moved to New Delhi with my wife and son, Tippy, who had just completed his engineering and had applied for post-graduation in USA. In March 1995, he finally left for higher studies to the US. While staying in New Delhi, I started preparing and appearing for all the exams of the DGCA for obtaining my Civil Pilot's licence. Finally, I obtained my ALTP licence on 20th July 1995, and applied for a job in civil airlines as a pilot. I received a response from Jet Airways and was required to appear for an interview in Mumbai on 7 September 1995. Before my interview, something fortunate had happened, thereby, changing my career path for the better. Air Cmde Kirpal Singh, a test pilot in the IAF, who knew me well, passed my name to Shri Naveen Jindal, who was looking for two experienced pilots for his company, Jindal Iron and Steel. Jindals had bought one Citationjet-525 twinjet aircraft with a capacity of two pilots and six passengers. I was totally unaware of this development until the HR Manager from Jindal Iron and Steel Company contacted me. He only told me about the above-mentioned development and, at the same time, called me for an interview. He also told me that Mr Naveen Jindal would like to see me in his office. My interview on 30 August 95 was a dramatic one. When I entered the interview room, I found Shri Naveen Jindal in the chair and Mr Verma, HR Manager, Mr Ahuja, the adviser and two more officers present there. I was prepared for a long interview but to my surprise, as soon I wished Shri Naveen Jindal, he got up from his chair, shook hands with me and said, 'Mr Sahota, your appointment is done. Do the nitty-gritty of pay and allowances with my officers'. Thereafter, he left the office. The officers present in his office fixed my pay and allowances and I was given my appointment letter at the same time. I was required to join my duty with effect from 31 August 1995. I was given three days to prepare myself and get ready to go to the United States for Conversion Flying Training in Cessna Centre at Kansas City. The Citationjet-525 was purchased from the same company. The other pilot employed was Wg Cdr Brar. We both left New Delhi on 4 September 1995 for Kansas City and reached on the same day.

Our training of ground subject started on 5 September1995 and we completed our simulator training and ground subjects at the same time. Flying Training commenced on our own aircraft (which was already purchased by Jindals). We had just flown two missions each;

our aircraft was being positioned by a technician in the hanger for night parking. He was late in putting the chocks (stoppers) behind the wheel of the aircraft. There was a slope towards the rear of the aircraft. By the time he brought chocks, the aircraft moved backwards and its elevator hit the beam of the hanger and got severely damaged. First, the inquiry and then the repair and claim from insurance company would take about 15 days. For all this, Wg Cdr Brar volunteered to stay at Kansas City. I took advantage of this time and quickly reached Fremont in California to my brother-in-law's house (my wife's younger brother Kalvinder Singh) so I could also meet Tippy, who was staying with him while doing his Bachelors Of Electrical Engineering.

After reaching Fremont the next day, I joined the San Jose Flying Club and completed my conversion on Beechcraft twin engine (propellers) within four days and received my certificate of completion. On the sixth day, I moved to San Diego and there I joined ATP Flying School, completed my ground subject for Cessna S-1 twin jet aircraft, completed simulator and commenced my training and completed all my training in record time of six days. For this achievement, I had to work day and night. I obtained my ATP (Air Transport Pilot) certificate from the FAA (Federal Aviation Administration). This American flying licence equivalent to Indian ALTP was an additional qualification, which I wanted to add to my already existing ones.

I spent a total of 13 days out of Kansas City and obtained two captaincies. On the 14th day, I reached back in Kansas City. Our aircraft was required to be cleared by the FAA, which took four more days as the aircraft was to be thoroughly inspected and was to be air-tested by a qualified representative of the FAA. As soon as the aircraft became available for flying training, I continued my further training. I used to be given simulator training at night. Both of us obtained our ATP licenses and instrument ratings on Type. I became captain on Type along with Brar. We also obtained 'Single Pilot' flying certification from the FAA for our aircraft and I also got endorsed as Commercial pilot for flying in the US after passing FAA exam.

Receiving keys and charge of Cessna-525 aircraft on behalf of
Jindal Iron and Steel Company

My company then hired an FAA pilot who was qualified for International Ferry of aircraft from the USA to various countries. After all the clearances and preparations, we started our Ferry from USA to India. The captain flew the aircraft from the left seat all the time, while Brar and I took turns on the right seat. Our route was a classic one; it went like this—Kansas city to Bangor (close to New York in USA)—Bangor to Goose Bay (in eastern most coast of Canada-night halt)—Goose Bay to Reykjavik (in Iceland night halt). Reykjavik to Plymouth, (in southern part of UK night halt). Plymouth to Athens in Greece (no night halt, only refuelling. Athens to Riyadh (no night halt, only for refuelling), Riyadh to Muscat (no night halt, only for refuelling)—Muscat to Delhi (our final destination).

For those days it was a great international exposure to fly around almost half the globe! We had plenty of canned food and soft drinks onboard. Our flights were usually very comfortable with a few incidents here and there. For instance, we landed in Iceland in heavy rainstorm during which our main compass packed up and we had to use standby compass to land. We had to go to Playmouth,

UK, to get the compass replaced from the Cessna Company there. We stayed the night in Playmouth and the next day, we started again on our flight to Athens where we stopped only for refuelling and clearances. Then from Athens we went to Riyadh and to Muskat with no night halt, but only stopped for refuelling the aircraft and for getting clearances from the respective airports. Our last leg of flight was from Muskat to Delhi International Airport, which was our final destination. This is how we brought the first aircraft for Jindal Iron and Steel Company.

We landed at Delhi airport on 20th October 1995 at 1100 hours. We were received by Jindal family and a couple of their friends. As we cleared our baggage from the aircraft, the DGCA sealed the aircraft for their inspection and preparation of inspection schedules. Our Technical Officer Mr Kalsi who was very experienced prepared these inspection schedules and was DGCA certified. All the pilot orders and some security orders were prepared by Brar and me as it was the DGCA requirement for Operation of aircraft in India.

After the DGCA was satisfied with our ground preparations, they released the aircraft for flying. Mr Kalsi prepared the aircraft for flying and I requested Shri Naveen Jindal to fly with us along with family members. The flight was planned from Delhi to Jaipur and then back to Delhi. Somehow, they were all busy in a family function, so, Shri Naveen Jindal told me to go ahead with the flight. He asked us to take our wives and one office manager, Mr Gupta, along for a ride with us. He said, 'Go and enjoy your first trip'. We flew to Jaipur, with Capt. Brar on the left seat and I was on the right seat. Our wives were mighty thrilled about the first flight. We all had coffee and snacks at Jaipur and spent about two hours there. Again, after obtaining the clearance, we took off for Delhi. This time I was on the left seat and Brar was on the right. The aircraft behaved well and it was a very memorable first flight. Thereafter, routine flights started and we stayed for six months in Delhi. During this time, Jindal company allotted both of us one Maruti AC car each as perks from the company.

Jindal's Cessna-525 aircraft, Mumbai India

We moved to Mumbai in March 1996 with our office materials. Air Works Engg-India provided ground support. Menon Brothers were running the organisation. They provided us an excellent and efficient ground maintenance support. There were other corporate aircrafts in Mumbai as well. Among all the corporate pilots, I was the senior-most and had become an authority in corporate flying. In fact, I was the highest paid pilot in Mumbai at that time with kind courtesy of Shri Sajjan Jindal, MD, Jindal Iron and Steel Company. I was the first captain in Mumbai who was cleared by the DGCA to perform Daily Inspections on my aircraft. Before that, for out-station flying, one Technical officer had to be with us on board. This meant there would be one seat less for corporate use. With my clearance, I saved one seat for my company's use. Within the next few months, I obtained the clearance from the DGCA to become an Instructor for conversion training of other young pilots. I also became an Instrument Rating Instructor. My status as an IRI in the IAF paid rich dividends. These two qualifications were extremely hard to obtain from the DGCA. A lot of midnight oil was burnt to qualify for these ratings.

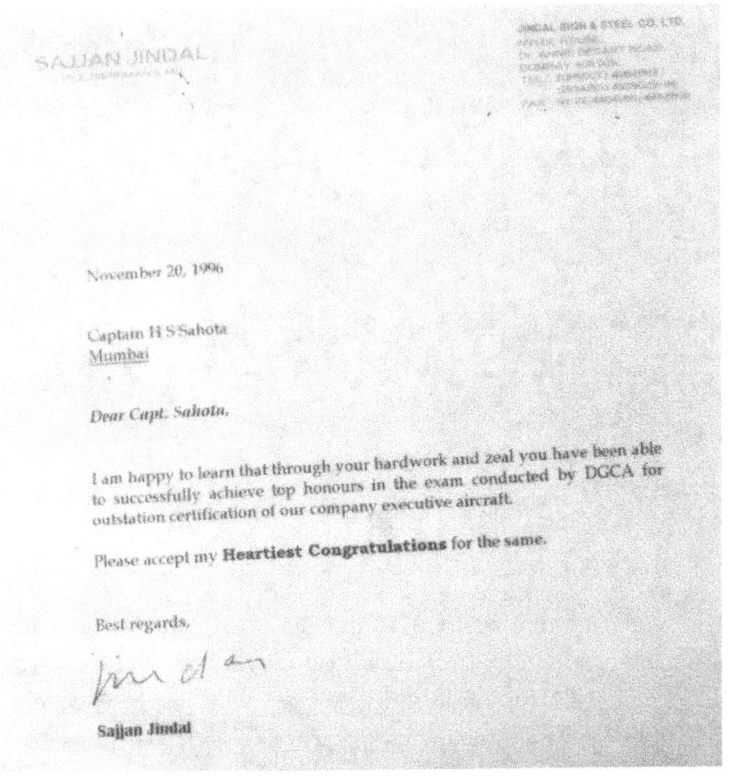

Letter of appericiation by Sajjan Jindal

With these qualifications, I had become a father figure in Mumbai for all the corporate sector pilots for six years. Capt. Brar had left us for beter job options, so now the other corporate pilots at Jindal were Capt. AD Sindhu, Capt. Lashkari, Capt. Mantur, Capt. Chandrashekhar, Capt. Tathgur, Capt. Paramjit Singh, Capt. Dhillon, Capt. Gupta, Capt. Sharma and Capt. Vinod.

I must mention my encounter with two fine gentlemen, whose hard work and efficiency impressed me during my tenure in JSW. After shifting from New Delhi to Mumbai for the operation of our aircraft, I needed a dedicated person who would make all the administrative arrangements for the passengers, looking after their reception and departure and their clearance through security. There would also be some provisions for soft drinks and eatables/snacks for the passengers depending upon their status. For this job the company detailed Mr

Ajay Kumar Hate. It took about three to four days to train him and he picked things up quite responsibly and professionally. So much so, he became a part of the crew team and worked very hard and sincerely with full dedication. His mannerism and communication skills were praiseworthy. Within a short time, he earned praises from almost all the VIPs travelling by our aircraft. And later, he was picked up by my MD Shri Sajjan Jindal to be his PA. I have fond memories of him.

Another person whom I would like to mention here is Mr Kirti Sodha. He was also with the corporate office at Mumbai and was a cricket player too. He was sent to me and I was amazed to see how he had learnt his job in a record time and proved to be an asset to the aviation department. I have recently learnt that he is continuing the same job with a much wider scope and has now completed 14 years of service with JSW, earning a feather in his cap.

Mr Sajjan Jindal, MD of Jindal companies in and around Mumbai, has a major factory in Bellary (Karnataka). Initially, when they had to go to Bellary, their aircraft could go only up to Bangalore and from there a tiring journey of almost four hours was taken by road to Bellary and the return used to be the same way. Mr Sajjan Jindal discussed the matter with me for making a runway at Bellary and asked me to carry out a feasibility study. I, along with engineers from Jindal Company, carried out the survey and found out that a runway, which would be sufficient for our operations, could be constructed. Thereafter, a firm was invited to survey and make a runway with clear approaches on both sides as Bellary factory was situated within a hilly terrain. I did my research to find out the source for construction of the runway as it is said, 'where there is a will, there is a way'. Then on one of our flights from Mumbai to Bellary, I observed from air that the Sahara company had their airport in a hilly terrain. Then I contacted them to find out who had done their construction. That's how Mone Associates were contacted for our job. Mone Associates from Pune did a wonderful job and made the runway in record time of approximately six months. I, on the other hand, was obtaining permission from the DGCA. This was the first time for me to be doing this job so it took some time to find my way with DGCA to get all the permissions for the construction of the runway. The airport was registered with DGCA as Vijaynagar airport, Vidyanagar Bellary, Karnataka.

A very unique work---Empowering the Brahm Sathall in Vijaynagar Steel Factory. Shri Sajjan Jindal and myself preparing for Pooja.

After the construction, the next job was marking of the runway and clearance from DGCA, Mumbai. Marking was done on the required specifications by taking technicians from the steel factory under my supervision. I was able to get all the support from the Jindal Steel factory because I was given a free hand for this job by Shri Sajjan Jindal.

Final inspection was completed by DGCA by end of April 1998. Our new runway was now complete and ready for our operations at Vijayanagar, and I as a pilot had the privilege for the first take-off and landing in May 1998. What a feeling it was! It's difficult to explain in words how proud I felt to fly on a runway and airport all designed by me. All my efforts in getting the runway operational at Vijayanagar were appreciated by Sajjan Jindal, Prithvi Jindal, Rattan Jindal, Naveen Jindal and their father Mr OP Jindal, who was an MP at that time and later had become a minister in the government of Haryana.

With Mr. Sajjan Jindal under the wing of Cessna Caravan—208.

For your knowledge, I must tell you that to get a runway operational for use, we had a structured plan, which was prepared under the following heads:

1) Construction
2) Infrastructure
3) Administration including manpower
4) Logistics
5) Operations
6) Maintenance
7) Security

Firstly, for the infrastructure, we needed navigational aids on the airport, namely, NDB (non-directional beacon) and VHF (very high frequency) VOR (omni-directional range). This is a type of short-range radio navigation system for aircraft, enabling aircraft with receiving unit to determine its position and stay on course by receiving radio signals transmitted by a network of fixed ground radio beacons. For this, I contacted AAI (Airport Authority of India), Delhi, for which they sent their teams to install the systems, which were eventually checked by me for operational use. Secondly, we started the construction of ATC (Air Traffic Control). The site and the design of the ATC were given by me because of my air-force experience. My pencil sketch was then designed to specifications by the civil engineers of the Jindal Steel Factory. After the construction of the ATC building, now came the task of making it operational for our use. Then I designed the deck for VHF communications for ground to air and vice versa. The local carpenter and engineers did a wonderful job. Finally, the ATC was ready for operations and now cropped the question, who was going to man this? Where would we find a trained ATC officer in Bellary? Since we were using our corporate aircraft here, I used to multitask my pilots as ATC officers one by one. On asking for a helping hand at ATC, we were sent Mr Prabhakar from Jindal Administration department. Mr Prabhakar was a very fast learner and was willing to undertake any job connected with airport. But he was a complete novice to airport operations so I took him under my wing and trained him specially for ATC duties. Because he was a good helping hand for all operations, he was involved in many activities at the airport like refuelling the aircraft, managing fuel storage from IOC (Indian Oil Corporation), obtaining clearances from ATC, Bangalore, arranging transport for pilots and looking after visiting aircraft of other corporates. He was my 'Man Friday' who seemed like a 'one-man army'. Then, after some time, when I felt that he was ready, I personally trained him and sent him to Hyderabad to do a certified course as ATC officer (ATCO). And, finally, we had a trained ATCO with us. I hear that recently, he has been awarded as one of the best ATC controllers in the corporate as well as civil sector. He is now regarded as an advisor and model for airport management. He manages Jindal Vijaynagar Airport operations single-handedly. I'm also proud to learn that he now has completed a master's degree in arts (MA) as well.

Managing refuelling of aircraft was another task for which I used to supervise Prabhakar until he had learnt the job in detail. I got the fuel bowser custom designed by Mr Bapu Patil's firm in Thane as per our requirements. We provided the chassis and they made the tanks and pumps for fuelling and defueling of aircraft.

Then a team of three people, including Prabhakar, started to manage it. To use our own designed bowser, we needed DGCA approval for which director DGCA, Mumbai region had come over to Vijaynagar airport to inspect all operations of the bowser. Mr Bapu Patil was also present during this inspection. And then finally we acquired the clearance for using it.

Until now we were able to use the runway for day operations only since there was no runway lighting system. So, the next phase of infrastructural addition was runway lighting, which was again planned and executed by me. The contract for the lighting was given to Mr Ashok Sawant of Kolhapur, who did an excellent job alongwith two assistants, namely Mr. Kusale and Abhijit Pore. So now life became convenient for us as we could operate at any time to and from Vijaynagar airport. At this time, we had two aircraft, namely, Cessna Citation Jet 525 and Caravan. And later on, two more aircrafts were inducted.

It had now become very convenient to travel from Mumbai to Jindal Vijayanagar airport and was a routine feature—flying between Mumbai and Vijayanagar. My MD, Shri Sajjan Jindal, and his family members travelled very often toVijayanagar. I was also used to convey all the company directors and executives for meetings to various places within India. I also undertook two international trips namely Sri Lanka and Maldives (Male).

Our operations were not at all easy as I encountered a very serious emergency on our second trip to Male at night, that too during a dark-night flying. While preparing to land at Male International Airport, I selected my undercarriage down. To my surprise, the undercarriage did not come down even when the hydraulic pressure was normal. I tried to operate the flaps; they too did not come down. I immediately informed the ATC at Male and climbed to a safe altitude with the permission from ATCO. At 5,000ft, I levelled out and tried to recycle the undercarriage. There was no response even though the indication of main hydraulic pressure was normal. Sensing that and going through the emergency checklist with my co-pilot who was too inexperienced, I lowered the undercarriage on the Emergency System. All three wheels got locked down and we got green indication. However, flaps were inoperative.

I returned to circuit and carried out ILS approach and without flaps, speed control was a bit difficult and landing speed was quite higher than normal. Male International Airport had a very long runway and I somehow managed to stop the aircraft and brought it to the taxiing speed. We cleared the runway and parked the aircraft in an isolated bay.

On the next day, our engineer along with one assistant flew in from Mumbai to Male. On inspection of the aircraft, they could not understand the emergency but managed to check one hydraulic valve that seemed to be inoperative. Our engineer did not have a spare valve, so, on the third day, the decision was taken to fly the aircraft with undercarriage in down position from Male to Mumbai via Trivandrum, Bangalore and Belgaum, and the final destination was Mumbai. I flew the aircraft with undercarriage in down position and carried out landings without flaps. And to my relief, after landing at Mumbai, the aircraft was handed over to Airworks Engineering for repairs.

After two years of normal operations, I encountered another emergency in the rainy season. My MD, Shri Sajjan Jindal, along with five more senior executives was travelling from Vijayanagar airport to Mumbai. My co-pilot, Sindhu, obtained all the clearances and we got airborne in Cessna-525 from Vijayanagar around 0200 hours. The flight time between both stations was generally 01 hour 15 to 30 minutes depending upon the winds. On this day, we experienced high clouds throughout the route. As we came close to Mumbai, we were informed that there was light drizzle over Mumbai Airport and warning was issued for heavy rain. Since the visibility was about 1.5 to 2 km, we carried on proceeding to Mumbai. As we descended to a lower altitude, we experienced turbulence and a thick wall of CB clouds. We were almost entering CB clouds, when Mumbai ATC reported heavy rain and visibility dropped to 500 metres. Due to heavy rain, there was a water film on the runway. The ATC Mumbai told us to divert to Ahmedabad Airport, which was our Primary Diversion Airport. Since we were carrying six passengers, we carried fuel just sufficient for Mumbai and to Ahmedabad Airport. We quickly climbed to the given altitude for the route and set course for Ahmedabad. As we came in contact with Ahmedabad ATC, they reported light rain over the Airport and visibility was 2,000 metres. We felt happy that all was well and we could make a comfortable landing. The flight time between Mumbai and Ahmedabad was 30 minutes. We were at a medium altitude and were rapidly consuming fuel. When we were about 10 minutes short of Ahmedabad in thick clouds, ATC reported heavy rain and visibility 300 to 400 metres. As we came overhead Ahmedabad Airport, we were in thick clouds and had water all over the front windscreen. We could not see anything outside. We were flying only on instruments. I commenced the ILS let down. As we came to the descent altitude for approach to the runway, our aircraft was behaving like a submarine in the Sea. ATC Ahmedabad kept reporting heavy rain and visibility dropping to nearly 50 metres. We were in thick rain and gusty winds were throwing our aircraft in unusual altitudes every now and then. We were on ILS approach at about 1,000 ft height, our glide stope disappeared and we could not see any ground features due to heavy rain. I descended to the height of 300 ft but still could not make contact with ground or runway. I started to goaround and climb to a safe altitude. Gusty winds were throwing the aircraft in unusual altitudes even during the climb. At this point, decision-making became very absolutely crucial. If I had delayed the second diversion to Baroda Airport, we would have landed in the fields for short of fuel (Engines flaming out). I diverted to Baroda Airport, which also had rain overhead, but visibility was 500 metres. I managed to land at Baroda with hardly any fuel left with us. Any mistake on my part would have jeopardised the safety of passengers, pilots and the aircraft. I personally feel that Waheguru was on our side. After landing, Shri Sajjan Jindal congratulated both of us and admired our cool handling of a potentially dangerous emergency.

At the beginning of 2006, Shri Sajjan Jindal took the decision to start commercial flying operations from Vijayanagar Airport. A beautiful glass building was constructed as Terminal Building. For the commencement of these operations, I was given the charge of the airport. It was a herculean task, which included clearances from BCAS, DGCA, AAI and Indian Met Department. All the security directives, orders and instructions were to be prepared. I prepared all these single-handedly. I used my experience of several years in the Air Force to get them ready and then compiled them together. We also required two scanning machines, one for checked baggage and one for hand baggage. These two were purchased by me from New Delhi and were transported to Vijaynagar airport.

I completed this task in a record time of three months along with my flying duties, as I was the only senior captain for Cessna citation jet-525. Before commissioning this airport, it was named as Vidyanagar Airport. The airport security was of utmost concern, so, in addition to local civil police force, Jindal administration department used to spare some guards for airport duty from the steel factory. Police for airport security duties specially trained these guards. Now we were to select an airline whose aircraft could operate from Vidyanagar Runway with a full load of passengers and baggage. The Kingfisher Airline had that aircraft and so was selected and contracted for one such aircraft operations between Bangalore and Vidyanagar Airport. Another major task was to take permission from government of Karnataka for starting operations of Kingfisher airlines. About four to five meetings were held between the officials of the airline and Karnataka government, with me as the sole representative of Vijaynagar airport.

The next requirement was meteorological reports for operation of airline aircraft. The second floor of the ATC building was utilised as Met. Office. For this, I approached the Meteorological Department of India in Delhi and managed to get a Met. Officer associated withVijaynagar airport from Karnataka area.

Kingfisher Flight Operations finally started on 15 May 2006. This flight became a great boon for all the people visiting Vijayanagar Dynasty— Hampi Ruins, which are, situated just about 30 to 35 km away from Vidyanagar Airport. These operations continued till 2009. Thereafter, an other airline started its operations. This way, Vidyanagar eventually became a business and tourism hub. This added one more feather in my turban.

Extract from *JSW Connect* magazine, issue 4, August 2008:

This captive airport at Vijayanagar was constructed to ferry senior personnel of Jindal Iron and steel company to the plant at Bellary factory site. This airport was subsequently opened for public operation to give air connectivity to the region. Today Jindal airport at Vijayanagar boasts of an international standard airport. Having thrown open the airport to public, JSW gave the much-needed boost to connectivity and economic activity in the region. At that time, Mr Sajjan Jindal explained that we did not build the airport to make money, but to give air connectivity to the region. Besides developing an IT-ITEs infrastructure around the airport, the Group plans to set up a flying club to train pilots and an aircraft maintenance facility. Mr Sajjan Jindal believes that building low cost airports are more essential by putting emphasis on the runway and instruments, than splurging on huge terminal buildings.

First flag hoisting by me at Vijaynagar airport on 15 Aug 2006

For quite some time our operations were going on smoothly. Since I was appointed an Instructor and Instrument Rating Examiner by the DGCA, I managed to convert eight pilots for operations on Citation Jet and Cessna Caravan. I also carried out Instrument ratings of many pilots from other corporate sectors. In fact, at one time, I was the only Instructor and IRE in Mumbai for five corporate sectors. I always feel that these kinds of achievements should make one humbler and I feel blessed to not let it get to my head.

During the normal course of operations, one more serious emergency took place. I was to take six passengers (five foreigners and Shri Sajjan Jindal) from Hyderabad to Delhi. Capt. Sindhu was my co-pilot. When passengers boarded the plane, Hyderabad had a 'weather warning' for heavy rain and gusty winds. But at that time, there was only light drizzle over the airport. We asked for permission to proceed to the runway in use. As we reached close to the runway in use, one aircraft was on final approach for landing. Pilot of that aircraft reported heavy rain on the approach and continued to land. As that aircraft landed, we asked for line up for take-off. The landing aircraft took a bit of extra time to clear the runway. In the meantime, partial rain had approached from the East and South East. We asked for take-off and started rolling. The downpour of rain with heavy downdraft came over us and covered the left window, that is, on my side and front windscreen. Since I was on the left seat, I lost contact with the runway. My co-pilot also could see through right window only. It was only with the help of instruments that I was able to keep the aircraft straight on the runway. I asked Sindhu to keep the right edge of the runway in contact and give me right or left direction so that I could keep the aircraft on the runway. At about halfway through the runway, we just had 70 kts of speed when Capt. Sindhu called 'Abort! Abort!' meant discontinue the take-off. Before I could even react to the call of my co-pilot, some godly power whispered in my ear, 'do not abort'. And so, I kept asking Sindhu to report right edge of runway in contact. He kept saying, 'Go left and go right' because strong wind from the left was pushing the aircraft to the right and I was only on instruments. I could not see the runway because of water film on the left window and on the front windshield. Due to heavy downdraft and heavy rain, we took almost 3/4th of runway to get airborne. As we got airborne, there was a great relief. Good thing that I did not 'abort my take-off'. Had I aborted, I surely would have entered the Katcha portion on the side of the runway. Because sudden deceleration due to quick closing of throttles would have given excessive pull to the left, there would have been very serious consequences if we had skidded on the runway. The 'godly whisper' saved us from a possible disaster. On the same mission, our weather radar had failed. Since the mission was of very urgent requirement for all officials in Delhi, we carried on with the flight. This being a rainy season, the CB clouds were all over along the route. As we reached our descent point, there was a wall of CB clouds. Delhi Airport was reporting CB clouds all over and there was light drizzle as well. We had no choice to change direction, as our weather radar was not available. We commenced our descent as per ATC's clearance. It was a dark night and lightning in the CB clouds was blinding us every now and then. I tried descending through a light CB cloud (less shine of lightning). However, at about 15,000 ft, we entered a thick, dark CB cloud. Soon after entering the cloud, our aircraft was struck by lightning. All the electrical instruments went off for a while and then got turned on, but not with very reliable indications. I only had reliable Airspeed Indicator and Altimeter. We reduced our speed and slowly descended to direct approach as advised by the ATC. On approach, I got glide slope indication, however, that could not be relied upon hundred percent. I carried on with chart approach and contacted the runway at a height of 500 ft. The reported visibility was 500 metres in rain. We finally made a safe landing and came to our parking bay. The aircraft was grounded for inspection and repairs for damage due to the lightning strike. It also needed clearance from the DGCA after all the inspections and repairs. We were lucky that there was no structural damage. God had saved us again, not just once, but twice!

In January 2006, Mr Sajjan Jindal, MD, appointed me as the Director of Aviation to deal with DGCA for all our aviation needs and requirements. I was staying in Mumbai with my family in a flat hired by Jindal Iron and Steel Company. We were staying in Andheri East and had a good stay there. My stay was made comfortable by my MD Mr. Sajjan Jindal, Mr Jain deputy MD, HR Head Mr Madhok and the head of Admin. Team - Mr Patil. Capt. Brar had left us for better job oppurtunities, there was a new team of respectable pilots with Jindal Aviation who carried on the work with impaccable skills and excellence. In April 2006, I shifted to Jindal Vidyanagar Township, near Bellary in Karnataka state. I was allotted Bungalow number 1 at Vidyanagar Township. Our house had huge lawns and many fruit orchard in the backyard. We also had a small kitchen garden from where we used to get organic fresh vegetables too.

All our aircraft operations started from Vidyanagar instead of Mumbai. I had a good bunch of pilots with me and I kept them so motivated that they were available for day and night operations on all days. They were very keen to take on any additional duties of running the airport too. At that time, the Jindal Iron and Steel Co. was renamed as Jindal South West (JSW) Limited. And around 2007, the airport was renamed as Vidyanagar Airport.

Now that we were based at Vidyanagar, we established an aviation office to handle all the correspondence related to flying. Mr Shaji Mathews was sent to me for aviation duty who was totally unaware of aviation functions and related matters. I trained him to handle all the correspondence and allied duties in connection with aircraft and pilot's movements. He was hardworking and sincere and in no time he learnt the job well. Later, he proved to be an asset to the aviation office.

My tenure here at JSW was very enriching and memorable one as we were very comfortable here, with excellent facilities provided for all JSW employees—accommodation, sports complex and very well stocked gym with well-trained instructors, club with two restaurants, man-made lake, walking tracks, children play area, very wellstocked market, multiplex, bakery, temple, museum-cum-meditation hall, cricket ground, school. Other than these, many social activities were also arranged for the families.

I would also like to mention that my stay was made further comfortable by my colleagues and friends at JSW—Mr Naval, Mr Bansal and Mr Lal. I would also like to mention Nanni and Narinder Sharma. Nanni and Capt. Sharma were both socially very active and were extremely helpful in organising social functions of the flying section. We did enjoy many meals together as Nanni was a great cook too. We are still in touch with them and they now have become like family members. Whenever we meet, we share fond memories of our stay together at Vidyanagar. His son Karan is following his father's footsteps and is now an airline pilot himself.

22

HOW I BECAME A HOMOEOPATH

In the year 1973, being in the Air Force, I was attending my Junior Commander course at Secunderabad. Something interesting and unique had happened. One day after our health run, I started to sneeze and had a runny nose. At the end of my class, I decided to see a doctor in Secunderabad. While looking for a doctor's clinic on Railway Road, I saw a Homoeopathic clinic. The name of the clinic was Sagar Homoeopathic Clinic. I entered that clinic; half the shop was full of Hompeopathy books and medicines while the other half was a clinic. A doctor was sitting at a table and on the opposite side; there was a vacant chair. I guessed that was for patients. As I went in front of the doctor, I saw his name plate (wooden block), on which was written Dr Shankar. I greeted him and he gestured me to take the seat. He asked me about my problem. After narrating my problem to him, he also asked me a few more questions for which I was feeling a bit irritated. He, anyway, gave medicine for three days and asked me to report to him again after three days of medication. He gave me one small plastic cylindrical bottle with white pills in it along with three small packets. The time for taking the medicine was written on the bottle and the packets. The first dose was given to me in his clinic itself. I returned home and the next day, I started the medication as per instructions. By evening, I felt slightly better and the next day, I was fully cured. I had no fever, no body ache and no sneezing. I felt so relieved that instead of waiting for the third day, I went back to Dr Shankar after two days to tell him that I was almost fully cured. Doctor advised me to complete third day's medicine also. I was so overjoyed that I could not wait for the third day. I was more interested in asking the doctor, 'what miracle drug had he given to me? He made me sit and talked about Homoeopathy in general. He also suggested me to read a book on Homoeopathy. I showed my interest in the subject and made friends with Dr Shankar. He took a lot of interest in teaching me the principles of Homoeopathy and Homoeopathic medicines. This way, I became interested in Homoeopathy and Alternative Medicines.

I did put in a lot of hard work to learn from books. After a couple of years, I started treating my family members and on various AF stations, the families and children of our domestic helpers too. I gave free medicines to all of them. I felt proud in curing some very complicated cases as well. The beauty of Homoeopathic medicines is that there are no side effects like some of Allopathic medicines. Reading more and more about Father of Homoeopathy, Samuel Hahnemann's work and discoveries, I got engrossed in Homoeopathy. However, all the time, I felt that I should have had formal training and some qualification in it. In fact, I had even joined one correspondence course in Homoeopathy when I was serving in the Air Force as Command Flight Safety and Inspection Officer at Shillong. However, I could not complete the course due to paucity of time then.

When I got posted as Air-1 at Southern Air Command at Trivandrum, this dream of earning a Homoeopathic degree appeared possible. At Trivandrum, I saw a Homoeopathic school, which used to take evening classes from 1800 Hours to 2100 Hours. It was also very convenient as it was just 8 kilometres away from my house. I met the principal of the institute Mavelil Homeo Mission and mentioned to him about my interest in Homoeopathy. So, at first, he wanted to see the case histories of the patients I had treated in the past. As I was maintaining a register with case histories including diagnosis and remedies given to each of the patients, I showed it to him. He looked at my meticulous work and got impressed and immediately admitted me for Diploma course in Homoeopathy and Biochemistry Training Classes. I mentioned to the principal about my busy schedule and heavy duties as Air-1 of a command and dealing with two naval commands and one army command. He gave me classes on three days a week (Wednesday, Saturday and Sunday). I took full interest and advantage of my time. I completed the course in a record time of three months. This included my practical training in his clinic in the Mission. I was awarded a certificate Regt. No. 8035/A by the Mission on 3rd December 1992. Thereafter, I completed the requirements of the INDIAN COUNCIL OF ALTERNATIVE MEDICINES. I was awarded the registration of R.M.P. (Registered Medical Practitioner) in Biochemical System of Medicine on 21st December, 1993. My interest in Alternative Medicines grew further as the results of my treatments were very encouraging and also life saving in certain cases.

Later on in 1996 at Jindal Iron and Steel Company, while taking my MD to Vidyanagar, I used to get a lot of time there. This time was utilized in treating many needy persons. I also used to educate most of the senior officers and technicians about alternative medicines and educate them to understand complicated medical terms, such as, the role of cholesterol. Many were not clear and would often ask, 'What is it and how does it work?' I consulted many medical books, prepared slides and explained the relationship of cholesterol with our body by giving a presentation. Our relationship with cholesterol is as complex and contradictory as our relationship with every other fat. We need it, but too much of the wrong kind can clog the arteries and cause harm. I explained cholesterol's function in the body—for better and for worse. Their questions were, 'what is good and bad cholesterol and how do they function in our body?'I would then begin to explain— Cholesterol is a fat-like substance that the body needs to build cells, make hormones and process fats; it travels inside lipoprotein molecules; LDL (low-density lipoprotein) carries cholesterol to cells; HDL (high-density lipoprotein) carries excess cholesterol back to the liver, which disposes it off.

Too much LDL cholesterol is considered bad because it is a major component of plaque that can form inside arterial walls, causing the arteries to narrow; high LDL levels are associated with heart disease. While high levels of HDL cholesterol are considered good because it is needed to rid the body of excess cholesterol: Low HDL levels are associated with heart disease. Triglycerides are the other lipoprotein routinely measured in evaluating heart disease risks; triglycerides are used by the muscles for energy and are stored as fat for later use; high levels in the blood are associated with risk of heart disease.

The next question would be, 'What do the numbers mean?' These numbers, I had obtained from a publication of U.S. Food and Drug Administration; American Heart Association. These are goals for the good, the bad and borderline levels of lipids in our bloodstream. All figures in mg/dL (milligrams per decilitre of blood).

	Desirable	Borderline	High
Total Colestrol	Less than 200	200 - 239	240+
LDL	Below 130	130 - 159	160+
HDL	60 or Higher	35 - 60	Below 35
Triglycerides	Below 200	200 - 400	400+

Next, they would ask about the working of cholesterol and associated diseases or problems. I explained the working of cholesterol. In Healthy bloodstream, cholesterol and triglycerides pass through without causing plaque to build. Cholesterol combined with other substances in the bloodstream forms plaque, which thickens the arterial walls, narrowing the inner channel and impeding blood flow; plaque can rupture, encouraging blood clots that can block the vessel entirely. In medical terms it is called, '*Arteriosclerosis*'. When arteries become clogged, blood can no longer carry enough oxygen or nutrients to heart muscles, causing some muscle tissue to die, if major branches such as left main coronary artery, left circumflex artery, left anterior descending artery and right coronary artery is blocked, a fatal heart attack is more likely.

Next they'd ask, 'What is a stroke?' I would start to explain—when plaque clogs arteries leading to the brain, part of the brain dies. This is one form of stroke.

The next question was, 'How does cholesterol enter the bloodstream?' I simply explained that it enters through the stomach as we digest foods that are rich in saturated fats. From there it goes to the liver, which produces cholesterol as well as helps to eliminate it. From there to the lungs and then to heart. That is why all the doctors recommend the regular check-ups of lipid profile.

Doctor of Medicine—Alternative Medicines

While I was working with JSW, I used to treat Officers and all other employees as well as their families and children. I also kept maintaining a register of case histories. Now I was fully confident to further my studies. I applied for the Doctorate Degree from the Indian Board of Alternative Medicines. This board is registered by the Government of West Bengal, affiliated with the Open International University for Complementary Medicines—Established under World Health Organisation, Alma Ata. USSR, Declaration, 1962 and recognised by the United Nations, Peace University constituted under Resolution No. 35/55/5/XII/80. The Board asked me to submit recent 50 case histories and appear for Examinations of the Board. I managed to pass all the examinations and final Interview by the Board Members held in Calcutta. Finally, I was awarded the 'Doctorate Degree of Doctor of Medicine (Alternative Medicines) (MD, AM) on 21st December 2001 in Calcutta—Registered no. IBAM/C/5967.

After my retirement from JSW (Jindal South West), I had planned to settle down in my good old village, Garhdiwala, in District Hoshiarpur, Punjab. Therefore, I applied for RMP (Registered Medical Practitioner) Registration for my village. This registration was awarded to me on 19th June 2003. I also obtained memberships and fellowship as given below:

- Member National Centre for Homeopathy, USA.
- Member International Homoeopathic Medical Society, USA (MIHMS).
- Member Mavelil Homeo Mission, India.
- Member Rural Health Society of India.
- Fellow World Society of Alternative Medicines, USA (FWSAM)

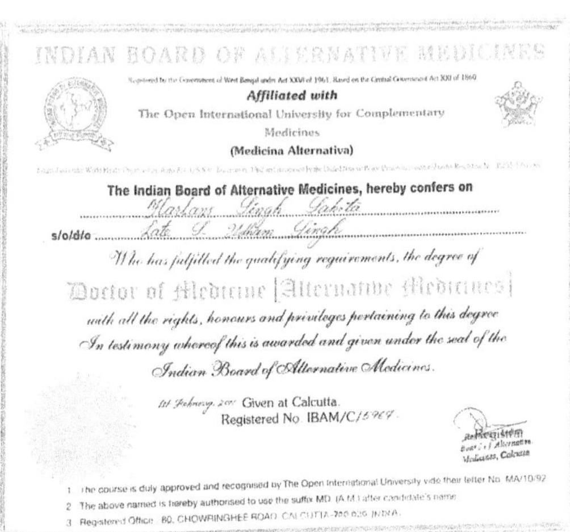

INDIAN BOARD OF ALTERNATIVE MEDICINES

Registered by the Government of West Bengal under Act XXVI of 1961. Based on the Central Government Act XXI of 1860

Affiliated with

The Open International University for Complementary Medicines

(Medicina Alternativa)

The Indian Board of Alternative Medicines, hereby confers on

Harbans Singh Sahota

s/o/d/o Late S. Udham Singh

Who has fulfilled the qualifying requirements, the degree of

Doctor of Medicine [Alternative Medicines]

with all the rights, honours and privileges pertaining to this degree
In testimony whereof this is awarded and given under the seal of the
Indian Board of Alternative Medicines.

1st February, 2001 Given at Calcutta.
Registered No. IBAM/C/5969.

Registrar
Board of Alternative
Medicines, Calcutta

1. The course is duly approved and recognised by The Open International University vide their letter No. MA/10/92
2. The above named is hereby authorised to use the suffix MD. (A.M.) after candidate's name.
3. Registered Office : 80, CHOWRINGHEE ROAD, CALCUTTA-700 020, INDIA.

INDIAN COUNCIL OF ALTERNATIVE MEDICINES

(AFFILIATED TO THE OPEN INTERNATIONAL
UNIVERSITY & REGD. BY THE GOVT. OF
W. B. BASED ON CENTRAL GOVT. ACT.)

172, ELIAS ROAD, CALCUTTA-58

(Council for the development of Alternative System of Treatment)

REGISTERED BY THE GOVT. OF WEST BENGAL

Registration No. 23,534

Certified that Dr. Harbans Singh Sahota
of vill. p/o Garhdiwala, Dist. Hoshiarpur, Punjab

has been Registered under the Byelaws of **INDIAN COUNCIL OF ALTERNATIVE MEDICINES** as a **R. M. P. (Registered Medical Practitioner)** in Alto - Calcutta
System of Medicine
Date of Issue 31st December 1993.

REGISTRAR

IMPORTANT DIRECTIVES

1) The Registered Medical Practitioner will only be declared as Qualified person to practise in India's own lines of treatment and shall not be considered or punished by any Government in India if the same is applicable to the State health Rules and he/she is proved to be of good moral conduct and honest to discharging his/her duty.

2) The practitioner's are eligible to issue medical certificate to only the genuine persons undergoing his/her treatment.

3) The practitioner must inform to council about any change in his/her address within 15 days, failing which his/her Registration may be cancelled.

4) Every Registered Medical Practitioners is advised to renew his/her Registration Certificate annually within 31st March of every year, otherwise his/her name may be struck off from the Register.

CERTIFICATE OF REGISTRATION

INDIAN BOARD OF ALTERNATIVE MEDICINES

Registered by the Government of West Bengal under Act XXVI of 1961. Based on the Central Government Act XXI of 1860

Affiliated with

THE OPEN INTERNATIONAL UNIVERSITY FOR COMPLEMENTARY MEDICINES

(Medicina Alternativa)

Established under World Health Organisation, Alma Ata, U.S.S.R., Declaration, 1962 and recognised by the United Nations Peace University constituted under Resolution No. 35/55-XII/80

Registration No. IBAM/RMP/ A-22776.

NAME	ADDRESS	DATE OF REGISTRATION	SYSTEM OF MEDICINE	RULE OF THE BOARD UNDER WHICH REGISTRATION IS ALLOWED
Dr Harbans Singh Sahota.	H. No-82, Ward No-8, Moh-Babbian Da, Vill & P.O-Garhdiwala, Hoshiarpur, (Pb.)	19-06-2003.	Alternative Medicines.	7 (a)

It is hereby declared that this Certificate reproduces the entries made in the Register of Registered Medical Practitioners of Alternative Medicines in respect of the name specified in the Certificate maintained by the Indian Board of Alternative Medicines.

Calcutta, the 19th June 20 03.

Registrar, Indian
Board of Alternative
Medicines, Calcutta

IMPORTANT DIRECTIVES

1. The Registered Medical Practitioner is declared as a Qualified Person to practise in Alternative Medicines lines of treatment as provided by the Rules and Regulations of the Indian Board of Alternative Medicines and shall not be convicted or punished by any Government in India if he/she is proved to be a man of good moral conduct and honest to discharge his/her duty as per Rule 7(f) of the Board.
2. The practitioner shall issue the medical certificate only to persons undergoing his/her treatment as per Rule 7(e) of the Board.
3. The practitioner should maintain the uniform code of conduct as determined by the Board (Rule 7(d) of the Board).
4. This Certificate is valid upto Life-Time.
5. Any change of address must be intimated promptly to the Registrar.
6. This Certificate is the property of the Board and issued to the above practitioner in accordance with Rule 7(a) of the Board.
7. REGISTERED OFFICE : 80, CHOWRINGHEE ROAD, CALCUTTA- 700 020, WEST BENGAL, INDIA.

23

LIFE WITH FAMILY IN USA

I continued my service with JSW Aviation as Chief Executive Pilot and Director of Aviation till 8th November 2008, and then after completing 65 years of age, I happily retired from my job. Just about a month before my retirement, I had received immigration papers from my son, Tipi, who was settled in USA. My son wanted us to be free to travel to the US to spend quality time with his children. I also felt that this was the time to bond with our grandchildren. Once the children grow up and become busy in higher classes, they will have less time for personal relationship with grandparents. For that reason, my wife and I migrated to the US and started living with our son and started fostering and bringing up the grandchildren (two daughters and one son, namely, Anaika, Ahana and Angad). I personally admire the foresight of my son and the right decision on our part. Now we are living a very happy life with all our grandchildren, our son and daughter-in-law (Ms Puneet Randhawa).

We realized that this was the right time to be with them. Within a few days, they got attached to me and we started spending even more time together. Anaika was in school in her second grade. I started driving her to school in the morning. At the end of her class, I used to pick her up too. Her school was only four miles away. She was very talkative and extremely inquisitive by nature. While playing around with me, she would ask far too many questions like, 'Dadaji, in India, what were you doing? Did you go to school? And after school, did you work?' I sensed that she would not stop with one or two answers. Before she used to go to sleep at night, I started telling her stories from my younger days, stories of my school and college. She would insist to listen more and more stories of my job and life. When I told her that I was a pilot in India, she asked, 'Dadaji where is your aeroplane now?'

These types of questions and answers went on for about three years. Then the other two siblings also started to flood me with their innumerable questions. It was in 2012 when my eldest granddaughter once told me,'Dadaji, you have so many stories of flying and other stories of your school and college, why don't you write a book?' That was when it really hit me hard that I had never thought of writing earlier. However, in the same year, I made the decision to write my life's story in the form of an autobiography. Hence, I began to write this book.

My elder granddaughter in USA graduated from high school in April 2019 and joined Medical College to become a doctor. This year (2020), I am going to present the book on my life story to all my grandchildren. My other granddaughter in India, Keerath, also joined a Medical College this year to become a doctor. And the younger one, Amanat, is in her 12th grade and she is aspiring to become an Airline Pilot just like her father, Harpreet Singh Basra, who retired from the Indian Air Force as Air Commodore and has become Captain in Air Asia Airline.

After my migration to USA, I continued flying a Cessna Citation jet-525 belonging to my friend Mr Don Morris in USA. It was very strange how we had become friends. This happened while I was working in Mumbai as a pilot. He had taken his aircraft to Mumbai with the help of an American Pilot. He wanted to take his aircraft from Mumbai to Pune. He, being a foreign pilot with foreign registered aircraft, was not cleared by the DGCA to go to Pune as that is a Defence Airfield. I was also operating a similar type of aircraft from Mumbai; so, he approached me for getting him the clearance for his aircraft to Pune. I asked him the purpose of going to Pune, and found that he had a very noble reason. He told me that he was born in Pune and had studied there up to fourth standard. His father owned a factory there, though it was being run by another owner, most of the old workers were still there. He wanted to give a ride to those workers, their families and children as a goodwill gesture. I explained to him the reasons for not getting the clearance for Pune. I got him the clearance to fly to

Vidyanagar Airport (my airport of operations belonging to Jindals) but I had to fly with him on the right seat as per the instructions by the DGCA. I found him to be a very kind-hearted person, so, at Vidyanagar, I made sure that he was treated like a VIP and I even had arranged a visit to the famous Hampi Ruins by a team detailed by me. From there, I got him the clearance for Mangalore and then back to Mumbai. After two days' stay in Mumbai, he with the help of an American pilot, returned to USA via Saudi Arabia. That is how we had become friends. In USA, he was staying in a city, which was about 30 miles away from my son's house. He had kept contact with my son. On my arrival, he requested me to fly for him as a job for which I would get paid, but I refused. I told him that I would fly with him on weekends but I would not charge any money. He was very happy and we kept flying on weekends for leisure visits to various places of his choice. I had a Commercial Pilot's Licence from the FAA, which remained valid along with my ALTP Licence from the DGCA, New Delhi, India. I obtained membership 0f AOPA (Aircraft Owners and Pilots Association). I kept flying in USA with Mr Don Morris until my ALTP expired in December 2011. So finally, I could fly no more after that and that was the end of my flying career. However, my flying passion will remain with me till the end.

Being Aviation minded and the love of flying and freedom
it brings—is a legacy worth passing on to future generations.

EPILOGUE

When I had joined the Indian Air Force, my enormous experience of farming had taught me to work hard and be regular in completing the given jobs. In my younger days, my father was my guide and a teacher. He always insisted on teamwork, sincerity, integrity and boldness. After my commissioning as a Fighter Pilot in the IAF, I explored all the teachings of my father and became a daredevil Fighter Pilot. I also started to work even harder to become a leader as well. Leadership is defined by various experts. To me, it is the skill, good judgement and polite behaviour that are expected from a person who is an achiever, developer, maximiser and excels in almost every unexpected, dangerous situation. From the very beginning of my career in the IAF, I started to work towards acquiring good communication skills, preparedness, punctuality, good work ethic, appropriate appearance and attire, especially my Uniform, writing and interpersonal skills, integrity and ambition. I know fully well that leadership is not something that is honed overnight. Rather, leadership behaviours are developed and honed over a long period of setting an example and display of courage and integrity.

The will to win, the desire to succeed, the urge to reach your full potential...
these are the keys that will unlock the door to personal excellence.

—Confucuis

It was not easy to get established in Corporate Sector Flying hierarchy. I had to struggle and work very hard and stand first in all the DGCA Examinations and in all tests in flying. It was my determination that had put me ahead of many stalwarts in the Corporate Sector Flying within a very short span of time. Fortunately, the Air Force Service, Corporate Commercial Flying and my Doctorate Degree (MD) provided me an excellent opportunity to learn and practice the many skills, traits and habits that define leaders. As I have mentioned earlier, Air Force service is one of the best among the defence services. Though the other two services, Army and Navy, are equally good in all respects. There are a lot of career opportunities for boys and girls in the Air Force.

Those who are interested, can contact:

DISHA CELL at Air Head Quarters,
Vayu Bhawan, Motilal Nehru Marg, New Delhi – 110106

Tel: 011-23013690, toll free no.: 1800-11-2448

website: https://careerindianairforce.cdac.in

What you really need to succeed:It doesn't matter if you did not receive the best academic training from a good university. A person with less education who has fully developed his Emotional Intelligence, Moral Intelligence and Body Intelligence can be far more successful than a person with an impressive education who falls short in Emotional, Moral and Body Intelligence.

—Keld Jensen

There is no discipline without character
There is no effectiveness without discipline!

No person lasts forever but the books and ideas can endure!

Memoirs

*Performed Bhangra Punjabi dance on 26th January 1980 celeberated
by Indian community in Enugu (Nigeria)—Myself, son, daughter and wife.*

Visit to--Sela and Tenga (Eastern Sector) Brigade Commander Brigadier Bali--Arranged local visit to Tenga Area and one game of Golf, which was won by me.

Visit to—Sikkim

With depty GOC Brigadier HPS Mann & Officers of No. 4 Div,
Vavuniya, Sri Lanka

Medals and Squadron Crests earned during service with IAF

Self, Gian, Tejinder and Tejpal
Family picture in January 1980

Amanat, Tejinder, Harpreet and Keerath, December 2019

Tejpal, Ahana (holding Mellow), Puneet, Angad and Anaika, December 2019

Our family House in Garhdiwala Distt. Hoshiar pur, Punjab, India

Back to roots with daughter-Tejinder

www.ingramcontent.com/pod-product-compliance
Lightning Source LLC
LaVergne TN
LVHW020049150726
843364LV00040B/1391